Corpus Linguistics and the

Corpus Linguistics and the Description of English

Hans Lindquist

Edinburgh University Press

© Hans Lindquist, 2009

Edinburgh University Press Ltd
22 George Square, Edinburgh

www.euppublishing.com

Reprinted 2010

Typeset in Janson
by Servis Filmsetting Ltd, Stockport, Cheshire, and
printed and bound in Great Britain by
CPI Antony Rowe, Chippenham and Eastbourne

A CIP record for this book is available from the British Library

ISBN 978 0 7486 2614 4 (hardback)
ISBN 978 0 7486 2615 1 (paperback)

The right of Hans Lindquist
to be identified as author of this work
has been asserted in accordance with
the Copyright, Designs and Patents Act 1988.

Contents

Figures

Tables

To readers

This book is written for university students of English at intermediate to advanced levels who have a certain background in grammar and linguistics, but who have not had the opportunity to use computer corpora to any great extent in their studies. Although the focus is on language, the book should also be interesting for students specialising in literature, especially the chapters on phrases, collocations, metaphor and gender.

The book gives brief introductions to the most important fields of English corpus linguistics with many step-by-step concrete examples and hands-on exercises. It is primarily about using existing corpora, not about making corpora. It gives the necessary information about how corpora have been constructed from a user's point of view, but it is not a handbook in compiling corpora. Readers who wish to go on and construct their own corpora are given references to handbooks and manuals that will give the necessary information in greater detail.

The organisation of the book is as follows. The first chapter gives the rationale behind corpus linguistics and discusses pros and cons of this methodology. The chapter also describes the main types of corpora and the best-known corpora in each category. The second chapter introduces some central concepts in corpus linguistics: frequency, representativeness and statistical significance, giving numerous authentic examples. The following eight chapters focus on specific areas of English: words, collocations, phrases, metaphors and metonyms, syntax, gender, and language change. The final chapter discusses the use of the web as a corpus. Each chapter is illustrated with a wealth of data from published articles or original research carried out for this book so that it is possible to follow the research process. At the same time the reader gets acquainted with a variety of corpora and methods. Each chapter ends with a number of study questions and suggestions for further reading. In addition, hands-on tasks for each chapter are available on the book's companion website.

These are all based on corpora which are freely available via links on the webpage. The exercises can be used in class, as essay topics or homework assignments.

My first contact with corpus linguistics was as a PhD student at Lund University in 1977. My supervisor, Jan Svartvik, was working on the digitalisation of one of the very first spoken corpora, The London-Lund Corpus, and I had a brief job manually tagging some of the material (more about tagging in Chapter 2). Working in the department at that time were also Karin Aijmer, Bengt Altenberg and Anna-Brita Stenström, among others, so it was an ideal environment for learning about corpus linguistics. However, my own dissertation was about translation from English into Swedish, and although I called it a corpus-based study it was really based on hand-collected examples on slips which were later put into a database. I did not get seriously into corpus work until 1994, when I started planning a project at Växjö University (now Linnaeus University) called Grammatical Trends in Moderns English (GramTime) with Jan Svartvik, Magnus Levin and Maria Estling Vannestål. I want to thank Jan for all the inspiration and support he has given me over the years, and Magnus and Maria for our very fruitful cooperation, which is still ongoing. Magnus read the whole manuscript of the book and made innumerable suggestions for improvements – some of which I have followed. Thanks to Magnus, the book is now much more student-friendly than it would otherwise have been. He also saved me from making a number of silly mistakes.

It is impossible to list all the friends and colleagues who have been important in different ways for the birth of this book, but I must mention a few: Gunnel Tottie, who at one time was my supervisor at Lund and has remained a supportive friend; Graeme Kennedy, with whom I have had many rewarding discussions in our shared office in Wellington and in his home; Michael Stubbs, who has illuminated many theoretical questions in corpus linguistics in his writings and at several visits in Växjö; and Christian Mair, with whom I have had the pleasure of co-editing a collection of papers and whose work is always an inspiration. I also owe a great debt of gratitude to Mark Davies and all other compilers of corpora used in the book, as well as to the large number of researchers whose work I quote.

The book would never have come about if it had not been for the original suggestion from Laurie Bauer and his good advice when I was preparing the proposal. Laurie also read the whole manuscript and made many useful comments. Similarly, I want to thank the series editor, Heinz Giegerich, for taking the proposal through the review process, the commissioning editors at EUP Sarah Edwards (who started the project) and Esmé Watson (who saw it to completion), and the copy-editor Fiona Sewell who did a great job on the typescript.

My final and warmest thanks go to my wife Agneta for always trying to lure me out of the study.

Abbreviations

ACE	Australian Corpus of English
AmE	American English
ANC	American National Corpus
ARCHER	A Representative Corpus of Historical English Registers
BNC	British National Corpus
BoE	Bank of English
BrE	British English
Brown	Brown Corpus
BYU	Brigham Young University
CEEC	Corpus of Early English Correspondence
CEN	Corpus of English Novels
CLAWS	Constituent Likelihood Automatic Word-tagging System
CLMET	Corpus of Late Modern English Texts
CMC	computer-mediated communication
Cobuild	Collins Birmingham University International Language Database
COCA	Corpus of Contemporary American English
COLT	Corpus of London Teenage Speech
DOE	*Dictionary of Old English*
EModE	Early Modern English
FLOB	Freiburg Lancaster–Oslo/Bergen Corpus
FRED	Freiburg English Dialect Corpus
Frown	Freiburg Brown Corpus
HC	Helsinki Corpus
ICAME	International Computer Archive of Modern and Medieval English
ICE	International Corpus of English (Subcorpora for countries are e.g. ICE-GB for British English, ICE-NZ for

	New Zealand English, etc.; ICECUP is the Corpus Utility Program.)
ICLE	International Corpus of Learner English
IND	*The Independent*
KWIC	keyword in context
LLC	London–Lund Corpus of Spoken English
LOB	Lancaster–Oslo/Bergen Corpus
LOCNESS	Louvain Corpus of Native English Student Essays
ME	Middle English
MED	*Middle English Dictionary*
MI	mutual information
MICASE	Michigan Corpus of Academic Spoken English
NLP	natural language processing
NYT	*The New York Times*
OE	Old English
OED	*Oxford English Dictionary*
OTA	Oxford Text Archives
PIE	Phrases in English
POS	part of speech
Time Corpus	Time Magazine Corpus
WSC	Wellington Spoken Corpus

1 Corpus linguistics

1.1 Introducing corpus linguistics

There are many "hyphenated branches" of linguistics, where the first part of the name tells you what particular aspect of language is under study: sociolinguistics (the relation between language and society), psycholinguistics (the relation between language and the mind), neurolinguistics (the relation between language and neurological processes in the brain) and so on. The stand of the present book is that corpus linguistics is not a branch of linguistics on a par with these other branches, since "corpus" does not tell you what is studied, but rather that a particular methodology is used. Corpus linguistics is thus a methodology, comprising a large number of related methods which can be used by scholars of many different theoretical leanings. On the other hand, it cannot be denied that corpus linguistics is also frequently associated with a certain outlook on language. At the centre of this outlook is that the rules of language are usage-based and that changes occur when speakers use language to communicate with each other. The argument is that if you are interested in the workings of a particular language, like English, it is a good idea to study English in use. One efficient way of doing this is to use corpus methodology, and that is what this book is about. We will see how the idea of using electronic corpora began around 1960, fairly soon after computers started becoming reasonably powerful, and how the field has developed over the last fifty-odd years. We will look at different types of corpora, study the techniques involved and look at the results that can be achieved. Since the field has grown phenomenally in the 2000s, it is impossible to cover every aspect of it, and what is presented in this book therefore has to be a selection of what I personally think a student of English should know. Throughout the book the focus will be on the joy and fascination that lie in the description and analysis of the English language, which after all is the purpose of all these efforts. The ultimate aim is to learn more about the language and to understand better how it works. In the next section we will retrace our steps a bit and think about how one can go about describing a language.

1.2 The professor's shoeboxes

Imagine that there were no grammars and no dictionaries of English and that you were asked to describe the language. How would you go about it? If you are a native speaker, you would perhaps begin by thinking about your own use of the language, and the kind of language you read and hear around you, and then start making lists of words and rules of grammar. And if you are not a native speaker, you would have to study the speech and writing of native speakers. There are still people who work from scratch like this, linguists who work in the field to describe those of the world's 6,000 or 7,000 languages that have not yet been described in detail. For English, of course, the situation is much more advantageous.

Dictionaries and grammars of English have been written for several hundred years and are continuously improved and updated (even if the first descriptions had been perfect, they would have had to be revised regularly, since the language keeps changing). Many of the earliest descriptions were quite biased, based on the compilers' own way of speaking and writing and on their own personal views on what constituted the correct use of the English language. However, over time scholars began to use more empirical material, a wider range of data. Perhaps the greatest example of all times was the monumental *A Modern English Grammar on Historical Principles* (1909–1949) by the Danish professor Otto Jespersen. In his autobiography he describes how his large villa outside Copenhagen gradually filled with shoeboxes containing hundreds of thousands of paper slips on which he noted examples of interesting English sentences from his copious reading of English literature. In every section of his grammar, under each construction treated, he gives authentic examples picked out of these shoeboxes.

The mind boggles at the thought of having to keep track of hundreds of thousands of slips, and finding the right slips for the writing of each chapter and section of the grammar book. No wonder that the project took many years, only to be finished by colleagues after Jespersen's death. And no wonder that there have been no further one-man projects on quite the same grandiose scale after Jespersen's, although some excellent grammars have been written using similar methods.

One thing that the work of Jespersen and his successors made clear was that comprehensive descriptive reference grammars of English need to be based on large amounts of authentic data, and preferably not only written literary texts but also written language from other registers and, importantly, spoken data as well. Here technological advances were to have a large impact.

1.3 The tape-recorder and the computer

One way of getting information about spoken language, apart from listening and taking notes, is to study the dialogue in plays and novels. But that is artificial spoken language, devoid of all or most of the hesitations, interruptions, false starts, incomplete sentences and hemming and hawing that is typical of authentic speech such as it appears when one listens to a taped conversation or reads a close, verbatim transcription of such a tape (for examples of this, see Figure 1.5 on page 12). In 1959, therefore, Randolph Quirk, later Lord Quirk, started the Survey of English Usage, which was to include both spoken and written language. For the spoken language, he and his collaborators made surreptitious recordings of private conversations and meetings.

At about the same time in the US, W. Nelson Francis and Henry Kučera at Brown University started to compile the first electronic collection of English texts to be used for linguistic research. They wanted to create a balanced and representative picture of printed, edited American English (AmE) in 1961, and proceeded to collect 500 samples of 2,000 words each from a selection of various text genres as listed in Table 1.1, thus getting a total of 1 million words. They called it the Brown Corpus. The word *corpus*, which is Latin for 'body', had been used before about the total works by an individual author or a certain mass of texts, as in "The Shakespeare corpus", and it can be used about collections of linguistic examples on cards or slips in shoeboxes as well (Kennedy 1998 calls those 'pre-electronic corpora'), but nowadays *corpus* is almost always synonymous with *electronic corpus*, i.e. a collection of texts which is stored on some kind of digital medium and used by linguists to retrieve linguistic items for research or by lexicographers for dictionary-making.

The make-up of the Brown Corpus is given in some detail here since it is a good illustration of how a number of leading linguists at the time tried to create a so-called balanced corpus, i.e. a corpus that gives a fair picture of the whole of the language. The model is especially important since it was later followed, first in a British version called the Lancaster–Oslo/Bergen Corpus (LOB) for 1961, and much later by a team in Freiburg who created "clones" based on material published

Table 1.1 The contents of the Brown Corpus

Text type		Number of texts	Proportion of the corpus (%)
A	Press: reportage (political, sports, society, "spot news", financial, cultural)	44	8.8
B	Press: editorial (including letters to the editor)	27	5.4
C	Press: reviews (theatre, books, music, dance)	17	3.4
D	Religion	17	3.4
E	Skills and hobbies	36	7.2
F	Popular lore	48	9.6
G	Belles letters, biography, memoirs etc.	75	15.0
H	Miscellaneous (mainly government documents)	30	6.0
J	Learned (academic texts)	80	16.0
K	General fiction (novels and short stories)	29	5.8
L	Mystery and detective fiction	24	4.8
M	Science fiction	6	1.2
N	Adventure and Western fiction	29	5.8
P	Romance and love story	29	5.8
R	Humour	9	1.8
	Non-fiction subtotal	374	75
	Fiction subtotal	126	25
	Grand total	**500**	**100**

Note: There is no category 'I'.
Source: Based on Francis and Kučera (1964)

thirty years later: the Freiburg Brown (Frown, actually based on 1992 material) and the Freiburg LOB (FLOB). The Freiburg corpora thus made it feasible to make comparisons between the two geographical varieties over time. At the moment work is going on in Lancaster to go back in time and create similar British corpora for 1931 and 1901 (called Lancaster1931 and Lancaster1901) and there are also plans for American counterparts.

In the five decades since 1961 there has been a tremendous boom in corpus compilation, in the writing of computer programs for retrieving and processing data, and in the development of linguistic theory relating to corpora. In the rest of this chapter we will discuss a number of different types of corpora that are now available and give examples of the kinds of data that you can get from them. First, however, we will return to the motivation for using corpora in the first place.

1.4 What can we get out of corpora?

Compiling corpora can take a lot of time and be quite expensive, so to justify the effort there must be considerable gains for the linguists. The major advantages of corpora over manual investigations are speed and reliability: by using a corpus, the linguist can investigate more material and get more exact calculations of frequencies. The results from corpora are usually presented in one of two ways: as a concordance or as frequency figures.

1.4.1 Concordances

Traditionally, a concordance is a list of all the contexts in which a word occurs in a particular text. For instance, people have compiled concordances of the Bible and of Shakespeare's work by hand in order for theologians and literary scholars to be able to study how certain words are used. To take an example, if you look up the word *globe* in a Shakespeare concordance you will find out that the bard used it 11 times in all. These can be displayed with the immediate context as in Figure 1.1.

Getting the information in this way is certainly quicker than reading through the complete works of Shakespeare, pencil in hand! A literary scholar could then go on by comparing, for instance, how Shakespeare used astronomical terms in his comedies and tragedies. In linguistics, the data are most often presented in so-called keyword-in-context (KWIC) concordances with about one line of context and the keyword centred, as in the example in Figure 1.2 from *The New York Times* 1990. The ten first lines are reproduced here.

Among other things we can see here that *globe* is used in talking about locations around the earth (e.g. 1), talking about travelling around the world (e.g. 6) and referring to a sphere representing it (e.g. 5). However, these are only the first 10 out of 502 tokens of *globe* in *The New York Times*, 1990. In order to get a better grip on the contents, in most concordance programs it is possible to sort the concordance lines in various ways. If, for instance, we are interested in travel verbs that can be used transitively with *the globe*, these can easily found by sorting the *globe* lines in alphabetical order first on the first word to the left and then on the second word to the left. Figure 1.3 shows a number of concordance lines that were found with this method.

Here, a quick manual scan of the alphabetically ordered concordance has made it possible to pick out the relevant tokens. The transitive constructions could then be compared with constructions like *travel*

1. No longer from head to foot than from hip to hip:
   she is spherical, like a **globe**; I could find out
   countries in her. *Comedy of Errors* [III, 2]

2. Ay, thou poor ghost, while memory holds a seat
   In this distracted **globe**. Remember thee? *Hamlet* [I, 5]

3. Why, thou **globe** of sinful continents, what a life dost
   lead! *Henry IV, Part II* [II, 4]

4. For wheresoe'er thou art in this world's **globe**,
   I'll have an Iris that shall find thee out. *Henry VI, Part II* [III, 2]

5. Approach, thou beacon to this under **globe**,
   That by thy comfortable beams I may
   Peruse this letter. *King Lear* [II, 2]

6. We the **globe** can compass soon,
   Swifter than the wandering moon. *Midsummer Night's Dream* [IV, 1]

7. Methinks it should be now a huge eclipse
   Of sun and moon, and that the affrighted **globe**
   Should yawn at alteration. *Othello* [V, 2]

8. Discomfortable cousin! know'st thou not
   That when the searching eye of heaven is hid,
   Behind the **globe**, that lights the lower world,
   Then thieves and robbers range abroad unseen *Richard II* [III, 2]

9. The cloud-capp'd towers, the gorgeous palaces,
   The solemn temples, the great **globe** itself,
   Ye all which it inherit, shall dissolve *Tempest* [IV, 1]

10. And then I'll come and be thy waggoner,
    And whirl along with thee about the **globe**. *Titus Andronicus* [V, 2]

11. And, hark, what discord follows! each thing meets
    In mere oppugnancy: the bounded waters
    Should lift their bosoms higher than the shores
    And make a sop of all this solid **globe**. *Troilus and Cressida* [I, 3]

Figure 1.1 Concordance for *globe* in Shakespeare's work.
Source: Based on http://www.opensourceshakespeare.org

1. to have 100 Planet Hollywoods around the **globe**. And he is working on other concepts,
2. over $11. Their inspirations girdle the **globe**. If the risotto I had recently was less al
3. China, 1898-1976, by Han Suyin (Kodansha **Globe**, $16). The former Prime Minister emerges as a
4. and 2,000 employees scattered around the **globe**. He said the company expected domestic sales
5. ery (admission $2.60), where I admired a **globe** made in 1622 by the Dutch cartographer Willem
6. e than 20 times, and circumnavigated the **globe** nearly four times. In 'Ice,' he wrote about
7. s many as 46 million children around the **globe** make goods for the United States market.\Fx0A
8. nd has sold 46 million copies around the **globe**.\Fx0A 'Without a doubt, the HBO special, we
9. he mid-80's.\Fx0A Whatever part of the **globe** her fictional superstar might inhabit, Nick
10. ithin its 840 acres resonate around the **globe**. Ms. Alves's relatives in Rio de Janeiro,

Figure 1.2 The first ten lines from the concordance for *globe* in *The New York Times*, 1990.

321 ur months' time required to circle the **globe** and of the minimum $30,000 to pay for it.
322 of stratospheric winds that circle the **globe** at the equator. These winds reverse direction
323 500 pounds each, that would circle the **globe** several hundred miles up in so-called low-
324 h hundreds of sailors have circled the **globe** alone and a dozen have made such a trip
325 last year Mr. Malamud has circled the **globe** seven times himself, logging 250,000 air
326 1976 Montreal Olympics. He circled the **globe** to hone his tactical skills and fitness. But
327 ng as some cosmonauts have circled the **globe**: 214 days and counting. They may be nameless
328 long as the applicant has circled the **globe**. At his death, Mr. Williams was president of
329 r who lives in Florida and circles the **globe** playing bridge. He reported the diagramed
330 spent his life restlessly circling the **globe**, moving in all the right robber-baron circles
331 o great former space foes circling the **globe** together has been hard to ignore.\Fx0A Even
332 e Pacific Ocean and circumnavigate the **globe**.\Fx0A Among regional projects linking small
333 thcoming attempt to circumnavigate the **globe** in a balloon.\Fx0A The Gordon Bennett
334 n a bet that he can circumnavigate the **globe** in 80 days. Fogg is aided and abetted by his
335 e first airplane to circumnavigate the **globe** without refueling, ponders his current and
336 than 20 times, and circumnavigated the **globe** nearly four times. In 'Ice,' he wrote about
337 reign patents, and circumnavigated the **globe** more than a dozen times as a highly sought
348 this: 'When I'm not crisscrossing the **globe**, honing my connoisseurship of the physical
439 ds a gang of provocateurs who roam the **globe** causing trouble, usually by stealing a great
440 ampbell, who intellectually roamed the **globe** examining the myths of the world and the
441 cting agendas as the company roams the **globe**.\Fx0A Already, within the United States,
471 world after all. You can't travel the **globe** now without finding a Bayer aspirin in the
472 bjects and works of art now travel the **globe** seeking buyers, the way young upper-class
473 tors. For seven years, he traveled the **globe** meeting and interviewing anybody he could
474 y of California at Davis, traveled the **globe** in search of the histories written on broken
475 at the same time she was traveling the **globe** in pursuit of tennis titles. 'To be
476 ast two years, he's been traveling the **globe** with Jagger, who has refashioned herself as a
477 The interesting wine list travels the **globe**, with many choices in the $20 to $40 per
478 on' that can enable us to traverse the **globe** without stirring from our living rooms, any
479 0 oil paintings a year, traversing the **globe** from his base in Brooklyn and, most

Figure 1.3 Selected concordance lines for *globe* in *The New York Times*, 1990, sorted on the first word to the left and the second word to the left.

around the world. These turned out to be much fewer: there were only one instance each of *dance, go, race, run* and *zip around the world.*

It is often possible to carry out your analysis based on the short context that the concordance line provides, but if you need a larger context most concordance programs let you have that through a simple mouse click. If, for some reason, you needed more context for example 479, it can easily be had, as can be seen in Figure 1.4.

Looking at these extracts from concordances of a randomly chosen word, *globe,* makes it clear that a concordance is nothing more than raw material for the linguist. Reading and analysing concordances skilfully to extract the semantic or grammatical information hidden in them is an important aspect of corpus linguistics and an art that requires some training.

479 ikhail S. Gorbachev seemed never to flag, droning on easily for four or five hours at Communist Party Congresses, outlasting summiteers years his junior, scoffing at jetlag.\Fx0A Yuri Gorbachev--the other Gorbachev, the famous one's strapping first cousin once removed-- produces upward of 100 oil paintings a year, traversing the **globe** from his base in Brooklyn and, most impressive of all, selling most of what he produces at an average of $5,000 apiece. A small sampling of his work is on display through Sept. 12 at the Vodka Bar, at 260 West Broadway at Sixth Avenue. \Fx0A 'Energy' is the word that makes its way most often into his conversation.\Fx0A 'I have to make people happy,' he said. 'It sounds banal, but it's energy, this positive energy, that frees people and has no pretensions.'\Fx0A

Figure 1.4 Expanded context for concordance line 479 for *globe* in *The New York Times*, 1990.

1.4.2 Frequency

Frequency is an important concept in linguistics. For instance, it is a major factor in language change, where irregular verbs like *speak–spoke–spoken* seem to resist regularisation thanks to their high frequency, and frequently used word combinations like *going to* tend to fuse in pronunciation (*gonna*) and acquire new meanings ('future'). One of the main advantages of computers is that we can easily get frequency data from large masses of text, which would be virtually impossible to achieve by hand. All through this book there will be examples of how frequencies can be compared in order to describe differences between genres, geographical varieties, spoken and written language, text from different time periods and so on.

1.5 Criticism from armchair linguists

Chomsky's short 1957 book *Syntactic Structures* had an enormous impact on the field of linguistics in the subsequent decades, and Chomskyan (generative) linguistics in its various later versions is still a very influential theoretical approach. One of the main theses of generative linguistics is that linguistics should study the mental grammar of an idealised speaker, i.e. what goes on inside his or her head. The central questions is: how is it that speakers know which sentences are grammatical and which are not? What kind of grammatical rules in the brain does this presuppose? The main data-gathering method for generative linguists has traditionally been introspection, hence the term *armchair linguist* coined by Charles Fillmore (1992). With such an agenda what can be found in corpora simply isn't interesting, and Chomsky himself has been very condescending towards corpus linguistics, claiming that its findings are trivial, as when he is reported to have said that the fact that *I live in New York* is more frequent than *I live in Dayton, Ohio* does not have any relevance for linguistic theory or description (cf. Halliday 1991: 42; Kennedy 1998: 23). It may be true that some findings presented by corpus linguists over the years have been trivial, but rarely on the New York–Dayton, Ohio level. In recent years, however, corpus linguistics has become more theoretically advanced, and there are many more friendly contacts between the camps.

Since generative linguistics was so successful and dominant in the 1960s and 1970s, many early corpus linguists almost felt as if they had to work in secret cells. This was the case, for instance, with the loosely organised International Computer Archive of Modern English (ICAME; later amended to mean International Computer Archive of Modern and Medieval English). It was started in Oslo in 1977 at Stig Johansson's kitchen table by a number of Scandinavian, British and American scholars, and until the mid-nineties it did not advertise its meetings and accepted participants by invitation only. One of the founding fathers of ICAME was Jan Svartvik. In 1992 he presented the advantages of corpus linguistics in a preface to an influential collection of papers. His arguments are given here in abbreviated form:

- Corpus data are more objective than data based on introspection.
- Corpus data can easily be verified by other researchers, and researchers can share the same data instead of always compiling their own.
- Corpus data are needed for studies of variation between dialects, registers and styles.
- Corpus data provide the frequency of occurrence of linguistic items.
- Corpus data do not only provide illustrative examples, but are a theoretical resource.
- Corpus data give essential information for a number of applied areas, like language teaching and language technology (machine translation, speech synthesis etc.).
- Corpora provide the possibility of total accountability of linguistic features – the analyst should account for everything in the data, not just selected features.
- Computerised corpora give researchers all over the world access to the data.
- Corpus data are ideal for non-native speakers of the language. (Svartvik 1992: 8–10)

However, Svartvik also points out that it is crucial that the corpus linguist engages in careful manual analysis as well: mere figures are rarely enough. He stresses too that the quality of the corpus is important. Here we might add some further caveats:

- Since the number of possible sentences in a language is infinite, corpora will never be big enough to contain everything that is known by a speaker of a language.
- Some of the findings may indeed be trivial.
- The intuition of a native speaker will always be needed to identify what is grammatical and what is not.
- Corpora contain all kinds of mistakes, speech errors etc. which may have to be disregarded.
- You will always need a theory of language to know what to search for in a corpus and to explain what you find.

In recent years, the relations between corpus linguistics and other types of linguistics have improved. On the one hand, corpus linguists have become more theoretically sophisticated and aware of the pros and cons of corpora. For instance, Tognini-Bonelli (2001) argued for corpus-*driven* linguistics. According to this view, the researcher should start working with the data with as few preconceived ideas as possible, and then arrive at an analysis inductively. In corpus-*based* linguistics, on the other hand, corpora are used to test hypotheses based on already existing theories. Among scholars who call themselves corpus linguists there is a spectrum between these two poles.

Corpora are also used by many linguists who do not primarily call themselves corpus linguists; for them, corpora and corpus methodology are just a set of data and research tools among many others. For instance, within cognitive linguistics the notion of usage-based grammar is compatible with corpus studies, and there is corpus work in systemic functional linguistics, historical linguistics, grammaticalisation studies and semantics. Even scholars with a background in the generative paradigm now recognise the value of corpus work, at least for testing hypotheses, e.g. Wasow (2002: 163): "given the abundance of usage data at hand, plus the increasingly sophisticated search tools available, there is no good excuse for failing to test theoretical work against corpora". We will return to some of these areas in the following chapters, but now we turn to the different types of corpora.

1.6 Types of corpora

Over the years, linguists have compiled a large variety of corpora for various purposes, and the number of corpora is growing rapidly. Table 1.2 gives the number of corpora of the English language listed in August

Table 1.2 English-language corpora

Type of corpus	N
Written language	29
Spoken language	34
Historical	27
First language learning	3
Second and foreign language learning	19
Specialised corpora	45
Parsed corpora (treebanks)	11
Multimodal corpora (including sound and/or film)	11

Source: Based on David Lee's webpage http://tiny.cc/corpora, August 2008

2008 on a webpage on corpus linguistics. The figures in the table are approximate since some of the categories are overlapping.

In some cases, for copyright or other reasons, these corpora have remained the property of an individual researcher or of a particular institution, without being generally available to others. In the following highly selective survey, however, the main focus will be on important corpora which are availably to anybody, at a fee or without cost.

1.6.1 Spoken corpora

The Brown/Frown and LOB/FLOB corpora described above are typical of corpora whose aim it is to represent general language at a particular point in time. Even so, they only cover certain uses of the language which were chosen by the compilers, while others are left out. One important area which is often under-represented in general corpora is spoken language. After all, most people speak more than they write and listen to others talking more than they read. Due to the fact that it is technically complicated, and therefore also more expensive, the compilation of spoken corpora has always lagged behind that of written ones. The London-Lund Corpus of Spoken English (LLC) was one of the first that was made digital, and for a long time it remained the one most frequently used. It contains approximately 500,000 words, i.e. it is half the size of e.g. LOB. The speakers were mainly faculty, staff and students at University College, London (who were afterwards told that they had been recorded and had the chance to withdraw their participation). The tapes were originally transcribed on paper slips not unlike those used by Jespersen, and filed together with the written part of the survey corpus in filing cabinets, but in the 1970s the transcriptions of spoken language were transferred to magnetic tape in a project lead

```
A    1 I'm ‖not - ‖ÒH∎  2 ‖THÀNKS∎  ·  3 ‖not really ᴧCÒMFORTABLE∎  ·  4 ‖like
     THÍS∎
b    5 ‖[m̀]∎ - - -  6 you got a ‖CÓLD∎
A    7 - 'INÒ∎  ·  8 just a ‖bit ᴧSNÌFFY∎  9 cos I'm - I 'ÌÀM CÓLD∎  10 and I'll ‖be
     all right 'once I've warmed ÙP∎ -  11 do I ‖LÒOK as though I've got a ᴧCÓLD∎
b    12 no I ‖thought you SÒUNDED as if you were
A    13 ‖[m̀]∎ - - -  14 «I ‖always DÒ a bit actually∎»  15 ‖CHRÒNICALLY∎
b    16 - - - ‖there you ÁRE∎
A    17 - - - ‖ÒH∎  18 ‖SÙPER∎
b    19 - - - ‖pull your CHÀIR up ▷close if you WÁNT∎ -  20 ‖is it - ☆«sylls»☆
A    21 ☆‖YÈS∎  ·  22 'I'll be all 'right in a MÍNUTE∎☆  23 it's ‖just that I'm
b    24 · «‖what have you GÒT∎»
>A   23 ᴧSTÙPID∎  25 I ‖had [ə] about ᴧfive 'thousand BÒOKS∎ -  26 to ‖take back
     to 'Senate HÒUSE YÉSTERDAY∎ -  27 and I got ‖all the 'way 'through the
     CÒLLEGE∎  28 to ‖where the CÀR was∎  29 at the ‖parking meter at the ᴧÒTHER
     end∎  30 and ‖realized I'd 'left my · ᴧCÒAT∎  31 in my ‖LÒCKER∎  32 and I
     ☆‖just couldn't☆ FÁCE∎  33 going ‖all the
b    34 ☆‖[m̀]∎☆
>A   33 way ᴧBÀCK again∎  35 with ‖this great · you know my 'IÀRMS were
     ▷aching∎
b    36 ‖[m̀]∎
A    37 - and I thought ‖WÈLL∎  38 I'll ‖get it on ᴧTÙESDAY∎ -  39 it's a bit ‖SÌLLY∎
     40 cos I ‖NÈED it∎
b    41 · ‖[m̀]∎ ·  42 it's gone ‖very CÒLD∎  43 ‖HÀSN'T it∎
A    44 ‖[m̀]∎ - - -  45 it's ‖FRÈEZING∎
b    46 ‖[m̀]∎ -  47 ☆I'm «‖syll SỲLL∎»☆
A    48 ☆«you're ‖KNÌTTING∎»☆ ·  49 ( - laughs) ‖what are you KNÌTTING∎
     50 ‖that's 'not a 'tiny GÁRMENT∎
b    51 ‖NÒ∎
```

Figure 1.5 Excerpt from a transcribed conversation in the London-Lund Corpus.

Source: Svartvik and Quirk (1980: 83)

by Jan Svartvik at Lund University, Sweden. Figure 1.5 is an excerpt from one of the transcribed tape-recordings in a book printed from the electronic version (two female undergraduates are chatting). A key to the complicated prosodic notation is given in Figure 1.6.

As shown in the excerpt in Figure 1.5, the London-Lund Corpus contains detailed prosodic information, so that the (trained) reader can see the beginning and end of tone units, rising and falling intonation and combinations thereof, stress, pauses, overlaps (simultaneous talk) and so on. All this makes the text a bit difficult to read, even though a fair amount of information was left out in the digitalisation compared to the original notation on paper slips (including tempo, loudness and voice quality).

The Survey of English tapes on which LLC is based were made

	Book	Slip	Tape	
Text Number	**S.2.3** **S.3.1a**	S.2.3 S.3.1a		Text number; small letter denotes subtext (example)
Speaker	**A**	A		Speaker identity (example)
	>A	(A)		Speaker identity; speaker continues where he left off (example)
	A, B	A, B		A and B (example)
	A/B	A/B		A or B (example)
	VAR	various		Various speakers
	?	?		Speaker identity unknown
	a	NSA		Non-surreptitious speaker (example)
	☆yes☆ +yes+	*yes* +yes+	042 ⎱ 043 ⎰	Simultaneous talk
	(laughs)	(laughs)	040 041	Contextual comment
	«yes»	((yes))	040 040 041 041	Incomprehensible words
Tone unit	■	*	035	End of tone unit (TU)
	‖	/	094	Onset
	{yes}	[yes]	123 125	Subordinate TU
Nucleus	yĕs	yès	092	Fall
	yÉS	yés	047	Rise
	yēs	yēs	061	Level
	yĚs	yès yês	092 047	(Rise-) fall-rise
	yÊs	yès yês	047 092	(Fall-) rise-fall
	yĕs yÉS	yès yés	092 047	Fall-plus-rise
	yÉS yĕs	yés yès	047 092	Rise-plus-fall
Booster	▷ yes	˙ yes	095	Continuance
	△ yes	:yes	058	Higher than preceding syllable
	△ yes	!yes	033	Higher than preceding pitch-prominent syllable
	△ yes	!!yes	033 033	Very high
Stress	'yes	'yes	039	Normal
	ˈyes	ˈyes	034	Heavy
Pause	yes · yes	yes · yes	046	Brief pause (of one light syllable)
	yes — yes	yes — yes	045	Unit pause (of one stress unit or 'foot')
	- ·	- ·	045 046	
	- -	- -	045 045	Combinations of pause
	- - ·	- - ·	045 045 046	
	- - -	- - -	045 045 045	

Figure 1.6 Key to transcription symbols.
Source: Based on Svartvik and Quirk (1980: 21–22)

Kenneth:	Come upstairs and listen to the tape? Blinding tape! do you wanna hear it?
Cliff:	Can't be bothered.
Kenneth:	Come on Cliff listen. It's funny [man I te=]
Cliff:	[Bring it] down here.
Kenneth:	Nah. It's better you got them speakers. It's enough funny man I'm telling ya! Come upstairs, play on the hi-fi. I I, bet you any money you'll laugh ... <nv>sniff</ > ... <nv>laugh</ > (135602: 34–38)

Figure 1.7 Excerpt from COLT.

Source: Stenström et al (2002: 144)

surreptitiously, but this is now illegal, so later spoken corpora have had to be made using other methods. When the spoken component of the British National Corpus (BNC; more about this corpus below) was compiled in the early 1990s, two different methods were used. One half, approximately 5 million words, was made up of recordings from various public events like lectures, sermons, radio shows etc., while the other half was collected by supplying people with portable tape-recorders (so-called walkmans) and asking them to tape their everyday conversations. The self-taped recordings were made by people selected through a demographic sampling so that people of all ages and from many different regions took part to cover England geographically and also socially.

When Anna-Brita Stenström wanted to investigate London teenage speech and started compiling the Corpus of London Teenage Speech (COLT) in 1993, she provided teenagers with a portable tape-recorder and a microphone in the same way. One might think that the microphone would inhibit people from speaking naturally, but numerous similar experiments show that people soon forget that they are being taped, or ignore it. In any case, the language on the COLT tapes is far from inhibited, as anyone can ascertain by listening to the tapes or reading the transcripts. An example is given in Figure 1.7.

We can see in the excerpt that the teenagers are aware of being taped but that the language seems natural enough (or *enough natural*, as 13-year-old Kenneth might say). In many other conversations the speakers use vulgar and sexually explicit language without inhibition.

These three spoken corpora thus differ in their coverage: LLC contains mainly academics in London talking about academic and general matters, BNC both informal conversation and various types of more formal speech by people of different ages and education in different parts of Britain, and COLT London teenagers talking to each other about boyfriends and girlfriends, parties and fights and so on. There are also publicly available corpora of transcribed conversation for Australian English (Australian Corpus of English, or ACE) and New Zealand English (Wellington Spoken Corpus, or WSC). For AmE the situation has been more problematic: there is the 5-million-word Longman Spoken American Corpus, which is used by some researchers but is not generally available, and the Santa Barbara Corpus, which is still not completed, but there has really been nothing else to be compared to LLC, the spoken component of the BNC and COLT. However, in 2008 the large Corpus of Contemporary American English (COCA) was made available, containing 78.8 million words of spoken English (the figure is from December 2008; the corpus is continually added to). The spoken language consists of transcripts of unscripted conversation from radio and TV programmes, so it is not fully comparable with the private conversations of the LLC and the BNC but more so with the parts of those corpora that come from public speaking.

The cost of recording and transcribing has made linguists resort to already available sources, for instance interviews which were recorded and transcribed for sociological research, transcriptions of radio and television shows etc. In the United States big corpora of telephone conversations in many languages have been collected. Such sources can supply linguists with larger amounts of data which can be very useful, and they have also been used in, for instance, the Bank of English (BoE; see below) and for the spoken component of the COCA, mentioned above. On the other hand there is the drawback that these transcripts are made for content rather than form, and that in the radio and television transcripts there is sometimes very little personal information about some of the participants.

1.6.2 General corpora

As we have seen, there are written-only and spoken-only general corpora, but there are also general corpora that contain both, such as the BNC, the BoE and COCA.

The Bank of English (BoE)
The BoE grew out of a corpus started in 1980 to be used for the making of the *Cobuild Dictionary* (Cobuild stands for Collins Birmingham University International Language Database). It has gone through several phases and has variously been referred to as the Cobuild Corpus and the Birmingham Corpus. While the original Cobuild corpus of 7.3 million words was carefully put together to be balanced between

different genres of spoken and written British English (BrE) and AmE it later developed into a so-called monitor corpus which is continually added to. The latest figure I have seen is 650 million words. The corpus is not freely available but can be used by researchers in Birmingham.

The British National Corpus (BNC)

The BNC is the result of a major commercial and academic project which started in 1991 and was run by Oxford University Press, Longman, Chambers, the British Library, Oxford University and Lancaster University. It is a 100-million-word corpus aiming at being a balanced representation of BrE in the 1990s, and is thus similar in aim to but 100 times bigger than the LOB corpus of 1961. In contrast to the earlier "standard" corpora it includes 10 per cent spoken language (10 million words), but this is hardly a true picture of all the language used by British people in a day or a year. Among the written texts, 25% are fiction and 75% non-fiction. The non-fiction covers a large spectrum of subjects in proportions roughly based on the number of books published in these areas. Texts were collected not only from books but also from periodicals, brochures and unpublished material, and care was taken to include material considered to be of "high", "middle" and "low" style. A major difference between the BNC and the Brown family corpora is that the BNC consists of longer text samples, often between 40,000 and 50,000 words. This is considered to be an advantage since texts to some extent contain different vocabulary and even different constructions at the beginning, in the middle and at the end. Its size and the care with which this corpus was compiled and documented, as well as its general availability through various free interfaces, make it a favourite with many linguists. For each example from the BNC quoted in the present book, the source text will be identified by means of the three-character code used in the corpus, e.g. '(BNC B7H)'.

The American National Corpus (ANC)

One drawback with the BNC is that it contains just BrE, and many researchers have wished for an American parallel to be able to make comparisons, just as between Brown and LOB and Frown and FLOB. And of course AmE is the single largest variety of native English and deserves to be investigated in its own right. In 1998, a number of scholars therefore proposed that an American National Corpus should be created, and started compiling it. The ANC is funded by a consortium of publishers and computer companies and shipped its first instalment of 11 million words in 2003. When completed, the ANC is planned to contain "at least" 100 million words, but unfortunately it will not be structured along the same lines as the BNC and therefore will not be directly comparable with the British corpus. So far (in August 2008) 22 million words have been released and the future of the project looks a bit uncertain.

Corpus of Contemporary American English (COCA)

This freely available corpus was created by Mark Davies at Brigham Young University and appeared on the scene in 2008 after only a year of preparation. It is an excellent, free-of-charge, user-friendly tool that offers many opportunities for interesting research. It contains 385 million words (in December 2008), is organised in sections of 20 million words per year from 1990 onwards, and will go on being expanded by 20 million words per year. The sources are American TV, radio, books, magazines, newspapers and journals, divided into five registers of equal size: (1) spoken (mainly transcribed conversation from television and radio), (2) fiction, (3) popular magazines, (4) newspapers (various sections) and (5) academic journals from a number of different fields. The COCA is an example of a new and promising way of creating large corpora by downloading texts from the web.

The International Corpus of English (ICE)

ICE was initiated by Sidney Greenbaum, then director of the Survey of English Usage, London, in 1988 with the aim of creating a number of 1-million-word corpora from countries all over the world where English is spoken as a first or second language, in order to make comparisons between these varieties possible. The size and the aims are thus similar to those of the Brown family, but the ICE corpora are unique in that they prioritise the spoken language: they contain 60% spoken and only 40% written material. The compilation of the corpora is the responsibility of research groups in various parts of the world, and not all the over 20 subcorpora planned have yet been completed. Table 1.3 lists those completed by 2008.

Teams of linguists are at the moment working on ICE corpora of English from the following countries: Canada, Fiji, Ireland, Jamaica, Malaysia, Malta, Nigeria, Pakistan, South Africa, Sri Lanka and the USA.

The set of ICE subcorpora provides a unique means to compare grammatical structures and certain frequent lexical items, but just as for the Brown family corpora, the size is too small for much work on lexis and on infrequent grammatical constructions. In addition, ICE-GB is one of the few parsed corpora which are easily available (more about parsing in section 2.7.2 below).

Table 1.3 ICE corpora completed by 2008

Name	Variety
ICE-GB	British English
ICE-NZ	New Zealand English
ICE East Africa	Kenyan and Tanzanian English
ICE India	Indian English
ICE Hong Kong	Hong Kong English
ICE Singapore	Singaporean English
ICE Philippines	Philippine English

1.6.3 Specialised corpora

The general corpora described so far can be used when you want to find out something about the language in general, since they aim to give a picture of the whole language. In most of them you can also restrict your searches to certain subcorpora, genres or registers, to study for instance academic language or the language of sports journalism. In many cases, however, researchers find it practical or necessary to create specialised corpora for the particular research questions they have, and sometimes they have made these corpora available to other scholars as well. I will mention a few such specialised corpora here.

The Michigan Corpus of Academic Spoken English (MICASE)

MICASE is a 1.8-million-word corpus of recorded and transcribed spoken American academic English collected at the University of Michigan 1997–2002. It is freely available on the web and can be searched by means of a dedicated search engine. In your searches you can specify a large number of parameters, so that for instance you can study the development of students' academic language from their freshman year to their senior year at university, differences between male and female students, or differences in the language of different situations like interviews, tutorials, supervision, lectures or classroom interaction.

The International Corpus of Learner English (ICLE)

At many universities all over the world researchers collect corpora containing spoken and written language produced by learners on various levels. The best-known project is the International Corpus of Learner English (ICLE). ICLE consists of a number of subcorpora of about 200,000 words of written English produced by learners of English in many different countries. So far, subcorpora containing texts written by English learners having the following first languages have been completed: Bulgarian, Czech, Dutch, Finnish, French, German, Italian, Japanese, Norwegian, Polish, Russian, Spanish and Swedish. The texts are student essays of roughly similar types (argumentative or expository), collected independently by teams in each country. The corpus makes it possible to compare the so-called interlanguage (i.e. the version of English that the learners have internalised and use in their writing) of learners with different native languages, and to see if they make different mistakes due to interference from their first language. Some very interesting research has come out of this, but one has to remember that the subcorpora are quite small and that there are some differences in the characteristics of the tasks given to students in different countries. The collection of subcorpora also contains a native speaker component, the Louvain Corpus of Native English Student Essays (LOCNESS), which can be used as a sort of standard to compare with the non-native data. One of the main purposes of the ICLE corpora and many similar ones that are being collected at universities around the world is to analyse learner performance in order to improve language teaching.

1.6.4 Historical (diachronic) corpora

Linguists are interested in how languages change over time, and to be able to study such change over longer periods they have always had to compare older texts with modern ones. This was traditionally done by manually perusing old manuscripts or text editions, but that work can now be complemented by work based on diachronic corpora. In a sense, the paired American and British Brown/Frown and LOB/FLOB corpora constitute diachronic corpora even though the time span is just thirty years at the moment. They will be even more useful when they are extended backwards in time to cover the series 1901-1931-1961-1991 (and forwards to 2021!). Similarly, newspaper CD-ROMs and other text archives which will be mentioned below can be used for diachronic studies. However, there are also a number of truly historical corpora which contain texts from older periods of English.

The Helsinki corpora
Pioneering work in the area of historical corpora was carried out in Helsinki by Matti Rissanen and his collaborators. Between 1984 and 1991 they compiled the Helsinki Corpus of English Texts: Diachronic Part. It contains 400 samples of text types such as diaries, letters, plays, sermons and legal documents from almost 1,000 years between 770 and 1700.

The production of historical corpora at Helsinki has continued, and there are now also the Corpus of Early English Correspondence, the Corpus of Middle English Medical Texts and The Corpus of Older Scots. We will return to some of these corpora in Chapter 9.

Lampeter Corpus of Early Modern English Tracts

This is a corpus of Early Modern English consisting of 120 texts from 1640 to 1740 taken from tracts and pamphlets available at the Founder's Library, University of Wales, Lampeter, and compiled by scholars from the University of Chemnitz, Germany. It can be freely downloaded from the Oxford Text Archives.

1.6.5 Parallel and multilingual corpora

All of the corpora mentioned so far contain only English-language texts. There are, however, also a growing number of corpora containing two or several languages. Usually they contain originals and their translations (which in translation studies are called source texts and target texts) or similar text types in different languages. Such corpora can be used both for comparative linguistic studies and for translation studies, but since this book is only about English we will not refer to parallel corpora again. For those who are interested, there are some references below under "Further reading".

1.6.6 Dictionaries as corpora

Electronic versions of dictionaries can be searched and used as corpora, but only if they contain authentic examples as illustrations. This is the case with historical dictionaries like the *Dictionary of Old English* (*DOE*, under construction at the University of Toronto), the *Middle English Dictionary* (*MED*) and the *Oxford English Dictionary* (*OED*). They contain a large number of short illustrative text excerpts which can be searched as a kind of corpus. The *MED* is freely available on the net, while the *DOE* and the *OED* have to be purchased on a CD-ROM or as a library service (the *OED* especially is available at many university libraries throughout the world). The *OED* comprises 2.5 million quotations from over 1,000 years, and it has been estimated that these contain 25–35 million words (Hoffmann 2004; Mair 2004:124). To a certain extent the *OED* is biased towards particular periods, genres and famous authors and can therefore be considered to be neither representative nor balanced. Still, it is a very useful complement to other, smaller historical corpora.

1.6.7 Text archives as corpora

Text databases are often called text archives rather than corpora, to indicate that they are collections of text which are put together for their own sake (i.e. their literary value or information content), and that they are not meant to be balanced in any way. However, they are often used for linguistic investigations and they can of course also be used by individual researchers to compile corpora of their own. Good examples of this are the freely available Corpus of Late Modern English Texts (CLMET) and Corpus of English Novels (CEN), which were compiled from such sources by Hendrik De Smet (2005). Text archives are often in compressed form so you have to unzip them after downloading. They are also normally untagged and you need a separate concordancing program like WordSmith Tools (Scott 2004) to search them.

Newspapers on line or on CD-ROM

Complete years of many newspapers can be bought on CD-ROM and are sometimes available in university libraries. Each year of a newspaper usually consists of 20 million to 50 million words, and since a paper contains many different kinds of text (news and sports reporting, commentary, feature articles, reviews, editorials etc.), it has become quite popular to use newspapers as data. However, the CD-ROMs are provided by different publishers and it is sometimes complicated to make linguistic searches on them. The CD-ROMs are also fairly expensive, so many researchers prefer to download material from the thousands of newspapers from all over the world that are available online and build their own corpus. This, however, takes some computer skills and a separate concordancing program to sort the data.

The Time Magazine Corpus

The Time Magazine Corpus (from here on the Time Corpus) gives free access to the *Time* archive 1923–2006. It is different from all the journals and newspapers that are available as text databases on CD-ROM or online in that it is available without cost, through a user-friendly web interface with a number of useful concordancing features created by Mark Davies. Since results can be specified decade for decade, it is a very handy tool for studying changes in AmE in the twentieth century. This corpus will be used frequently in this book.

The Oxford Text Archives (OTA)

The Oxford Text Archives (OTA) is an organisation that stores several thousand electronic texts and corpora in English and other languages.

Here you can find books by individual authors, the Bible and many standard reference works, the majority of which can be downloaded without cost. In this way it is possible to compile a corpus of a certain period or genre. OTA also stores and distributes whole corpora, like the Lampeter Corpus mentioned above.

Project Gutenberg

Project Gutenberg is similar to OTA in that it provides electronic access to many fiction and non-fiction texts (over 25,000 titles), but different in that it is based on voluntary work. Anyone can upload the text of, for instance, a literary, philosophical or religious text as long as it is old enough to be out of copyright, which means that it was published before 1923 or that seventy years have passed since the death of the author. The nature of the set-up means that one cannot be 100 per cent certain of the quality of the text versions that are accessible, but for most linguistic purposes it is quite sufficient.

1.6.8 The web as corpus

One of the most exciting corpus developments in the first decade of the twenty-first century is the exploitation of the world wide web as a source for linguistic investigations. We will look at occasional examples of this throughout this book and devote all of Chapter 10 to this new and expanding field.

1.7 Very large and quite small corpora

Is there an ideal size for a corpus? While general corpora tend to get bigger and bigger, new, small corpora of special areas keep being made. Graeme Kennedy (1998) has said that corpora tend to be either too small or too big: either you get too few examples of what you are looking for, or far too many. The key, then, is to get the right size (and of course the right type) for the particular question you want to answer. This is often difficult to know in advance. For the most frequent structures in spoken and written English, corpora of a million words often suffice. For less frequent structures, 100 million words or more may be needed. For lexical studies on word formation or phraseology, 500 million words or more might be ideal. It is therefore necessary to choose the right corpus for each research project (or to compile a new one). Alternatively, and less attractively, you have to adjust your research question to the corpora you have available. If you think you need a really big corpus, you may need to use text archives or the net.

1.8 Summary

In this chapter we have covered a lot of background information which was necessary before we move on to the more technical questions in Chapter 2 and the examples of studies in the following chapters. We started by discussing the rationale for using corpora in the description and analysis of the English language and surveyed a little bit of the history of corpus linguistics. Some criticisms of corpus linguistics were also mentioned. We then looked at different types of corpora including spoken and written corpora, general corpora, specialised corpora, historical corpora, parallel and multilingual corpora, dictionaries as corpora, text archives as corpora, newspaper CD-ROMs as corpora and the web as corpus, ending with a short discussion of very large and quite small corpora. A general conclusion that can be drawn from this chapter is that there has been a very dynamic development in the field of corpus linguistics over the last fifty years, and that for most, if not all, investigations you want to make, there is now a suitable corpus available.

Study questions

1. What are the main advantages and disadvantages of using corpora for linguistic research?
2. What are a concordance and a concordance line? Why are concordances useful?
3. What are the extra complications with corpora of spoken language?
4. Why is it not always possible to compare data from different corpora?
5. What is the difference between corpora proper and text archives?

Corpus exercises

Hands-on exercises related to this chapter are available at the following web address:
http://www.euppublishing.com/series/ETOTELAdvanced/Lindquist.

Further reading

Jespersen's methods are described in Jespersen (1938/1995) and Meyer (2008). The art of reading concordances can be learnt from the do-it-yourself guide provided by Sinclair (2003) and in Wynne (2008). The early days of corpus linguistics and the beginnings of ICAME are described in Svartvik (2007) and Johansson (2008).

For cognitive corpus studies, see Mukherjee (2004) and Gries and Stefanowitsch (2006); for corpus studies in systemic functional linguistics, see Thompson and Hunston (2006); and for corpora and grammaticalisation studies, see Lindquist and Mair (2004). The compilation of the BNC is described in Aston and Burnard (1998) and Hoffmann et al. (2008). General questions of spoken corpora are discussed in Leech, et al. (1995).

Theoretical and practical aspects of parallel corpora are dealt with in Johansson and Oksefjell (1998) and Aijmer (2008), and surveys of the use of corpora in contrastive linguistics are given in Johansson (2003, 2007). Text archives as corpora are dealt with in Hundt (2008). Practical tips about using newspaper corpora are given in Minugh (2000). Granger (1998) contains a number of papers based on the ICLE learner corpora, and Granger (2008) gives an overview of learner corpora.

Up-to-date information on all the corpora mentioned in this chapter and many more, including parallel and multilingual corpora, can be found on David Lee's webpage, *http://tiny.cc/corpora*. A very comprehensive survey is also given in Xiao (2008). Baker et al. (2006) contains brief definitions of many terms related to corpus linguistics.

Survey articles by leading experts on many other issues in corpus compilation and corpus research can be found in Lüdeling and Kytö (2008, 2009). This handbook appeared too late to be taken into account to any great extent in the present volume; however, some references to it have been made when relevant.

2 Counting, calculating and annotating

2.1 Qualitative and quantitative method

The great advantage of computers over human beings is the speed and accuracy with which computers can search for material in huge databases and collections of text, manipulate data and make calculations of various sorts. In the present chapter we will see how this can be exploited in linguistic research. But first we need to say a few words about the difference between qualitative and quantitative methods.

It is common to distinguish two main types of scientific method in linguistics (and in general): qualitative and quantitative. If you use a qualitative method you make close analyses of, for example, individual texts or grammatical constructions that you know from introspection or get from other sources. Through these analyses you arrive at theories about language by induction, or test hypotheses which you have set up in advance. Typical proponents of the qualitative method are the schools of generative linguistics emanating from Chomsky's work, but here also belong, at least traditionally, many other schools of linguistics.

Quantitative methods, on the other hand, as the name implies, count things and use frequencies and percentages to describe language and to formulate hypotheses and theories. There were quantitative studies before computers, but since hand-counting is hard work they were not very common and could never be very large in scope. With the arrival of computers, however, it became much easier to deal with large masses of text, and corpus linguistics was born. Corpus linguists have sometimes been accused of just counting what can be counted, regardless of whether it is linguistically interesting or not. It may be true that some of us have been guilty of such misdemeanours, but on the whole one now sees less and less of such tendencies.

But it is important to stress that all quantitative studies also must include an element of qualitative method. First of all, in order to be able to decide what to count, you need categories, which must be based on a qualitative analysis. For instance, even if you decide to do something as superficially simple as counting words per sentence in broadsheets (quality papers) and tabloids (popular papers) to see if there is a difference, you have to decide what qualifies as a word (more about this below) and what qualifies as a sentence (e.g. is a one-word heading like *Obituaries* a sentence or not?). Similarly, if you are interested in the frequency of different types of adverbials you probably need to make a thorough analysis of what adverbials are before you start.

Second, most good corpus studies do not stop with frequency tables and statistical analyses. In order to make the best use of the figures, it is vital to go back to individual examples from the corpus to look at the reality behind the figures. For instance, a surprisingly high frequency of a particular construction in one part of the corpus can often be explained by unforeseen circumstances which are disclosed by a close analysis. We will see examples of this further on in this book

Finally, corpora can be used as sources of illustrative examples for studies which are basically qualitative. A number of different terms have been created to describe these various approaches: 'corpus-driven' if you start with as few preconceived theoretical concepts as possible, 'corpus-based' if you use corpora and quantitative methods to investigate a problem which is formulated within a particular linguistic theory (this is the most common type), and 'corpus-aided' or 'corpus-supported' if you use corpora mainly to find illustrative examples.

In the rest of this chapter we will look at some examples of quantitative investigations.

2.2 Frequency

Let us start with the intuitively simple concept of frequency. What are the most frequent words in the English language? This can be good to know for various reasons. Many applications in language technology make use of frequency information. One example is the texting program in your mobile phone which "guesses" which word you intend when you touch a series of keys, each of them having at least three characters associated with them. When I touch the following keys on my mobile: GHI + MNO + TUV, the first alternative suggested by the text program is *got* rather than the less frequent *hot*, the abbreviation *gov*, or any nonexisting but possible words like *int* or *hov*. This is because *got* is the most frequent of the alternatives, and this saves my thumb some work!

Furthermore, teachers and textbook writers use knowledge about frequencies when they decide in which order they are going to present new words to pupils and students (and the same goes for the frequency of different constructions). Frequency is not the only factor they take into account, but it is certainly relevant. In the old days, they had to trust their intuition and common sense. But it has been shown that native speakers often have rather vague notions about the relative frequency of different words. If you are a native speaker of English, you probably have a feeling that *hand* is more frequent than *toe* because we have more opportunities to talk about hands than about toes. But what about *hand* and *eye?* And what verbs and adjectives are the most frequent in the language? Which is most frequent, *big* or *large?* The answers to these questions are given below in Tables 2.3 and 2.5.

Before computers and corpora, frequency counts had to be made by hand and were very laborious; now they can be made almost with a mouse click. The following tables are from frequency tables based on the contents of the 100 million word BNC, which are freely available on several different websites. Table 2.1 shows the fifty most frequent words in the corpus. The column 'POS tag' gives the part of speech (word class); a key is given below the table. We will deal in more detail with POS tags in section 2.7.1 below.

Note that some word forms occur several times, distinguished by different POS tags, like *to*, which is both an infinitive marker at rank 6 and a preposition at rank 10. This illustrates the usefulness of POS tags – without them these two *to*'s would have been counted together, as would for instance the modal verb *can* (rank 48) and the noun *can* 'container' (with a much lower rank, not in the table).

Another observation that can be made is that all the words on the top fifty list are so-called function words: pronouns, prepositions, conjunctions, determiners, modal verbs. There are no words from the classes of content words: nouns, adjectives, adverbs and lexical verbs. Most of these function words will occur on the top fifty list no matter which corpus the calculations are based on, but the rank order may differ somewhat depending on the nature of the texts. Content words, on the other hand, vary greatly depending on the type of text.

In Table 2.1, *be* and *was* are counted as separate words, but in a sense they are of course instances of the same word, just as *walk* and *walked* can be said to be the same word, only used in different tenses. In order to allow for this fact, a corpus can be 'lemmatised'. This means that all word forms which are just different inflected forms of the same word are grouped with that word, so that for instance the verb forms *kick*, *kicks*, *kicked* and *kicking* are grouped together as the lemma *kick* (lemmas are often written in small caps: KICK). The same goes for irregular verbs: *sing*, *sang* and *sung* all belong to the lemma SING. Lemmatisation can affect all word classes: *car* and *cars* make up the noun lemma CAR; *big*, *bigger* and

Table 2.1 The fifty most frequent words in the BNC

Rank	Word	POS tag	N
1	the	at0	6,187,267
2	of	prf	2,941,444
3	and	cjc	2,682,863
4	a	at0	2,126,369
5	in	prp	1,812,609
6	to	to0	1,620,850
7	it	pnp	1,089,186
8	is	vbz	998,389
9	was	vbd	923,948
10	to	prp	917,579
11	I	pnp	884,599
12	for	prp	833,360
13	you	pnp	695,498
14	he	pnp	681,255
15	be	vbi	662,516
16	with	prp	652,027
17	on	prp	647,344
18	that	cjt	628,999
19	by	prp	507,317
20	at	prp	478,162
21	are	vbb	470,943
22	not	xx0	462,486
23	this	dt0	461,945
24	but	cjc	454,096
25	's	pos	442,545
26	they	pnp	433,441
27	his	dps	426,896
28	from	prp	413,532
29	had	vhd	409,012
30	she	pnp	380,257
31	which	dtq	372,031
32	or	cjc	370,808
33	we	pnp	358,039
34	an	at0	343,063
35	n't	xx0	332,839
36	's	vbz	325,048
37	were	vbd	322,824
38	that	dt0	286,913
39	been	vbn	268,723
40	have	vhb	268,490
41	their	dps	260,919
42	has	vhz	259,431

Table 2.1 (continued)

Rank	Word	POS tag	N
43	would	vm0	255,188
44	what	dtq	249,466
45	will	vm0	244,822
46	there	ex0	239,460
47	if	cjs	237,089
48	can	vm0	234,386
49	all	dt0	227,737
50	her	dps	218,258

Note: Key to POS (part-of-speech) tags: at0 = article, cjc = coordinating conjunction, cjs = subordinating conjunction, cjt = *that* when it introduces a relative clause, dps = possessive determiner, dt0 = general determiner, dtq = *wh*-determiner, ex0 = existential *there*, pnp = personal pronoun, pos = possessive marker, prf = the preposition *of*, prp = preposition, to0 = infinitive marker, vbb = present tense form of *be*, vbd = past tense form of *be*, vbi = infinitive form of *be*, vbn = past participle form of *be*, vbz = the -*s* form of *be*, vhb = the finite base form of *have*, vhd = the past tense form of *have*, vhz = the -*s* form of *have*, vm0 = modal auxiliary, xx0 = negative particle.

Source: Based on Adam Kilgarriff's webpage 'BNC database and word frequency lists', http://www.kilgariff.co.uk/bnc-readme.html

biggest the adjective lemma BIG. Normally, the forms in a lemma must belong to the same word class, so the noun *kick* and its plural *kicks* make up a different lemma from the verb KICK – we could call them KICK$_n$ and KICK$_v$. Table 2.2 shows the fifty most frequent lemmas in the BNC. As can be seen, lemmatisation creates a slightly different list.

As mentioned already, the relative frequency of content words is more dependent on the type of corpus than the frequency of the function words. In the BNC, the most frequent noun lemmas are the ones given in Table 2.3. Note that in this table the frequencies are given per million words.

Returning to the questions about frequencies which were put at the beginning of this chapter, we can see in Table 2.3 that the most frequent body-part nouns in the BNC are *hand* (532 per million), *head* (402) and, in third place, *eye* (392). The three most frequent nouns overall are *time*, *year* and *people*.

Let us now look at the top fifty verbs, which are given in Table 2.4. In Table 2.4 auxiliaries are not separated from so-called lexical verbs, and we can see that six out of the top seven verbs are auxiliaries, which are a kind of function words in the verb category. The auxiliaries in the table have been italicised. Looking at lexical verbs, the ten most frequent are

Table 2.2 The fifty most frequent lemmas in the BNC

Rank	Word	Word class	N
1	the	det	6,187,267
2	be	v	4,239,632
3	of	prep	3,093,444
4	and	conj	2,687,863
5	a	det	2,186,369
6	in	prep	1,924,315
7	to	infinitive marker	1,620,850
8	have	v	1,375,636
9	it	pron	1,090,186
10	to	prep	1,039,323
11	for	prep	887,877
12	i	pron	884,599
13	that	conj	760,399
14	you	pron	695,498
15	he	pron	681,255
16	on	prep	680,739
17	with	prep	675,027
18	do	v	559,596
19	at	prep	534,162
20	by	prep	517,171
21	not	adv	465,486
22	this	det	461,945
23	but	conj	459,622
24	from	prep	434,532
25	they	pron	433,441
26	his	det	426,896
27	that	det	384,313
28	she	pron	380,257
29	or	conj	373,808
30	which	det	372,031
31	as	conj	364,164
32	we	pron	358,039
33	an	det	343,063
34	say	v	333,518
35	will	modal	297,281
36	would	modal	272,345
37	can	modal	266,116
38	if	conj	261,089
39	their	det	260,919
40	go	v	249,540
41	what	det	249,466
42	there	pron	239,460

Table 2.2 (continued)

Rank	Word	Word class	N
43	all	det	230,737
44	get	v	220,940
45	her	det	218,258
46	make	v	217,268
47	who	pron	205,432
48	as	prep	201,968
49	out	adv	201,819
50	up	adv	195,426

Source: Based on Adam Kilgarriff's webpage 'BNC database and word frequency lists', http://www.kilgarriff.co.uk.bnc-readme.html

Table 2.3 The fifty most frequent noun lemmas in the BNC

Noun	N per million words
time	1,833
year	1,639
people	1,256
way	1,108
man	1,003
day	940
thing	776
child	710
Mr	673
government	670
work	653
life	645
woman	631
system	619
case	613
part	612
group	607
number	606
world	600
house	598
area	585
company	579
problem	565
service	549
place	534
hand	532

Table 2.3 (continued)

Noun	N per million words
party	529
school	529
country	486
point	484
week	476
member	471
end	458
state	440
word	438
family	428
fact	426
head	402
month	398
side	398
business	394
night	393
eye	392
home	390
question	390
information	387
power	385
change	384
per_cent	384
interest	376

Note: Some multi-word units, such as *per cent*, are counted as one lemma in the BNC. This is marked by an underscore between the words.
Source: Based on Leech et al. (2001)

say, get, make, go, see, know, take, think, come and *give*. What do these verbs have in common? Most of them are fairly general and vague in meaning and can occur in a number of different contexts and phrases. Later on, we will take a closer look at some of these contexts (note the use of *take* in the phrase *take a look* in this sentence!).

In the next table, Table 2.5, we see the most frequent adjectives.

Few people would probably guess that *other* is the most frequent adjective in English, since for most of us prototypical adjectives are descriptive ones like the adjectives that come after *other* in the list: *good, new, old* etc. Referring to our question at the beginning, it turns out that *large* is 39% more frequent than *big* in the BNC (471 against 338 tokens per million words).

Table 2.4 The fifty most frequent verb lemmas in the BNC: auxiliaries italicised

Verb lemma	N per million words
be	42,277
have	13,655
do	5,594
will	3,357
say	3,344
would	2,904
can	2,672
get	2,210
make	2,165
go	2,078
see	1,920
know	1,882
take	1,797
could	1,683
think	1,520
come	1,512
give	1,284
look	1,151
may	1,135
should	1,112
use	1,071
find	990
want	945
tell	775
must	723
put	700
mean	677
become	675
leave	647
work	646
need	627
feel	624
seem	624
might	614
ask	610
show	598
try	552
call	535
provide	505
keep	505
hold	481
turn	465

Table 2.4 (continued)

Verb lemma	N per million words
follow	460
begin	440
bring	439
like	424
going	417
help	416
start	414
run	406

Source: Based on Leech et al. (2001)

Table 2.5 The fifty most frequent adjective lemmas in the BNC

Adjective lemma	N per million words
other	1,336
good	1,276
new	1,154
old	648
great	635
high	574
small	518
different	484
large	471
local	445
social	422
important	392
long	392
young	379
national	376
British	357
right	354
early	353
possible	342
big	338
little	306
political	306
able	304
late	302
general	301
full	289

Table 2.5 (continued)

Adjective lemma	N per million words
far	288
low	286
public	285
available	272
bad	264
main	245
sure	241
clear	239
major	238
economic	236
only	231
likely	228
real	227
black	226
particular	223
international	221
special	220
difficult	220
certain	220
open	219
whole	216
white	207
free	200
short	198

Source: Based on Leech et al. (2001)

The frequency figures given in Tables 2.1–2.5 tell us how many instances of a particular word or lemma there are in the corpus. Linguists call this the number of 'tokens'. The question "How many words are there in the BNC?" can have two answers. If we ask about the number of tokens, the answer is: approximately 100 million. We must say approximately, for the answer depends on our definition of word. One problem area is how to deal with compounds. Is *blow torch* two words when it is written with a space – *blow torch* – and one word when it is written solidly – *blowtorch*? And what about when it is written with a hyphen: *blow-torch*? There are no final answers to these questions; they are matters of definition. Incidentally, the frequencies for these forms in the written component of the BNC are: *blowtorch* 19, *blow torch* 7, *blow-torch* 3. For AmE, the written component of the COCA gives the following figures: *blowtorch* 93, *blow torch* 16, *blow-torch* 9. The frequencies

Table 2.6 Word forms in the BNC

	N
Word forms occurring 10 times or more	124,002
Word forms occurring 5–9 times	62,041
Word forms occurring 4 times	28,770
Word forms occurring 3 times	46,459
Word forms occurring twice	98,774
Word forms occurring once	397,041
Total	757,087

Source: Based on Leech et al. (2001: 9)

of the spellings here suggest that *blowtorch* is becoming an established compound (especially in AmE). Note that the transcribed spoken components of the corpora cannot be used for this kind of argument: the spellings found there depend on the transcribers' personal preferences, or on general instructions given to them.

If we ask about 'types' rather than 'tokens', on the other hand, we are interested in how many *different* words the corpus contains. According to one count, there are 757,087 different word forms in the BNC. More than half of those only occur once, as can be seen in Table 2.6.

Note that the category of word forms occurring only once especially includes thousands of odd abbreviations and strings of characters and misspelt words, many proper names such as *al-Hashemi*, scientific substance names such as *3,3-diaminobenzidinetetrahydrochloride*, figures and measurements such as *39-metre-high*, and foreign words such as *ankus* in (1).

(1) For example, many Westerners are indignant when seeing an Indian mahout raise high his **ankus** (an iron rod with a hook at one end) and bring it down smartly on the head of his inattentive elephant. (BNC B7H)

There are also large numbers of very rare English words, such as the adjective *ajangle* 'jangling' in (2) and infrequent compounds like the verb *alarm-quack* in (3).

(2) Alix brought a chrome bowl out of an open cupboard, set it down **ajangle** with instruments of torture and turned on the generator for her machines. (BNC AD9)

(3) We were near enough to compare the drake's greenish-yellow bill, with his mate's orange (it is the female mallard which **alarm-quacks** the loudest). (BNC F9H)

In this section we have discussed various ways of calculating the frequency of individual words or word forms in a corpus. In later chapters we will study the frequency of combinations of words (collocations, Chapter 4) and more or less fixed phrases (Chapter 5).

2.3 Comparing frequencies

Knowing the frequency of something in a particular corpus, like a certain word, is fine for some purposes, as mentioned in the previous section. But most of the time we are interested in how frequencies differ between corpora or parts of corpora (usually called subcorpora). Such comparisons can be made to investigate a number of phenomena, for instance differences between the language of men and women (see Chapter 8), the development of language over time (see Chapter 9) or the differences between regional varieties (see Chapter 10). In order to be able to draw safe conclusions from such comparisons, a certain level of statistical awareness is needed.

Very often we feel that the figures "speak for themselves" – it seems obvious that there is a difference between two numbers or that a particular curve indicates a clear change or tendency. Although this is certainly true in many cases, there are also instances where figures can be somewhat misleading. This is often due to the fact that the total number of tokens is too low. In statistics, several methods have therefore been developed to measure the 'statistical significance' of quantitative findings, i.e. the likelihood that the differences we see in the figures are due to real differences in the world and not just to chance. The degree to which corpus linguists use such methods varies greatly. This is probably due to the fact that courses in statistics have not traditionally been part of the training of language scholars, as they have, for instance, in the social and natural sciences. Recently, some researchers have complained about the low level of statistical expertise in corpus studies (e.g. Gries 2006) and called for greater sophistication. The situation is likely to improve in the future even if it is the case that the statistical experts themselves do not fully agree about which statistical measures are most suitable for corpus studies. Some of the methods are quite complicated, at least if you want to understand the mathematical reasoning behind them, and we will not discuss them in this introductory book. There are two kinds of statistics, however, that everyone using corpus data should know about. The first is significance testing, which tests whether observed patterns and figures are meaningful, and the second is the measurement of the strength of lexical associations. We will deal with the most frequently used measure for significance testing, the chi square

Table 2.7 Frequency of *but* and *however* in COCA, 1990–1994, compared with 2005–2007: per million words

	1990–1994	2005–2007	Total
but	4,443	4,466	8,909
however	410	314	724
Total	4,853	4,780	9,633

test, here and look at a number of tests for lexical associations in the next chapter.

With the chi square test, you can test whether the measured difference in some respect between two groups is statistically significant or likely to be due to chance. To apply the test you need to have two independent variables and a number of dependent variables in your study. The independent variables could be male/female, BrE/AmE, 1950s/2000s, 30-year-olds/60-year-olds, working-class speakers/middle-class speakers, sentence-initial/sentence-final position, fiction/non-fiction – any categories that you want to compare. Let us say that you are interested in the frequency of the conjunctions *but* and *however* in AmE over time. Have they increased or decreased recently? Searching for *but* and *however* in COCA, we get the figures given in Table 2.7.

We can be certain that these differences hold for the corpus we have investigated. But to be able to generalise to the whole population (in this case, the total mass of AmE) we need to submit the figures to a statistical test of significance. The chi square test compares the observed frequencies with the frequencies we would expect if there were no relationship between variables (i.e. the time periods) in the whole population (AmE). To perform a chi square test on the results in Table 2.7, we need to go through the following steps.

1. Decide the level of significance that we are willing to accept. In linguistics this is usually that there is 1 chance in 20 or 1 chance in 100 that the results are due to chance. These probabilities are expressed as $p < 0.05$ or $p < 0.01$.

2. Chi square compares the observed frequencies in each cell with the frequencies expected if the variants were evenly distributed (this is called the 'null hypothesis'). The expected frequency has to be calculated for each cell. For *but* in 1990–1994 this is done in the following way: multiply the row total by the column total and then divide by the sum total: $(8,909 \times 4,853)/9,633 = 4,488$. Next, the expected frequency for *but* in 2005–2007 is calculated in the same manner: $8,909 \times 4,780/9,633 = 4,421$. And so on for all the other cells. The results are given in Table 2.8.

Table 2.8 Observed and expected frequency of *but* and *however* in COCA, 1990–1994, compared with 2005–2007: per million words

	1990–1994	*2005–2007*	*Total*
but observed	4,443	4,466	8,909
but expected	4,488	4,421	
however observed	410	314	724
however expected	365	359	
Total	4,853	4,780	9,633

We can now compare the observed frequencies with the expected frequencies. For instance, we can see that there are fewer *however* in the 2005–2007 period than expected, and slightly more *but*. But we still do not know if the figures are significantly different, or if the differences could be the result of chance. We therefore need to move on to the next step.

3. Compute the chi square for each cell by means of the following operation. (i) Subtract the expected frequency from the observed frequency. (ii) Square the difference (this is done to get a positive figure even if the difference is negative). (iii) Divide the squared difference by the expected frequency. For our table we will get the following results:

but 1990–1994 $(4,443 - 4,488)^2/4,488 = 0.451$
but 2005–2007 $(4,466 - 4,421)^2/4,421 = 0.458$
however 1990–1994 $(410 - 365)^2/365 = 5.548$
however 2005–2007 $-(314 - 359)^2/359 = 5.640$

4. We then add up all the chi square values to get a total of 12.097. But this figure does not mean anything in itself – it needs to be interpreted. To do this we must first establish a figure called the 'degree of freedom'. This is a measure of how many cells in the table are free to vary, and is arrived at by multiplying the number of columns minus one by the number of rows minus one, in our case: $(2 - 1) \times (2 - 1) = 1 \times 1 = 1$. So the degree of freedom is 1. When we have the degree of freedom we can compare the total chi square value with the so called 'critical values of significance', which can usually be found in a table at the end of statistics books or on the web. Table 2.9 gives the values for 1, 2 and 3 degrees of freedom.

Since our degree of freedom (df) is 1, we read on the first row and find that our total chi square value of 12.079 exceeds the critical value of even 0.001, which means that there is less than 1 chance in 1,000 that our

Table 2.9 Chi square critical values of significance

	Significance level					
	0.20	0.10	0.05	0.025	0.01	0.001
df 1	1.64	2.71	3.84	5.02	6.64	10.83
df 2	3.22	4.61	5.99	7.38	9.21	13.82
df 3	4.64	6.25	7.82	9.35	11.34	16.27

Source: Based on Oakes (1998)

Table 2.10 Distribution of a selection of adjectives over subcorpora in COCA: per million words

	Spoken	Fiction	Magazines	Newspapers	Academic	Total
appalling	3.5	3.1	3.3	3.5	2.3	3.2
bizarre	17.3	12.2	13.4	11.0	6.5	12.3
conceptual	0.7	0.9	5.0	2.7	50.4	11.9
purple	7.2	42.1	27.2	15.0	5.8	19.7

results on *but* and *however* are due to chance, and we can confidently say that the figures in Table 2.7 are significant at the $p < 0.001$ level.

This exercise was done to illustrate what lies behind figures like $p < 0.05$, $p < 0.01$ and $p < 0.001$ in corpus-based linguistics papers. However, it should be stressed that the chi square test is not reliable for very small samples, and that with very large samples it is easy to get significant figures. And with simple tables like the one we looked at here it is often possible to judge the significance with the naked eye anyway.

2.4 Distribution in the corpus

There is one important aspect related to representativity (cf. section 2.6) that we have not touched upon yet: distribution (also know as dispersion). A word, phrase or collocation can get misleadingly high frequency figures in a corpus by being frequent in just one or a few texts or genres, while it is absent in all the others. This could be either because the item is closely connected to a very limited genre or topic, or because it is characteristic of one or just a few writers/speakers. Table 2.10 shows the distribution of a selection of adjectives in COCA.

Table 2.10 shows that while the evaluating adjective *appalling* happens to be quite evenly dispersed over the corpus, the other adjectives are not. The descriptive and evaluating *bizarre* is most frequent in the spoken subcorpus, the abstract and technical *conceptual* is very typical of

Table 2.11 Distribution of *out* and *out of* in spoken and written British material

	out		*out of*	
	N	%	N	%
Spoken	232	72	88	28
Written	198	20	804	80

Source: Based on Estling (1998, 1999)

the academic subcorpus, and *purple* occurs most often in magazines and fiction, where there are many descriptions of fashion and design. It is quite clear that a corpus with a different make-up could yield different figures and therefore a different picture of the use of these adjectives. For instance, a corpus without an academic component would have shown *conceptual* as a much rarer adjective than the totals in Table 2.10 suggest.

2.5 Using percentages and normalising

In presenting your results it is important to remember what the original research question was, and how it can be answered in the clearest possible way. In a study of the competition between the simplex preposition *out* and the complex preposition *out of*, Estling (1998) noticed, among several other things, that the forms were differently distributed in the written and spoken parts of her corpora. Since she was interested in the relation between the two possible forms, it was appropriate to report the proportions as percentages, as in Table 2.11.

The percentages are counted on the horizontal rows here and show that in the spoken British material, *out* was used in 72% of the cases and *out of* in the remaining 28%, while for the written material the situation is very much the reverse. The figures thus suggest a strong influence of the channel (spoken/written) on the choice of form. Examples of the two variants are given in (4) and (5).

(4)   [...] I heard banging, and I looked **out the window** and they were hacking at my fence [...] (BNC KB8)

(5)   [...] when you and me look **out of the** same **window**, we do not see the same things [...] (BNC BIC)

Note that Estling also gives the absolute frequencies (usually marked by the symbol N) so that the reader can judge whether the percentage figures are based on reasonably large absolute figures or not. This is extremely important. You must never give only percentages – for all

Table 2.12 Frequency of noun-*to*-noun patterns with identical body-part nouns: per 100m words

Phrase	BNC	New York Times
face to face	798	498
side to side	375	113
back to back	159	449
hand to hand	136	56
head to head	78	248

Source: Based on Lindquist and Levin (2009)

the reader knows, they may otherwise be based on just a few chance examples which are not statistically significant at all.

The frequencies of the adjectives in different subcorpora of COCA were given per million words in Table 2.10 above, rather than as absolute frequencies. This method is called 'normalising' and should always be used when you compare frequencies in two corpora or subcorpora of different sizes. Doing this, it is, for instance, possible to compare results from a corpus of 100 million words with results from a corpus of 300 million words, as was done in Lindquist and Levin (2009), where we looked at the frequency of constructions consisting of a body noun + the preposition *to* + the same body noun, as in Table 2.12.

Since the *New York Times* corpus consisted of 300 million words, giving the absolute frequencies would have been potentially confusing, and normalising to 100 million words seemed the most natural thing to do. Note that one usually normalises downwards to a figure close to the size of the smallest corpus. If you have 3 tokens of a certain phenomenon in a 1-million-word corpus it is not correct to normalise this figure to 30 per 10 million words, since that would give the impression that you have actually found 30 tokens – but your 3 tokens may be the only ones existing in the whole world!

2.6 Representativity

We tried to answer the question "Which is the most frequent word, noun, verb etc. in English?" by making frequency counts in the BNC. But the only thing we can be absolutely certain of with that method is which the most frequent words in that particular corpus are. The BNC is meant to give a fair picture of the English language in Britain around 1990, but we must be aware, which the compilers certainly were, that this can only be achieved up to a point. It is true that they made efforts to make the proportion of the different printed text types (newspaper text, popular novels, science texts) in the corpus similar to the proportions of the total number of works published in the relevant years, and that they included several types of spoken language. But spoken language is costly and complicated to collect since it has to be recorded and then transcribed, and it is therefore under-represented in the corpus. And no matter how much written text is included, there will always be genres and text types which are left out. Another problem is the difference in impact that different texts have. If included in a corpus, an utterance from a radio programme with 100,000 listeners gets the same weight as an utterance made by one speaker to another in a private conversation, and sentences from best-selling novels get the same weight as sentences from flyers about the local charity bazaar, once they are in the corpus. And there is also the problem of status: general corpora have had a tendency to favour 'high' culture over 'low'.

The conclusion must be that representativity is relative: it varies between corpora and it is never absolute. This means that when we discuss and evaluate results based on a corpus we must always consider the extent to which they can be generalised to the language as a whole, or to a genre or text type as a whole. If the investigation is based on a corpus of twenty crime novels from the 1990s, can we be certain that what we find holds generally for English in the late twentieth century, for English in the 1990s, or just for crime novels in one of those periods? Or do we only know things about these particular twenty novels? In a number of studies, researchers at my university have studied the difference between BrE and AmE by comparing *The New York Times* from 1990, 1995 and 2000 with the British newspaper *The Independent* from the same years. We have argued that we have seen signs of real differences in some areas, but we have also acknowledged that in theory these differences might be due to different editorial policies and style preferences in the two papers, and not to national differences. In some instances we checked with the *Los Angeles Times* and *The Times* of London, and found that the differences remained. This made us more certain that the differences were real. But they were still only differences in the language of quality newspapers. Making similar studies based on other types of corpora, like Brown/Frown and LOB/FLOB or COCA and the BNC, would certainly make the findings more reliable.

2.7 Corpus annotation

2.7.1 Part-of-speech tagging

Many of the searches behind the results presented as exemplification so far have made use of part-of-speech tagged corpora, i.e. corpora where each word has a tag, like a price tag, stating its part of speech (word class). Being able to use these tags simplifies the linguist's work enormously. Let us say that you are interested in the lexical variation between the nouns *can* and *tin* referring to a metallic container in different varieties of English, and want to start by checking the frequencies of these lexical items in a few different corpora. A search for the word forms *tin* and *can* in *The New York Times*, 1990, gives the frequencies 540 and 15,993, respectively. But if you look at the actual concordance lines, you will find that only about 0.2 per cent of the *can* examples refer to containers – all the others are instances of the modal verb *can*! So you need a way of getting at the container instances. There are some tricks to get around the problem in an untagged corpus. For instance, you can search for combinations of words where the noun use of the words is more likely than the verb use, such as *tin of* and *can of.* That will eliminate most of the verbal contexts and give you only container meanings (twenty of them). Or add the definite article *the can* – that will give you another four instances.

These examples illustrate how one can work with so-called lexical templates to get at grammatical categories (in this case nouns). But this can be quite clumsy and time-consuming. In addition, neither 'precision' nor 'recall' is particularly good. Precision is a measure of how large a proportion of your hits actually consist of the thing you were looking for. If half of the hits are irrelevant rubbish, the precision is 50% and you need to carry out a lot of manual post-editing. Recall is a measure of how many of the relevant tokens in the corpus you actually retrieve in your search. Ideally, of course, both precision and recall should be 100%. In our case, you would like to have all the container instances of *tin* and *can*, and none of the verb instances (and ideally none of the instances where *tin* means 'kind of metal', either). However, precision is rarely perfect. In addition, if the search word is used metaphorically, as in (6) where *can* means 'jail', those tokens will have to be dealt with manually.

(6) "If someone has done something illegal, charge them, convict them, put them in the **can**," Mr. Feinstein said. (*New York Times*, 1990)

To alleviate this problem, part-of-speech (POS) tagging was introduced at a very early stage of corpus development. If our corpus had been tagged, we could have searched for *can* with the tag 'noun' and would have avoided all the other hits. So POS tagging is extremely useful. There are some complications, however. It is not always obvious what the correct tag should be. In the sentence *He looked after the children*, is *looked* an intransitive verb and *after* a preposition, or is *looked after* as a whole a particle verb? Anybody who has analysed and parsed naturally occurring written language knows that it is often hard to fit authentic language into categories set up by a grammatical theory. And in transcribed spoken corpora the situation is much more complicated than with written material. The theoretical differences of opinion can be even deeper. For instance, most traditional grammars and most existing taggers would call *before* in (7) a conjunction and *off* in (8) an adverb.

(7)   We left **before** the meeting ended.
(8)   He darted **off.**

But Huddleston and Pullum in their *Cambridge Grammar of the English Language* (2002: 598–617) include both in the preposition category. If you agree with Huddleston and Pullum's arguments for their new view on word classes, the tags in corpora tagged according to another system may not be very helpful. There are even some linguists (notably John Sinclair) who argue that one should always use untagged corpora since tagged corpora force you to accept someone else's analysis. However, the majority of corpus linguists prefer tagged corpora when they are available. But it is good to be aware of the principles according to which your corpus was tagged.

The second problem is that the tags must be put there in the first place. Very small corpora can be hand-tagged by an individual or a group of researchers. If you have a tagging team, the team has to be trained to tag in the same manner. As you get above half a million words or so, however, you really need an automatic tagger, i.e. a computer program, to do the job. Much ingenuity has been put into the development of automatic taggers, which make use of different techniques including grammatical rules and probabilities. The taggers also have a lexicon of common words and their tags. As we saw in Table 2.1 above, the taggers work with a more fine-grained classification of the words than just calling them nouns, adverbs and so on. Table 2.13 shows the C5 tagset used by the CLAWS (Constituent Likelihood Automatic Word-tagging System) tagger for the BNC. This is an abbreviated set with only 60 tags – larger versions have up to 160 tags and more.

As can be seen in Table 2.12, this tagset distinguishes the unmarked form of adjectives from comparatives and superlatives, while unmarked and compared adverbs are subsumed under the same tag, AV0. This is presumably because compared adverbs are relatively rare. Note also that some words have individual tags of their own: the conjunction *that*, existential *there*, the preposition *of*, the infinitive marker *to*. These words do not fit easily into any larger categories, and it is useful to be able to specify them in corpus searches. Note also that the verbs are tagged for

Table 2.13 The C5 tagset for the CLAWS tagger

Tag	Explanation	Forms
AJ0	adjective (unmarked)	e.g. *good, old*
AJC	comparative adjective	e.g. *better, older*
AJS	superlative adjective	e.g. *best, oldest*
AT0	article	e.g. *the, a, an*
AV0	adverb (unmarked)	e.g. *often, well, longer, furthest*
AVP	adverb particle	e.g. *up, off, out*
AVQ	*wh*-adverb	e.g. *when, how, why*
CJC	coordinating conjunction	e.g. *and, or*
CJS	subordinating conjunction	e.g. *although, when*
CJT	the conjunction *that*	
CRD	cardinal numeral	e.g. *3, fifty-five, 6609* (excl. *one*)
DPS	possessive determiner form	e.g. *your, their*
DT0	general determiner	e.g. *these, some*
DTQ	*wh*-determiner	e.g. *whose, which*
EX0	existential *there*	
ITJ	interjection or other isolate	e.g. *oh, yes, mhm*
NN0	noun (neutral for number)	e.g. *aircraft, data*
NN1	singular noun	e.g. *pencil, goose*
NN2	plural noun	e.g. *pencils, geese*
NP0	proper noun	e.g. *London, Michael, Mars*
NULL	the null tag (for items not to be tagged)	
ORD	ordinal	e.g. *sixth, 77th, last*
PNI	indefinite pronoun	e.g. *none, everything*
PNP	personal pronoun	e.g. *you, them, ours*
PNQ	*wh*-pronoun	e.g. *who, whoever*
PNX	reflexive pronoun	e.g. *itself, ourselves*
POS	the possessive (or genitive morpheme) 's or '	
PRF	the preposition *of*	
PRP	preposition (except for *of*)	e.g. *for, above, to*
PUL	punctuation left bracket	i.e. (or [
PUN	punctuation general mark	i.e. . ! , : ; ? . . .
PUQ	Punctuation quotation mark	i.e. ' ' "
PUR	punctuation right bracket	i.e.) or]
TO0	infinitive marker *to*	
UNC	"unclassified" items which are not words of the English lexicon	
VBB	the "base forms" of the verb *be* (except the infinitive)	i.e. *am, are*
VBD	past form of the verb *be*	i.e. *was, were*

Table 2.13 (continued)

Tag	Explanation	Forms
VBG	-*ing* form of the verb *be*	i.e. *being*
VBI	infinitive of the verb *be*	
VBN	past participle of the verb *be*	i.e. *been*
VBZ	-*s* form of the verb *be*	i.e. *is, 's*
VDB	base form of the verb *do* (except the infinitive)	
VDD	past form of the verb *do*	i.e. *did*
VDG	-*ing* form of the verb *do*	i.e. *doing*
VDI	infinitive of the verb *do*	
VDN	past participle of the verb *do*	i.e. *done*
VDZ	-*s* form of the verb *do*	i.e. *does*
VHB	base form of the verb *have* (except the infinitive)	i.e. *have*
VHD	past tense form of the verb *have*	i.e. *had, 'd*
VHG	-*ing* form of the verb *have*	i.e. *having*
VHI	infinitive of the verb *have*	
VHN	past participle of the verb *have*	i.e. *had*
VHZ	-*s* form of the verb *have*	i.e. *has, 's*
VM0	modal auxiliary verb	e.g. *can, could, will, 'll*
VVB	base form of lexical verb (except the infinitive)	e.g. *take, live*
VVD	past tense form of lexical verb	e.g. *took, lived*
VVG	-*ing* form of lexical verb	e.g. *taking, living*
VVI	infinitive of lexical verb	
VVN	past participle form of lexical verb	e.g. *taken, lived*
VVZ	-*s* form of lexical verb	e.g. *takes, lives*
XX0	the negative *not* or *n't*	
ZZ0	alphabetical symbol	e.g. *A, B, c, d*

Source: Based on the webpage 'CLAWS part-of-speech tagger for English', http://ucrel.lancs.ac.uk/claws

tense, in order to make it possible to search for sentences with different tenses in the corpora.

Automatic taggers often claim to have a 97–98% success rate, which is not bad. But the rate is boosted by the 100% success rate with common unambiguous words like *the* and *a*. This means that if you are working with an automatically tagged corpus which has not been manually post-edited, you must expect to find quite a few wrongly tagged items in the output, since, after all, 97% correct tags means that 3% or one in 33 words is incorrectly tagged. For instance, a search for the noun *fine* in COCA returned fifty hits, the first ten of which are shown in Figure 2.1 with my manual analysis given in square brackets.

Half the concordance lines do not contain *fine* as a noun and are thus irrelevant if we are analysing nouns. A closer look shows that all the

1. No, but you can't get the government into **fine**- tuning (Spoken) [ADJ]
2. Finally, minors may be cited with a mail-in "parking ticket" **fine** of $25 for possession of tobacco products (Magazines) [N]
3. Yeah, all right, **fine**- in Southern California, of course. (Spoken) [ADJ]
4. 2:4593@-**fine**. -but let me ask you, Mr. Scannell, you certainly can't say (Spoken) [ADJ]
5. One shows Michael all dressed up, a **fine**- looking man heading out to a party, ready for a good time. (Spoken) [ADJ]
6. You know, I think you'd even make a **fine**- yeah, I could make you my chief (Spoken) [ADJ]
7. Often officials pocket part or all of the "excess birth" **fine** of $280, a figure exceeding the per capita annual income in the village (Newspapers) [N]
8. The proposed Infinity **fine** would cover the same programs, which also aired on WXRK-FM in New York (Newspapers) [N]
9. There was no guarantee, but a paid **fine** was to be a positive development. (Academic) [N]
10. In fiscal year 1991, the average corporate **fine** was $502,000. (Academic) [N]

Figure 2.1 The first ten concordance lines for *fine* (noun) in COCA, with manual analysis.
Note: Subcorpus is given in parentheses, with manual part-of-speech analysis in brackets.

incorrect tags occur in the spoken part of the corpus – apparently the automatic tagger had problems with the grammar of spoken language. The proportion of errors depends on how difficult your search item is to disambiguate for the tagger, but very commonly it is a matter of 5–15 items per 100. A search for the noun *dance* in the same corpus was more successful: out of the first 100 lines, only 9 (i.e. 9 %) contained mistaggings, as shown in Figure 2.2.

Again, we see examples from spoken English and fiction dialogue. These examples show that if you want a set of 100 relevant tokens to analyse, you should always make a pilot search to determine the approximate error rate and then search for more tokens than you need, so that you can manually delete the irrelevant tokens to arrive at the desired number of relevant tokens.

2.7.2 Parsing

Tagging for word classes and subclasses of word classes is really just the first step towards a complete grammatical analysis of a corpus. The next step is parsing, i.e. assigning a syntactic analysis to the corpus. Parsing has not yet been as successful as POS tagging, which is because it is a more difficult undertaking, not least because it is even more dependent on which linguistic theory you subscribe to. The most common type of parsing has been phrase structure analysis, where phrases and

> 9 dance company because they're beautiful dancers and all they want to do is **dance**. (Spoken)
> 37 favorite because it demanded more from me and I had to, you know- **dance** or, you know, get the hook. (Spoken)
> 51 singing That's Mr. Bojangles / Call him Mr. Bojangles / Mr. Bojangles / Comeback and **dance**, dance, dance, dance. (Spoken)
> 55 Squeezing hands, we had watched Tamara Toumanova **dance** Phedre. (Fiction)
> 65 Then if you don't get up and **dance**, they say, (Fiction)
> 80 some girls dancing with coloured men, de first time a see white woman **dance** wit coloured man (Fiction)
> 84 You come often and see me **dance** and buy me drinks, okay? (Fiction)
> 85 just answer this man, who is only one more man who saw me **dance** naked. (Fiction)
> 87 The next Saturday Mr. Fontenot does not come and see me **dance** naked. I sit at the bar with my clothes on (Fiction)

Figure 2.2 The nine concordance lines with incorrect tagging out of the first 100 concordance lines for *dance* (noun) in COCA.
Note: Subcorpus is given in parentheses. All these tokens of *dance* are verbs.

clauses are given functional labels such as adverbial clause, adjective phrase, temporal noun phrase, past participle clause etc. A corpus with this kind of annotation is called a treebank (since the structures can be represented as tree diagrams even if they are normally printed as series of brackets). Automatic parsing is especially important for a number of technical applications in the field of natural language processing (NLP), where it can be used in machine translation, speech-to-text conversion etc. The treebank that has been most widely used by linguists is probably the parsed version on ICE-GB and its interface ICECUP.

2.7.3 Other types of corpus annotation

Apart from POS tagging and syntactic parsing, corpora can be given other annotations, for instance semantic, pragmatic/discourse or prosodic annotation. These are also fields where considerable efforts are being made. However, we will not make use of such corpora in this book.

2.8 Summary

This was the second preparatory chapter, where we focused on methodology, underlining the difference between qualitative and quantitative method. We noted that for studies of frequency it is important to define carefully what is being counted and to be aware of the notion of statistical significance. We saw that frequencies can be presented in different ways, as absolute figures, as normalised figures and as percentages. The notion of representativity was also discussed. In the final section we saw how corpora can be tagged for part of speech, parsed for grammatical structure, or annotated for semantic, pragmatic/discourse or prosodic features.

Study questions

1. What is the difference between qualitative and quantitative methods? How can quantitative methods be combined with qualitative analysis?
2. What is lemmatising? How does it influence frequency counts?
3. Why is it important to normalise frequencies when you compare results from different corpora?
4. What arguments are relevant when we discuss whether a corpus is representative or not?
5. What are the main types of corpus annotation? Why is it important to know the principles behind the tagging of a corpus that you are using?

Corpus exercises

Hands-on exercises related to this chapter are available at the following web address:

http://www.euppublishing.com/series/ETOTELAdvanced/Lindquist.

Further reading

It is hard to find easy-to-digest information on statistics. Even Oakes (1998), which is specifically for corpus linguistics, is rather tough going, and the chapters on statistics in introductory books on corpus linguistics such as McEnery and Wilson [1996] (2001), Biber et al. (1998) and Meyer (2002) are quite brief. A clear but somewhat technical introduction is given in Baroni and Evert (2009). There are also tutorials on the web.

Aston and Burnard (1998) deal with some of the questions raised here, including representativity. The classic paper on representativity is otherwise Biber (1993). The best introduction to corpus annotation is still Garside et al. (1997), especially the first two chapters. More detailed and up-to-date treatments of questions related to annotation can be found in Lüdeling and Kytö (2008: 484–705). Treebanks are treated in Wallis (2008). Nelson et al. (2002) describe the philosophy behind the parsed version of ICE-GB and give many examples of studies that can be made by means of the special search program ICE-CUP.

3 Looking for lexis

3.1 The role of the lexicon in language

The traditional distinction between the grammar and the vocabulary of a language is reflected in the fact that we have separate grammar books and dictionaries. Generative linguistics in the second half of the twentieth century emphasised this separation and strove to describe grammatical structures in which lexical items were inserted only at a late stage in the derivation (construction) of a sentence, when the grammatical structure had already been decided. The lexicon in such a model has a peripheral role as a storehouse of words, idioms and oddities that cannot be described by rules.

In many alternative linguistic models, however, the lexicon is given a more central role. In these models, lexical items or small classes of lexical items are believed to have not only their own meaning but also their own "local" grammars, which can be discovered by the close study of language in use. The ideal method to carry out such studies is to use corpora. It is therefore reasonable that in this book we devote several chapters to the lexicon. We will begin by saying a few words about using corpora in the production of dictionaries.

3.2 How lexicographers use corpora

In the old days, lexicographers collected slips of paper with text excerpts for all the words they were going to include in their dictionary, just as Jespersen did for his grammar. The editors of the *OED*, for instance, had hundreds of correspondents who collected and sent in slips with citations of interesting new words or new uses of old words. In the end there were hundreds of thousands of handwritten slips in the purpose-built pigeonholes in the garden shed of the editor, James Murray, in Oxford (where a large number of helpers were busy sorting them for him). This was very cumbersome work, so computers have been a great invention for dictionary-makers. As mentioned in Chapter 1, the Cobuild corpus was originally compiled for lexicographical purposes, and today all major British dictionary publishers have their own corpora (many of which unfortunately are not accessible to outside researchers). The editors use concordances to find out the typical meanings and constructions in which each word is used, and try to evaluate which of these are worth mentioning in the dictionary. Many dictionaries also quote authentic examples from corpora, either verbatim or in a slightly doctored form. It is also possible for modern lexicographers to get a good grip on differences between genres and registers by studying specialised corpora or subcorpora. Finally, corpora give rich information on common words like *take*, *go* and *time*, which often have very many meanings and uses which tend to be overlooked in introspection and by human citation collectors. In the next section we will look at a dictionary entry and compare it with findings from a corpus which is different from the one that the dictionary is based on.

3.3   The meaning of words

As mentioned in the discussion about tagging, the easiest way into a corpus is to search for lexical items. But even that is not always totally straightforward. First we must decide whether we are interested in a word form or a lemma. If we are interested in the verb *squeeze*, we are probably interested in all the forms of that verb: *squeeze*, *squeezes*, *squeezed* and *squeezing*. These forms together constitute the verb lemma SQUEEZE. We might also decide to study the noun lemma SQUEEZE as in *one squeeze* and *several squeeze*s. Remember that lemmas are often written in small caps. Before we go on, try think of all the meanings of the verb *to squeeze* that you know. You probably have a general idea of the meaning, and some contexts probably crop up in your mind, maybe something like *She squeezed my arm* or *He squeezed out the last of the toothpaste*.

Let us now see what the *Longman Dictionary of Contemporary English*, a learner's dictionary, says about the verb *squeeze* (Figure 3.1).

The *Longman Dictionary of Contemporary English* is a corpus-based dictionary, so the definitions given here are already based on corpus findings. As you can see, the dictionary lists no fewer than six meanings plus a number of phrases like *squeeze sth out* and *squeeze up*. Clearly, describing the meaning of even a relatively simple verb like *squeeze* is far from easy, and it would be extremely difficult to arrive at all these meanings by introspection only.

To get a feeling of what kind of material lexicographers work with, we will now compare the description given in the dictionary with what can find in a corpus. In Figure 3.2 the first twenty concordance lines

> **squeeze¹** /skwiz/ *v* **1 PRESS** [T] to press something firmly together with your fingers or hand: *She smiled as he squeezed her hand.* | *He squeezed the trigger, but nothing happened.*
> **2 PRESS OUT LIQUID** [T] to get liquid from something by pressing it: *Squeeze the oranges.* | **squeeze sth out** Try to squeeze a bit more out. | **squeeze sth on/onto sth** *Squeeze a bit of lemon juice onto the fish.*
> **3 SMALL SPACE** [I, T always + adv/prep] to try to make something fit into a space that is too small, or to try to get into such a space (cf. **squash**): [+**into**] *Five of us squeezed into the back seat.* | [+**through/past**] *He had squeezed through a gap in the fence.* | **squeeze sb/sth in** *We could probably squeeze in a few more people.*
> **4 squeeze your eyes shut** to close your eyes very tightly
> **5 JUST SUCCEED** [I always + adv/prep] to succeed, win, or pass a test by a very small amount so that you only just avoid failure: *Greece just squeezed through to the next round.*
> **6 LIMIT MONEY** [T] To strictly limit the amount of money that is available to a company or organization: *The government is squeezing the railways' investment budget.*
> **squeeze sb/sth in** <-> also **squeeze sth into sth** *phr v*
> to manage to do something although you are very busy: *How do you manage to squeeze so much ino one day?* | *I can squeeze you in at four o'clock.*
> **squeeze sth** <-> **out** *phr v*
> **1** to do something so that someone or something is no longer included or able to continue: *If budgets are cut, vital research may be squeezed out.*
> **2** to squeeze something wet in order to remove the liquid from it: *Squeeze the cloth out first.*
> **3** to squeeze sth out of sb to force someone to tell you something: *See if you can squeeze more information out of them.*
> **squeeze up** *phr v BrE*
> To move close to the person next to you to make place for someone else

Figure 3.1 Dictionary entry for the verb *squeeze*.
Source: Longman Dictionary of Contemporary English [1978] (2003: 1606–1607)

containing the infinitive form of the verb *squeeze* found in the 1990s section in the Time Corpus are given. They have been ordered according to the five different meanings given in the dictionary.

Meaning 1: PRESS

The two examples given in the dictionary entry are both about concrete things being pressed together (a hand, the trigger of a gun), but among our twenty Time Corpus tokens only one, example (1), is of this kind. Examples (2)–(5) are about (political) forces applying pressure on a country and its ruler. This metaphorical meaning is not mentioned in the dictionary (for a definition of metaphor, see Chapter 6). Example (6) is about a period of time which is made shorter by compression, so to speak. Examples (2)–(6) illustrate the fact that many words and expressions which are originally based on physical phenomena (and which we think of as physical) are more often used metaphorically about abstract phenomena. Dictionaries tend to begin with the physical explanation, and sometimes leave it at that.

Meaning 2: PRESS OUT LIQUID

There were no examples concerning liquids among our twenty concordance lines, but instead a number of metaphorical uses that seem to fit best under this heading: (7)–(10), where the stuff that is pressed

1. gun to your head and say, "I'm gonna **squeeze** it five times, and if there's not a bullet
2. confronts Saddam Hussein, encircles Iraq and Kuwait, and begins to **squeeze**.
3. As an international embargo begins to **squeeze**, Saddam adds American diplomats to his collection of Western hostages
4. the view that the economic embargo, if it could ever **squeeze** Saddam sufficiently to cause his unilateral withdrawal from Kuwait, would
5. their best tactic is to **squeeze** Saddam between rebellious Kurds to the north and hostile Shi'ites
6. Part of the solution: **squeeze** the interval between final editing and distribution of the magazine
7. From so little they glean so much: **squeeze** the last ounce of joy from a flower with no petals
8. He did manage to **squeeze** out of Israel an agreement that might finesse the problem of
9. the contender who reminds no one of a President, might **squeeze** victory out of the state's mercurial mood.
10. The struggle to **squeeze** more aid dollars out of a finite pool brings with it
11. (RUC) and British intelligence forces had too often managed to **squeeze** information out of its members.
12. second performance for all the healers and spiritualists who were unable to **squeeze** into the auditorium for the first one.
13. The time traveler would have to survive the crushing pressure inside a black hole and somehow **squeeze** through an opening smaller than a single atom.
14. They have found a way to **squeeze** up to 45 billion bits of data onto a square inch
15. Budget Director Richard Darman was able to **squeeze** under the Gramm-Rudman-Hollings deficit target of $64 billion but only by
16. How many hits can a movie mogul **squeeze** into a box office?
17. He managed to **squeeze** in concern for the middle class about as often as Bob
18. He will also try to **squeeze** in a drama workshop at Los Angeles' Mark Taper Forum
19. much time for relaxation, but he claims to be able to **squeeze** in trips to the opera and other cultural events.
20. Saddam's dictatorship can and will **squeeze** the civilian economy as hard as may be necessary to maintain

Figure 3.2 The first twenty concordance lines for *squeeze* (verb) in the Time Corpus, 1990s, ordered according to meanings given in the *Longman Dictionary of Contemporary English* [1978] (2003).

out is *joy, an agreement, victory* and *aid dollars.* Example (11) is related to these, although "to force someone to tell you something" has been given a place of its own under the phrase **squeeze sth out 3** in the dictionary (see below).

Meaning 3: SMALL SPACE

The examples in the dictionary are all about physical space, like our examples (12)–(14). In addition, however, we have examples (15)–(17), which are about various metaphorical spaces, and (18)–(19), which are squeeze[2] *n* |C| **1 a (tight) squeeze** a situation in which there is only just enough room for things or people to fit somewhere: *It will be a squeeze with six people in the car.* **2** an act of pressing something firmly with your fingers: *Marty gave her hand a little squeeze.* **3 squeeze of lemon/lime etc.** a small amount of juice obtained by squeezing a fruit **4** a situation in which wages, prices, borrowing money etc. are strictly controlled or reduced: [+on] *cuts due to the squeeze on public sector spending* | *a credit squeeze* | *All manufacturers are feeling the squeeze* (=noticing the effects of a difficult financial situation. **5 put the squeeze on sb** *informal* to try to persuade someone to do something **6 sb's (main) squeeze** *especially AmE* someone's BOYFRIEND or GIRLFRIEND

Figure 3.3 Dictionary entry for the noun *squeeze*.
Source: *Longman Dictionary of Contemporary English* [1978] (2003: 1607)

about fitting something into a tight schedule. The schedule meaning is given separately in the dictionary under the phrase **squeeze sb/sth in**.

The dictionary categories 4 and 5 do not occur in our small sample, but example (20) belongs to Meaning 6: LIMIT MONEY. Note that this mini-study was made on just the infinitive form; similar studies of the other verb forms indicated that different meanings dominate different tenses, so that there is a difference between the progressive *squeezing* and the simple past *squeezed*. For lack of space we will not go into that here. Instead we will turn to the meanings given for the noun *squeeze* in the dictionary, which are in part parallel to the verb meanings. The dictionary entry is given in Figure 3.3.

The twenty first concordance lines from the corpus have been ordered according to these meanings in Figure 3.4.

The results in Figure 3.4 are a bit surprising at first. There were no examples of tight physical squeezes with just enough room, and no physical squeezing of things (but in example (21), not on the list, there was one, referring to the handling of a gun: *those rapid-fire guns that require a single squeeze of the trigger for every round discharged*). Examples (1)–(3), however, might be seen as metaphorical extensions of physical squeezing. There was no squeezing of fruit either, and no instances of the phrases **put the squeeze on sb** or **sb's main squeeze**. Instead, all the remaining seventeen examples fit more or less well under the dictionary's Meaning 4, a situation in which wages, prices, borrowing money etc. are strictly controlled or reduced. These examples indicate that the noun *squeeze* has become part of a number of fixed compounds, e.g. *money squeeze, budget squeeze, financial squeeze* and *energy squeeze*. In the next chapter we will return to the phenomenon of words tending to co-occur or collocate frequently with certain other words.

The fact that some of the meanings from the dictionary did not turn up in our sample, and that some other meanings were heavily over-represented, can be explained by two circumstances. First of all, the

1. To overcome Shamir's qualms, Bush and Gorbachev staged a diplomatic **squeeze** play.
2. Arafat is also caught in a political **squeeze**.
3. of the railroads, such schemes were unlikely to break Moscow's **squeeze**.
4. Or if he can, you get caught in a "short **squeeze**," in which the stock gets bid up to even
5. but they did just that when a money **squeeze** threatened to shut down twelve of the city's 25 branches
6. other regimes also confront a money **squeeze** as Soviet funds dry up.
7. A cash **squeeze** was in fact one element in the pressure that Washington put
8. Post-secondary institutions are feeling both an economic and a demographic **squeeze**.
9. While the **squeeze** has so far been greatest in New England and neighboring states
10. tighter capital is beginning to put the **squeeze** even on healthy industries!
11. This **squeeze** on families bodes ill for children.
12. is battling its most awesome and implacable enemy: the defense budget **squeeze**.
13. But the budget **squeeze** has sparked a debate about whether the U.S. can afford three
14. Democrats feared that the budget **squeeze** on other domestic programs, already harsh, would be still
15. but a NASA budget **squeeze** killed the project.
16. Crimes Statistics Act is already caught up in the Government's financial **squeeze**.
17. In the U.S. the scientific community is beset by a budget **squeeze** and bureaucratic demands, internal squabbling, harassment by activists
18. devastated by corruption and the financial **squeeze** applied by the U.S. during the final two years of Noriega
19. While the energy **squeeze** is far less severe than the shocks of the '70s
20. Symptoms of an energy **squeeze** are breaking out all over.

Figure 3.4 The first twenty concordance lines for *squeeze* (noun) in the Time Corpus, 1990s, ordered according to meanings given in the *Longman Dictionary of Contemporary English* [1978] (2003).

Time Corpus is biased towards some registers, such as politics and arts, but contains less of others, such as recipes (squeezing of lemons), and virtually no authentic spoken everyday conversations. This shows that a multipurpose learner's dictionary has to be based on a very varied corpus. Second, twenty concordance lines are far too few. How many concordance lines a lexicographer needs to write an entry for a word depends on how many different meanings the word in question has, but twenty is seldom enough.

In searches for lexical items quite often some of the hits consist of names of people, organisations etc. Such hits should normally be discounted, so that if you intend to investigate 100 examples of a particular word and it turns out that 5 are proper nouns (i.e. names), these 5 tokens should be excluded and another 5 relevant ones added (using the same sampling method) so that the total number of relevant tokens is 100. The easiest way to avoid extra work is to make a quick pilot search first and check the rough proportion of names in your data, and then make your search big enough so that you will have enough examples even after the names have been deleted. Out of the first 100 hits in a search for the colour noun *green* in the BNC, for instance, 11 referred to people by the name of *Green* and another 4 referred to places (*Blade Bone Green, Dock Green, Abbey Green* and *Juniper Green*). To be certain to retrieve the right number of colour nouns, therefore, about 25% should be added to the figure in this case.

However, sometimes it can be interesting to see how a particular word has been used to name companies, rock bands and so on. Such an example is (1) from the *squeeze* search.

(1)   [. . .] by presenting such offbeat performers as Sinead O'Connor, Neil Young and **Squeeze**. (Time Corpus, 1990s)

Squeeze here refers to a 1970s British New Wave band. In all, the *squeeze* exercise has shown that the meaning of a word can only be ascertained by looking at the contexts in which it occurs.

3.4 Semantic preference, semantic prosody and evaluation

We saw in the last section that the meaning of a word depends on its context, so that the meaning of a verb like *squeeze* depends on both its subject and its object. It may also be the case that words acquire a sort of hidden meaning, which was not there from the beginning, from the words they frequently occur together with. This has been called 'semantic prosody'. Semantic prosody is part of a system of lexical relations suggested by Sinclair (1998) and explained by Stubbs (2009: 22) in the following way (the wording has been slightly simplified):

> COLLOCATION is the relation between a word and individual word-forms which co-occur frequently with it.
> COLLIGATION is the relation between a word and grammatical categories which co-occur frequently with it.
> SEMANTIC PREFERENCE is the relation between a word and semantically related words in a lexical field.
> SEMANTIC PROSODY is the discourse function of the word: it describes the speaker's communicative purpose.

We will return to colligation and collocation in the next chapter and will not discuss semantic preference further, since it is a concept that has not been widely used in corpus linguistics. Semantic prosody, however, is frequently referred to. A famous example used by Sinclair is the phrasal verb *set in*. Basically, it means just 'begin', but Sinclair claims that looking in a corpus one will find that most of the things that *set in* are negative. Figure 3.5 shows the first ten concordance lines with the relevant sense of *set in* in COCA for the 2000s.

1. There was a whirlwind for 24 hours, and then reality **set in**
2. a bit of effort to sweeten it after the bad, vengeful habits have **set in.**
3. Panic hasn't **set in** yet
4. economic depression, lawlessness and authoritarianism **set in**
5. the drift had arguably already **set in.**
6. the postwar years when the cold war **set in,**
7. So far, that spiral has not **set in.**
8. In addition to financial worries, the psychological toll of unemployment has **set in.**
9. As physical changes such as arthritis **set in,**
10. But by the 1980s, a reaction would **set in**

Figure 3.5 The first ten concordance lines for *set in* in COCA, 2000s.

These results support Sinclair's claim about *set in*. Six cases are clearly negative, while four are unclear either because the contexts are too short or because one can have genuinely different opinions about the things that set in. *Reality* in (1), which is about a couple who met through a dating programme on television, could be argued to be a good thing, but here it is contrasted to the romantic whirlwind of the first 24 hours on a cruise ship and so probably it is seen as something bad; *drift* in (5), which is about a TV series, could be neutral, but here it is about a drift towards lower quality; *spiral* in (7) is about a negative development on the housing market; and, finally, *reaction* in (10) is about a reaction against the westernisation of Turkey, a reaction which might be considered to be positive by some but in the context is clearly intended to be taken as negative.

The phenomenon is called 'semantic prosody' because meanings spread over the words in a sentence in a way similar to intonation in prosody, and speakers and writers can use it to convey negative or (much less frequently) positive evaluation without stating their views explicitly. Corpus searches can be useful in confirming or disconfirming hunches about semantic prosody, and it is also possible to investigate groups of words, for instance synonyms or near-synonyms, for possible semantic prosodies. However, most cases are less clear than *set in*, and often it is hard to decide what is positive and what is not – after all, it is the researcher who must decide. Therefore, the concept is controversial and some scholars prefer to talk about 'evaluation', which is inherent in some lexical items. Channell (1999), for instance, talks about 'evaluative lexis'. One of her corpus examples is that *regime* does not only mean 'method or system or government', as she found in dictionaries, but rather 'method or system of government which I, the speaker, dislike'.

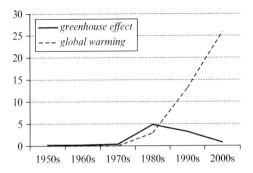

Figure 3.6 Frequency of *greenhouse effect* and *global warming* in *Time*, 1950s–2000s: per million words.

3.5 How words change in frequency over time

The lexicon of a language changes all the time. To be able to talk about new inventions, new concepts and new ways of organising society it is necessary to create new terms, borrow words from other languages or use old words in new ways. There are many different causes of language change, and we will come back to these in Chapter 9. Here we will just take a look at some recent changes pertaining to words, starting with two compounds relating to the environment. We are all familiar with the *greenhouse effect* and *global warming*. But how recent are these terms? Figure 3.6 shows their frequency in *Time* magazine decade by decade from the 1950s. There were no occurrences in the 1920s–1940s.

It is hard to see in the diagram, but the first mentions of *greenhouse effect* in *Time* occurred in the 1950s, while *global warming* did not appear on the scene until the 1980s. What can be clearly seen, however, is that *greenhouse effect* had a short period of popularity with a peak in the 1980s, and that it is being replaced by *global warming*, which has a steeply rising frequency curve. The only three mentions of *greenhouse effect* from the 1950s occurred in the same issue (28 February 1956) and are shown in (2)–(4).

(2) This "**greenhouse effect**" traps heat and makes the earth's surface considerably warmer than it would [. . .]

(3) The **greenhouse effect** will be intensified. Some scientists believe that this is the cause of recent [. . .]

(4) More water will evaporate from the warm ocean, and this will increase the **greenhouse effect** of the CO_2.

Note that the new term is given within inverted commas in the first mention, and then, when it has been established in the text, without inverted commas. It took more than four years before *Time* wrote about the greenhouse effect again, and when this happened, in the issue of 4 April 1960, the inverted commas were back, as can be seen in (5).

(5)   They fear that the added CO_2 will have a "**greenhouse effect**," trapping solar heat at the earth's surface and raising its temperature [. . .]

The story of the term *global warming* in *Time* begins on 21 February 1986. The three first occurrences, from 1986–1988, are shown in (6)–(8).

(6)   [. . .] but its consequences – air pollution, acid rain and the threat of **global warming** caused by the *greenhouse effect* – will limit its use.
(7)   [. . .] now capturing far more of the earth's excess heat, resulting in **global warming**.
(8)   Ultimately, they would like to learn how the oceans will influence the **global warming** trend, known as the *greenhouse effect*, and how they will be influenced by [. . .]

Note that here the new term is explained by means of the older one. According to (6), global warming is caused by the greenhouse effect, while according to (8) the two terms are synonymous. This cursory look at the actual examples told us something about how the words were used and about their relationship, something that the pure figures did not. No investigation of lexis should stop at the statistics – you should always take a close look at the word in context.

Greenhouse effect and *global warming* are terms that are related to topical issues in politics and science, and their use is strongly influenced by the debate. But less obtrusive words change too. If you look up the word *maybe* in a dictionary you are likely to get the meaning given as 'perhaps', and if you look up *perhaps* it will be explained with 'maybe'. They seem to be more or less synonymous. Figure 3.7 shows their frequency over the years in *Time*.

The curve for *perhaps* is a bit squiggly, starting high and ending at approximately the same level, around 200 tokens per million words. *Maybe* is very different, with a steady climb from a very low frequency in the 1920s to almost the same level as *perhaps* in the 2000s. *Maybe* is obviously gaining ground, at least as far as *Time* goes. What could be the reason for this? Is it just fashion? This would take much further work to investigate, but a quick look at the genre distribution of the two words in COCA, another American corpus, gives a hint. The figures are given in Table 3.1.

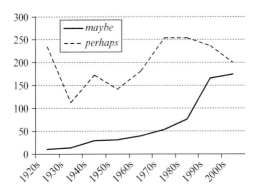

Figure 3.7 Frequency of *maybe* and *perhaps* in *Time*, 1920s–2000s: per million words

Table 3.1 Frequency of *maybe* and *perhaps* in COCA: per million words

	Spoken	Fiction	Magazines	Newspapers	Academic
maybe	398	593	150	158	28
perhaps	198	264	211	161	262

Table 3.1 shows that *maybe* is more frequent than *perhaps* in two subcorpora (spoken and fiction), equally frequent in one (newspapers) and less frequent in two (magazines and academic). The change shown in Figure 3.7 could possibly be caused by a general change in the language, but Table 3.1 suggests another solution, namely either that *Time* has started to include more fiction and reported speech over the years or that more informal and spoken-like language has seeped into the general writing of the magazine. The latter explanation would square well with a process which has been observed elsewhere in English and which has been dubbed 'the colloquialisation of the language', which, for instance, can be seen in the more frequent use in print of contracted forms like *isn't* for *is not*, and the gradual replacement of formal prepositions like *upon* with more neutral forms like *on* (Mair 2006a: 183–193).

But the big difference between *maybe* and *perhaps* in the academic subcorpus should also make us look more closely at the data. A possible clue to the answer can be found in searches for the simple word *may* and the word combination *may be* (written as two words) in the corpus. The results are given in Table 3.2.

While *maybe* is quite rare in the academic subcorpus, as we saw in Table 3.1, Table 3.2 shows that the modal verb *may* and the combination *may + be* are more frequent in the academic subcorpus than in the

Table 3.2 Frequency of *may* and *may be* in COCA: per million words

	Spoken	Fiction	Magazines	Newspapers	Academic
may	795	283	1,087	791	1,556
may be	224	52	271	182	458

other subcorpora. It seems then that academic style disfavours *maybe* and prefers either *perhaps* or a construction with the modal verb *may* plus a verb, as illustrated in (9) and (10).

(9) **Maybe** it's expensive, **maybe** it's difficult, but it is reversible. (COCA Spoken)

(10) It **may be** difficult to teach children that history is both important and uncertain [. . .] (COCA Academic)

The words *maybe* and *perhaps* and the phrase *may be* in (10) express epistemic meaning, which means that they say to what extent something is likely or possible. In a larger investigation, one could go on and investigate all the ways that likelihood and possibility are expressed in the subcorpora, including other adverbs like *possibly* and clauses like *it is possible that*. . . It seems likely that the subcorpora have different preferred ways of expressing epistemic meaning.

3.6 How words spread between varieties of English

With access to diachronic corpora, i.e. corpora from a longer stretch of time with details about the date when each token occurred, it is possible to study the spread and development of individual lexical items. In a study I carried out with a colleague (Lindquist and Estling Vannestål 2005) we were interested in how the word *fatigue* was used in combination with other nouns. We had noted that there were not only the traditional *battle fatigue* (afflicting soldiers) and *metal fatigue* (afflicting nuts and bolts in aeroplanes and bridges) but also new ailments like *Clinton fatigue* (afflicting news consumers) and *museum fatigue* (afflicting museum visitors), and decided to see what we would find in *The New York Times* (NYT) and *The Independent* (IND) from 1990, 1995 and 2000, thus investigating both development over time and difference between two geographical varieties: American and British English.

Using newspapers for this kind of investigation is well motivated, since they provide reasonably comparable data from AmE and BrE. They are also good sources for innovative language, since journalistic prose has been shown to be a "fast" (Mair 1998: 155) or "agile" (Mair

Table 3.3 Corpora used in the investigation of *fatigue*

Newspaper and year	Number of words (millions)
New York Times, 1990	60
New York Times, 1995	53
New York Times, 2000	67
Independent, 1990	35
Independent, 1995	35
Independent, 2000	45

and Hundt 1999) genre which picks up new trends quickly. Ideally, more than one newspaper from each regional variety should have been searched, but in this particular case we did not think it likely that the results were influenced by editorial policies and house styles. As mentioned in Chapter 1, newspaper CD-ROMs are not created for use by linguists and searching them can be somewhat cumbersome. For *The Independent*, the search engine Freeway supplied by the CD-ROM provider Chadwyck-Healy was used to retrieve all articles containing *fatigue*, which were then saved in their entirety to disk as text files. In the next step, these text files were searched by means of the concordance program WordSmith Tools to create concordances. *The New York Times* CD-ROMs, on the other hand, could be searched directly by means of WordSmith Tools.

One further drawback with newspaper CDs is that the publishers do not provide figures for the total number of words, which means that the statistics have to be treated with a certain amount of caution. The figures for the number of words given in Table 3.3 are based on figures and discussion we found in the literature.

Since we were interested in new types of fatigue – that is, new things that were connected to fatigue – we decided to look at noun phrases with *fatigue* as head, consisting of noun + noun. We found 439 such combinations, i.e. 439 tokens, which we then analysed. After having sifted through all the tokens for a while, we could distinguish some different categories, and classified the constructions into four groups according to the meaning expressed by the nominal premodifier in the phrase:

1. DIRECT CAUSE ('exhausted from (taking part in, practising etc.)')
   battle fatigue, compassion fatigue, conference fatigue, flight fatigue

(11) [. . .] Major Pincus rattled off statistics to highlight concrete damage caused by what past generations variously called shell shock, **battle fatigue** or combat stress. (NYT, 1995)

(12) So much literature of and about India is mired in despair that it has contributed to an unhealthy **compassion fatigue** in the West [...] (NYT, 1995)

> 2. INDIRECT CAUSE ('fed up with (being exposed to/hearing about)')
> *Chardonnay fatigue, Clinton fatigue, corruption fatigue, green fatigue, nineties fatigue*

(13) Of course, voters may grow weary before September finally arrives. The campaigners should think seriously about **election fatigue**. (IND, 2000)

(14) Even the policemen are suffering from **fashion fatigue**. (NYT, 1995)

> 3. EXPERIENCER ('X is exhausted' or 'the exhaustion is located in')
> a. human   *commuter fatigue, donor fatigue, pilot fatigue*
> b. body part   *muscle fatigue, nose fatigue, palate fatigue*
> c. material   *metal fatigue, masonry fatigue*

(15) The safety board studied 107 accidents, analyzing them to determine which ones had **driver fatigue** as a factor [...] (NYT, 1995)

(16) There is a built-in problem with juices: **pucker fatigue**. Your mouth gets tired of citrus. (NYT, 1995)

(17) **Metal fatigue** is difficult to spot, Mr. Holl said, although rust or cracks are the usual telltale signs of a weakening piece of metal. (NYT, 1995)

> 4. TIME (point in time at which exhaustion occurs, or, sometimes, which causes exhaustion)
> *morning fatigue, daytime fatigue*

(18) Mr Belind also conceded that *Kate*, which opened in November, is also suffering a bit from **April fatigue**, when handfuls of productions open and older shows get less attention than newcomers. (NYT, 2000)

It must be noted that this classification of the premodifying noun had to take context into account. In isolation, cases like *travel fatigue, battle fatigue, war fatigue* and *museum fatigue* can be analysed as either direct or indirect cause, i.e. approximately 'exhausted by' or 'fed up with'. In unclear cases we chose the direct cause meaning.

Table 3.4 shows the frequency distribution of these *fatigue* compounds in *The Independent* and *The New York Times* in 1990, 1995 and 2000.

As can be seen in Table 3.4, the frequency of the standard, established

Table 3.4 Frequency of *fatigue* compounds in *The Independent* and *The New York Times*, 1990–2000: absolute numbers

		IND			NYT			
		1990	1995	2000	1990	1995	2000	Total
Noun	Direct cause	25	23	21	18	23	20	130
	Indirect cause	8	21	36	7	7	49	128
	Experiencer	31	15	47	14	37	25	169
	Time	1	3	4	1	1	2	12
Total		65	62	108	40	68	96	439

use of *fatigue* in direct cause constructions (e.g. *battle fatigue*) remains quite stable in both IND and NYT. Indirect cause (e.g. *fashion fatigue*) shows a steady increase in IND and a sharp rise from 1995 to 2000 in NYT (this is so even if the 28 instances of *Clinton fatigue* are deducted[1]). The figures for Experiencer (e.g. *commuter fatigue*) show great fluctuations, and conclusions are hard to draw for this category; the Time category, finally, is very small.

Through the method we chose, we were able to see *fatigue* suddenly spread from contexts which have been established and probably stable for a long period (Direct cause) to new, innovative uses (Indirect cause) like the ones from *The New York Times* in (19)–(20):

(19) People have **chicken fatigue**, burger boredom and are tired of pasta and pizza as alternatives, said Al Tank, chief executive of the National Pork Producers Council, based in Des Moines. (NYT, 2000)

(20) The Republicans think this plays into **Clinton fatigue**, said Chris Lehane, Mr. Gore's press secretary. (NYT, 2000)

Our data thus indicated that the vogue use of *fatigue* is an innovation that spread from BrE to AmE, where it caught on approximately five years later than in the UK. The *fatigue* words are therefore an exception to the well-known trend that most lexical influences today go from the US to the UK.

---

[1] Clinton still seems to lead the *fatigue* league, at least among politicians, but Obama is catching up quickly. A Google search on 11 March 2009 yielded 14,900 *Clinton fatigue*, 9,970 *Bush fatigue* and 12,700 *Obama fatigue*. There were only 496 *Blair fatigue* (*Brown fatigue* cannot easily be searched for since most hits will refer to *fatigue* as an article of clothing modified by the colour adjective *brown*).

3.7 How authors use words

So far we have seen how corpora can be used to describe the English language as a whole, or the language of registers like newspaper language or spoken conversation. But it is also possible to use corpus techniques to study the language of individual writers, or specific literary works. This is a branch of quantitative stylistics, or electronic text analysis. Literary stylistics is the study of the linguistic means by which authors produce literary effects. Many such "tricks", like the repetition of certain phrases or structures, the use of long or short sentences, the insertion of numerous adjectives or strange metaphors, and so on, the analyst can easily see with the naked eye. Even if that is the case, as Stubbs (2005) has pointed out, electronic text analysis can add a descriptive basis for what may be an already accepted literary interpretation. But Stubbs also claims that electronic analysis can identify linguistic features which have not been recognised before. In his analysis of Joseph Conrad's short novel *The Heart of Darkness*, one of Stubbs's starting-points is that literary scholars have long noted that the text contains many references to vagueness. But Stubbs can provide the figures. There are more than 150 tokens expressing vagueness: *dark/ly/ness* 52, *shadow/s/y* 21, *gloom/y* 14, *shape/s/d* 13, *smoke* 10, *fog* 9, *shade* 8, *dusk* 7, *mist/y* 7, *blurred* 2, *haze* 2, *murky* 2, *vapour* 1. Here Stubbs was able to substantiate the claims made by literary scholars. He mentions that such scholars often pick up on lexical words, but frequently ignore grammatical words which may have the same effect. His further searches showed that the novel contains more than 200 instances of the vague pronouns *something, somebody, sometimes, somewhere, somehow* and *some*.

However, neither the figures for vague nouns, adjectives and adverbs nor the ones for vague pronouns mean anything as long as we do not know what is normal for a novel. Style is always defined by differences against the average or some other measure. The figures have to be compared to a standard. Stubbs therefore compared the frequencies of the pronouns in *The Heart of Darkness* with the frequencies in two corpora: Fiction in the Brown, LOB, Frown and FLOB corpora (710,000 words) and the written component of the BNC sampler (a short 1-million-word version of the BNC containing various kinds of written text, not just fiction). The results are shown in Table 3.5.

Table 3.5 shows that these vague pronouns are indeed more frequent in *The Heart of Darkness* than in the other corpora, and Stubbs's hypothesis is thus supported. His case would have been even stronger if he had compared Conrad's novel with a corpus made up of novels from the same period rather than present-day English, but in this particular example this is probably not a serious problem.

Table 3.5 Vague pronouns: per 1,000 words

Pronoun	Heart of Darkness	Fiction corpus	BNC sampler written
some	2.6	1.5	1.5
something	1.3	1.0	0.4
somebody	0.2	0.1	0.05
sometimes	0.6	0.2	0.2
somewhere	0.2	0.2	0.03
somehow	0.2	0.1	0.04

Source: Stubbs (2005)

A slightly different method is called 'keyword analysis'. It has been popularised by Mike Scott, who created the corpus analytic tool WordSmith Tools (Scott 2004). By means of this program, it is possible to find out which words are special for a certain text compared with some norm. This is done by calculating statistically which words are more frequent (positive keywords) and less frequent (negative keywords) than expected according to the norm. The method can be used to investigate typical traits of any text or group of texts or genre. Obviously, it is important to choose a relevant norm. For instance, it would be reasonable to compare all Conrad's novels with a representative collection of other novels from the same period to see what is typical of Conrad's style. It is also possible to compare different parts of the same text. In a study of characterisation in Shakespeare's *Romeo and Juliet*, Culpeper (2002) used WordSmith Tools to compare the speech of each of the six main characters in the play with the speech of all the other characters in the same play. Table 3.6 shows the top positive keywords for the six characters (a minimum frequency was set at 5, so that words which occurred less frequently than that do not appear in the table).

Culpeper underlines that it is necessary to undertake a qualitative analysis by examining the individual occurrences of these words before one can be certain that they have something to say about characterisation. For instance, it is important that the words are reasonably well dispersed over all of a character's lines and not just due to the topic of a particular scene. Some of Culpeper's conclusions are summarised here:

- Romeo's keywords match our picture of him as the lover of the play: *beauty, blessed, love* and *dear* belong in this sphere, as does the mention of body parts such as *eyes* and (further down the list, not reproduced here) *lips* and *hand*.

Table 3.6 Top ten positive keywords for six characters in *Romeo and Juliet*: frequency of occurrence given in brackets

Romeo	Juliet	Capulet	Nurse	Mercutio	Friar Laurence
beauty (10)	if (31)	go (24)	day (22)	a (85)	thy (51)
blessed (5)	or (25)	wife (10)	he's (9)	hare (5)	from (23)
love (46)	sweet (16)	thank (5)	you (55)	very (11)	thyself (5)
eyes (14)	be (59)	ha (5)	quoth (5)	of (57)	Mantua (6)
more (26)	news (9)	you (49)	woeful (6)	he (20)	part (7)
mine (14)	my (92)	t (5)	God (12)	the (85)	heaven (10)
rich (7)	night (27)	Thursday (7)	warrant (7)	o'er (5)	forth (5)
dear (13)	I (138)	her (29)	Madam (10)		her (30)
yonder (5)	would (20)	child (7)	Lord (11)		alone (6)
farewell (11)	yet (18)	welcome (5)	Lady (16)		time (10)

Source: Based on Culpeper (2002: 19)

- Juliet's top keyword is *if*, and together with *yet* it suggests that Juliet is in a state of anxiety for much of the play.
- Capulet's top keyword is *go*, usually imperative and used in commands to members of his household, which is typical of his social role.
- The nurse is emotional (*woeful*, *God*) and either addresses or talks about people of higher status (*Madam*, *Lord*, *Lady*). She also likes to gossip about what other people have said (*quoth*).
- Mercutio's keywords indicate that he has a less interactive and more written-like style, with more noun phrases than the others (*a*, *of*, *the*).
- The fact that Friar Laurence has *thy* and *thyself* among the three top keywords leads Culpeper to a special investigation of the characters' use of personal pronouns, but we will not go into that here.

Culpeper's study shows that the keyword method can give interesting results as long as it is complemented by close analysis of the individual text passages. Again we see that quantitative and qualitative analyses need to be combined.

3.8 Summary

In this chapter we have seen that corpora can be used as very useful resources for studying various aspects of the lexicon. For lexicographers, large numbers of authentic examples in context, ordered in concordances, make it possible to make informed judgements about which meanings and constructions to include in dictionaries. Comparing corpus searches with actual dictionary entries, we noted that our results did not fit the description in the dictionary perfectly, which is probably due to the choice of corpora. The notion of semantic prosody was introduced and we saw that corpus searches can be used to check hunches about hidden evaluative meanings in phrases like *set in*. It is a well-known fact that some words suddenly become popular, and then fade away again. The compound *greenhouse effect* seems to be such a word, at least according to the frequency figures for the second half of the twentieth century in *Time* magazine. We also used corpora to investigate differences in word use between written and spoken language and between genres (*may/perhaps*) and the spread of innovations between geographical varieties like AmE and BrE (*fatigue*). Finally we saw that corpus methodology can also be applied to the study of literary style.

Throughout the chapter we discussed advantages and disadvantages of different corpora, and difficulties related to the comparison of different corpora, and noted that size is often important in lexical studies – for all but the most common words you need big corpora to get sufficient numbers of tokens.

Study questions

1. What are the main advantages of corpus-based lexicography compared to the old way of collecting examples by hand?
2. What does "semantic prosody" mean? Do you know other examples of words which have hidden meanings?
3. What does "the colloquialisation of English" mean? Can you think of any further examples?
4. The chapter gives some examples of how corpus methods can be used in literary studies. Do you think this is a good way to study literature? Are there other aspects of literature that could be investigated by means of corpora?

Corpus exercises

Hands-on exercises related to this chapter are available at the following web address:
http://www.euppublishing.com/series/ETOTELAdvanced/Lindquist.

Further reading

A comprehensive practical guide to computer-based lexicography is Atkins and Rundell (2008), which also has a chapter on corpora and dictionary-making. The fascinating story of the *OED* is told in Murray (1977) and Winchester (1988, 2003). Heid (2008) surveys the field of corpus linguistics and lexicography.

Stubbs (2001) is a central work on lexis and meaning. A good basic introduction to electronic text analysis is Adolphs (2006). Further examples of textual and literary corpus studies are given in Scott and Tribble (2006), Starcke (2006) and Mahlberg (2007).

4 Checking collocations and colligations

4.1 Two types of collocations

As pointed out by e.g. the psycholinguist Alison Wray, the tendency in speakers to use groups of words together as multi-word units or phrases is a phenomenon which has been acknowledged by linguists like de Saussure, Jespersen, Bloomfield and many others over the years (cf. Wray 2002: 7 for references). Wray is looking for the rationale behind this human inclination to use "words and strings of regular as well as irregular construction" (2002: 279), and suggests that the explanation lies in the human learning and storing process on the one hand and the retrieval process on the other (2002: 100–102). The ability to combine words in the right way is the key to native-like fluency. Even speakers of English as a second language with an almost perfect command of the language often make small mistakes in the choice of words which mark them as non-natives.

The first important work on word combinations using the term 'collocation' was the pedagogically motivated *Second Interim Report on English Collocations* by the educationalist H. E. Palmer, published rather obscurely in Japan in 1933. It offers the following definition:

> A collocation is a succession of two or more words that must be learnt as an integral whole and not pieced together from its component parts. (1933: title page)

Palmer classified the collocations according to a number of patterns. Figures 4.1 and 4.2 illustrate how the collocations were presented in his book.

I think the reader will recognise all or most of these word combinations as phrases that it would be useful for a learner to master. They all consist of a more or less fixed string, sometimes with an open slot where there is some variation.

The British linguist Firth used the term 'collocation' in a rather

---

31214.2

Pattern

VERB x SPECIFIC N$_2$ x PREP x N$_3$

Note. N$_3$ is generally represented here by *it*.

To get the best of x N$_3$
To have a hard time of it
To have the best [worst, *etc.*] of N$_3$
Not [Never] to hear the last of N$_3$
To hear something [anything, nothing, *etc.*] of [about] N$_3$
To know something [anything, nothing, *etc.*] of [about] N$_3$
To make no bones about N$_3$
To make no mistake about N$_3$
To make a point of N$_3$
To see something [anything, nothing, *etc.*] of [about] N$_3$
To take one's word for N$_3$
To think nothing [little, *etc.*] of N$_3$

Figure 4.1 A verb pattern in H. E. Palmer ([1933] 1966: 62).

35124

The category number 35124 (or 3512.4) stands for all other adverbials of the 3512 type. They may conveniently be subdivided according to their patterns as follows:

Noun x PREP x SAME NOUN

Step by step
One by one
Little by little
Inch by inch
Bit by bit
Face to face
Back to back
Arm in arm
Hand in hand
Word for word

Figure 4.2 Excerpt from a noun pattern in H. E. Palmer ([1933] 1966: 154).

---

different sense, and his statement that "[y]ou shall know a word by the company it keeps" (1957: 11) is often quoted. As the quotation suggests, Firth put greater stress on how the *meaning* of individual words is influenced by other words that it frequently occurs together with. Firth's ideas inspired early computer-based work on collocations by Halliday and Sinclair in the 1960s. Their work resulted in the famous OSTI (Office for Scientific and Technical Information) report in 1970, which was not published until 34 years later (Sinclair et al. 2004). In this tradition, a working definition of collocation can look like this:

> The more-frequent-than-average co-occurrence of two lexical items within five words of text. (Krishnamurthy in Sinclair et al. 2004: xiii)

If we compare this definition with Palmer's given above, it becomes clear that we are dealing with two very different concepts. This has caused considerable confusion, since linguists use the term in either the Palmerian or the Firthian way and do not always make clear which. We will deal with one type at a time, beginning with the Firth/Sinclair type, which I will call 'window collocations', and then return to 'adjacent collocations', which are more like H. E. Palmer's original collocations.

4.2 Collocations in a window

This type of collocation refers to words, called 'collocates', which occur in the vicinity of the keyword but which do not necessarily stand in a direct grammatical relationship with it. The space to the left and right of the keyword that is included in the search for such collocations is called the window. The span of the window can be of varying size depending on the aim of the study. Very commonly it is four or five words to the left and to the right, which is expressed as "− 4 to + 4" or "− 5 to + 5". However, as Sinclair has pointed out (Sinclair et al. 2004: xxvii), "the wider the span, the lower is the significance in general". It should be mentioned that the span does not have to be equally wide to the left and to the right. For some purposes, for instance if you are looking for subjects of certain verbs, it can be better to just look at the five words to the left: − 5.

But let us start with a symmetrical window. If we investigate the verb collocates of the noun *dog* within a window of five words to the left and five words to the right in the BNC, we find that the most common verbs that occur there are the ones given in Table 4.1.

The frequencies given are the number of collocations with the word in question, i.e. the number of times these verbs occur within five words to the left or right of *dog*. The verbs all belong among the most frequent verbs in the language, and knowing that they occur near the word *dog* is not very exciting − it may even be the case that they have nothing at all to do with *dog*, as in (1).

(1)   A man who adored his pet **dog was** told by a nurse: "I've run it over." (BNC CH6)

Table 4.1 Verb collocates of *dog* in the BNC: frequency

Rank	Collocate	N
1	was	2,546
2	is	2,482
3	's	1,698
4	had	1,282
5	have	952
6	be	801
7	do	706
8	would	613
9	said	608
10	has	544

Table 4.2 Verb collocates of *dog* in the BNC: MI score

Rank	Collocate	N	MI value
1	wag	58	7.70
2	barking	253	7.48
3	wagged	36	7.25
4	wags	25	7.21
5	barked	139	7.21
6	wagging	57	7.14
7	barks	643	6.81
8	yapping	191	6.81
9	petting	452	6.52
10	sledding	20	6.52

Was in (1) is counted as a collocate of *dog* since it occurs within five words to the right of it, in spite of the fact that it is the poor man who was told something, not the dog.

To get around the frequency effect, i.e. the fact that very frequent words will frequently occur near any word by sheer chance, there are a number of statistical measures which calculate the frequency of words near the keyword in relation to their total frequency in the corpus. By means of such calculations we get lists of words which occur close to the keyword more often than expected. Using one of these methods, the mutual information (MI) score, we instead get the list of verb collocates for *dog* given in Table 4.2.

Note that it is not necessary for a collocation to have a high frequency to get a high MI score. *Wag, wagged* and *wags* get top positions because out of all instances of these words, a high proportion occur near *dog*

Table 4.3 Noun collocates of *dog* in the BNC: frequency

Rank	Collocate	N
1	dog	384
2	cat	140
3	man	118
4	food	103
5	owners	90
6	dogs	75
7	pet	72
8	time	72
9	police	70
10	guide	67

(about 15%). That words which denote actions that are typical of dogs occur in connection with the word *dog* does not come as a surprise. If we make a search for noun collocates we already get similar results when we order the collocates according to absolute frequency, as in Table 4.3.

Note that *dog* is the most common collocate of *dog*. When we talk about a topic we usually mention it several times, so very often the keyword occurs as a collocate of itself, as in (2).

(2)   The Rottweiler is a working **dog**, a cattle **dog**. (BNC AR5)

Most of the other words in Table 4.3 are semantically related to *dog* and therefore tend to be used in the same context. This is a direct result of the way the world around us is, as illustrated in (3).

(3)   His **cat** was chased by a **dog**, he says, before finding refuge at the top of a concrete lamp post. (BNC K54)

In other cases the words are actually adjacent, as in the compounds in (4) and (5).

(4)   Right you stay there, mummy get the **dog food**. (BNC KBH)
(5)   **Dog owners** in Cleveland have been warned they will have to pick up the tab if their pets go walkabout. (BNC CFA)

Finally, we should note again that some nouns have such a high overall frequency that they occur as collocates of many keywords without having any special relation to them at all. In Table 4.3, *time* is such an example, as in (6).

(6)   This **time** the **dog** didn't come back. (BNC ABX)

Table 4.4 Collocates of *educational* in the BNC (window −5 to +5): by absolute frequency

Rank	Collocate	Total in the BNC	Total as collocate
1	the	6,054,237	2,037
2	,	5,026,136	1,670
3	and	2,621,932	1,620
4	of	3,049,275	1,463
5	.	4,722,094	1,033
6	in	1,946,866	802
7	to	2,599,307	628
8	for	880,715	488
9	an	337,725	389
10	a	169,250	382

In the BNC, *time* is the most frequent noun of all, with 18,330 occurrences (as we saw in Table 2.3), so it is likely to occur close to many words by chance.

To take another example, let us say we want to know which words of any word class occur most frequently together with the adjective *educational* in the BNC, within a span of five words to the left and five words to the right (−5 to +5). Before you go on to read the relevant tables, make a guess, and then see if you were close! Table 4.4 shows the ten most frequent items which occur within the set window.

Since commas and full stops are searchable in the corpus, they turn up as words, but we do not need to bother with them here. As a result of their high general frequency, the most frequent function words dominate the list: out of the eight real words in the table, seven are among the twelve most frequent words in the corpus. The table therefore tells us very little about the word *educational*. It is not very interesting to learn that *the*, *and* and *of* are the words that collocate most often with *educational*! Again, we therefore use the MI score to arrive at the more relevant results in Table 4.5.

The MI formula measures the collocational strength, i.e. the ties between the node word and each collocate. One drawback with this measure, however, is that it gives too much prominence to rare combinations. As can be seen in Table 4.5, the top collocate *non-broadcast* is in fact not very frequent in real numbers (and besides, all the collocations with this word occur in one and the same text, so they are very unevenly dispersed as well). There are a number of other measures that to a varying extent avoid the problem that low-frequency collocates come

Table 4.5 Collocates of *educational* in the BNC (window −5 to +5): by MI
score

Rank	Collocate	Total in the BNC	Total as collocate	Number of texts	MI value
1	non-broadcast	21	11	1	10.7
2	technologist	41	8	2	9.3
3	attainments	76	13	13	9.1
4	technologists	92	15	2	9.0
5	psychologist	518	65	31	8.6
6	Heinemann	82	7	6	8.1
7	establishments	830	54	49	7.7
8	psychologists	862	50	27	7.5
9	interpretive	92	5	2	7.4
10	attainment	910	45	30	7.3

Table 4.6 Collocates of *educational* in the BNC (window −5 to +5): by
z-score

Rank	Collocate	Total in the BNC	Total as collocate	z-score value
1	psychologist	518	65	161
2	needs	19,909	150	150
3	non-broadcast	21	11	135
4	special	21,852	351	132
5	provision	8,744	180	107
6	establishments	830	54	105
7	institutions	6,440	141	98
8	psychologists	862	50	96
9	technologists	92	15	88
10	qualifications	2,304	73	85

high on the list. We will look at the output of two of them, beginning
with z-score in Table 4.6.

Comparing the outcome of the MI test and the z-test, we can see that
most of the collocates which occur high on the z-score list have a higher
absolute frequency than those that come high on the MI list. Intuitively,
then, the z-score list represents the important collocations with *educational* better than the MI list. Let us look at one more table, Table 4.7,
which is based on the outcome of yet another statistical test, called the
log-likelihood test.

As seen in Table 4.7, the log-likelihood formula gives a result which
looks like a compromise between absolute frequency and the z-score

Table 4.7 Collocates of *educational* in the BNC (window −5 to + 5): by log-likelihood

Rank	Collocate	Total in the BNC	Total as collocate	Number of texts	Log-likelihood
1	and	2,621,932	1,620	599	5467
2	the	6,054,237	2,037	521	4755
3	of	3,049,275	1,463	438	4210
4	needs	19,909	382	90	3784
5	,	5,026,136	1,670	570	3758
6	special	21,852	351	55	3349
7	in	1,931,797	802	290	2002
8	provision	8,744	180	77	1802
9	system	44,195	232	130	1690
10	an	337,725	389	228	1689

figure. It allows some frequent lexical words, including function words, to get onto the list, but not the same ones as those that figure on the MI and z-score lists.

From these illustrations it should be clear that the interpretation of collocation data has to take into account which statistical measure has been used, and that before choosing a measure one has to decide what the purpose of the exercise is. Similarly, when you read about the most important collocations of a particular word, you need to know by which measure the collocations were calculated.

4.3 Adjacent collocations

Adjacent collocations are different from the collocations we have just looked at in that the collocates occur immediately to the right or to the left of the keyword (or sometimes with an empty slot in between). This kind of collocation is therefore closer to real linguistic structures and not a statistical phenomenon to such a high extent as the "window collocations".

Each time we choose a word in speaking or writing, we are influenced by the words we have just uttered or written, and also by the words we are planning to speak or write next. There is certainly some truth in the expression "one word led to the next". Of course the strength of this influence depends on the circumstances, how imaginative you are as a speaker and what you want to say. But there is a statistical probability which makes some choices more likely than others. For instance, if you have just said *go to*, the most likely noun to follow is *bed*, at least

Table 4.8 Right collocates of *go to* in the BNC

Collocation	N
go to bed	638
go to sleep	329
go to school	283
go to work	214
go to church	124
go to the toilet	118
go to London	88
go to the police	85
go to court	93
go to hell	69
go to prison	74
go to war	58
go to hospital	50
go to university	57
go to France	43
go to the loo	43
go to the bank	47
go to the cinema	41
go to the hospital	41
go to America	39
go to college	39
go to the doctor	39

according to statistics from the BNC. Table 4.8 gives the twenty-two most likely words or phrases to come after *go to* in the BNC.

Since most of these collocations describe events that occur frequently in British everyday private or public life and are therefore talked about a lot, the words referring to those events occur often, and get associated with each other. This does not mean that we cannot put any word we like after *go to* if it pleases us. If we are going to Bristol and not to London we will say *go to Bristol* (*go to Bristol* occurs five times in the corpus); *go to the gym* occurs three times, as does *go to the horse*, and so on.

The "binding" between the node word and its collocate can go in either direction: forwards from left to right as we have just seen, or backwards from right to left. Let us consider one of the words in Table 4.8. What usually comes before *bed*? Looking at combinations of three words, the ten most frequent collocations in the BNC are given in Table 4.9.

The prepositional phrases *on the bed* and *of the bed* are most frequent, but then *go to bed* turns up again in third place. If we add up the different

Table 4.9 Three-word combinations ending in *bed* in the BNC

Collocation	N
on the bed	753
of the bed	493
go to bed	638
went to bed	343
going to bed	267
in the bed	205
up in bed	171
back to bed	162
to the bed	153
gone to bed	144

forms of the lemma GO in the corpus (*go, went, going, gone* and *goes*) we arrive at the figure 1,438. Clearly, this is the verb most commonly used in connection with *bed* in the BNC.

Let us now turn to collocations with another frequent noun: *hand*, dealt with in Lindquist (2009). In the BNC, the lemma HAND occurs approximately 532 times per million words, and is thereby the most frequent body term noun and the twenty-sixth most frequent noun overall (Leech et al. 2001). In spite of the fact that we have two hands, the singular form *hand* is twice as common as the plural form *hands*, with approximately 355 occurrences per million words against 177. Apart from being used for simple reference to a part of the body, *hand* occurs frequently with extended and metaphorical meanings (for more about metaphors, see Chapter 6). Table 4.10 shows the most frequent left collocates of *hand* in the BNC.

Note that the genitive *'s* is counted as a word in the BNC, and that the same holds for the complex preposition *out of.* The POS tags help us organise the collocates in a number of types:

Preposition + noun: *in hand, to hand, by hand, at hand, out of hand, on hand*
Possessive pronoun + hand: *his hand, her hand, my hand, your hand*
Adjective + noun: *other hand, right hand, left hand*
Article + noun: *a hand, the hand*
Cardinal number + noun: *one hand*
Genitive *'s* + noun: *'s hand*

In the following section, we will take a closer look at the collocations with prepositions, and in particular four whose meanings overlap in

Table 4.10 Left collocates of the noun *hand* in the BNC

Collocation	N	POS tag
other hand	5,564	AJ0 NN1
his hand	3,859	DPS NN1
her hand	2,610	DPS NN1
one hand	2,536	CRD NN1
a hand	2,105	AT0 NN1
in hand	1,306	PRP NN1
the hand	1,246	AT0 NN1
's hand	1,135	POS NN1
right hand	1,102	AJ0 NN1
my hand	953	DPS NN1
left hand	896	AJ0 NN1
your hand	644	DPS NN1
to hand	540	PRP NN1
by hand	517	PRP NN1
at hand	482	PRP NN1
out_of hand	363	PRP NN1
on hand	361	PRP NN1

Note: See notes to Tables 2.3 and 2.13.
Source: Based on Phrases in English (PIE). For more information on PIE, see Chapter 5, section 5.3

quite intriguing ways: *at hand, in hand, on hand* and *to hand.* These collocations show signs of lexicalisation as fixed sequences (which will be the subject of the next chapter) in that they lack definite articles or possessive pronouns and in that they are in fact much more frequent than the more regularly formed strings *at the hand, at his hand* etc. For instance, there were only 15 instances of *at the hand* in the corpus, compared to the 564 instances of *at hand.* Similarly, plural forms are much less frequent than singular. For instance, there were only 24 instances of *in hands.*

The four collocations have a number of meanings ranging from the straightforwardly literal to the non-literal or figurative. The most relevant meanings given by the *OED online* for the four sequences are given in Figure 4.3.

As can be seen in the *OED* excerpts in Figure 4.3, there is a certain overlap in the meanings. In order to see how the collocations were used in the corpus, 200 random tokens of each 2-gram (i.e. identical sequence of two words) were analysed to see what kind of items were described as being *at hand, in hand, on hand* and *to hand.* These were categorised as belonging to one of the categories Humans, Animals, Inanimate concrete items and Abstract items. An overview of the results is given in Table 4.11.

25. **at hand. a.** Within easy reach; near; close by. (Sometimes preceded by *close, hard, near, nigh, ready.*) **b.** Near in time or closely approaching. (Sometimes qualified as prec.)

29. **in hand. a.** *lit.* (Held or carried.) (---) **d.** In actual or personal possession, at one's disposal; (---) **f.** In process; being carried on or actually dealt with in any way. (---) **h.** *in hand:* under control, subject to discipline. (Originally a term of horsemanship, cf. b.)

32. **on hand, upon hand. a.** In one's possession; in one's charge or keeping: said of things, or of work or business which one has to do. (---) **e.** At hand; in attendance (*U.S.*).

34. **to hand. a.** Within reach, accessible, at hand; (---)

Figure 4.3 Selected meanings of *at hand, in hand, on hand* and *to hand* in the *OED online.*

Table 4.11 Items described as being *at hand, in hand, on hand* or *to hand*

Item	at hand	in hand	on hand	to hand	Total
Humans	32	19	151	11	213
Animals	3	1	1	1	6
Inanimate concrete items	55	49	30	123	257
Abstract items	110	131	18	65	324
Total	200	200	200	200	800

Humans, Animals and Inanimate concrete items are relatively straightforward categories, while the category Abstract items subsumes a number of different subcategories, some of which will be discussed below. As seen in Table 4.11, there is some specialisation as regards the type of item that is referred to: *at hand* and *in hand* are similar in being used mainly about abstract things, *on hand* is used mainly about humans and *to hand* about inanimate concrete items. However, there is also considerable overlap: as will be shown below, several of the phrases can be used in identical contexts with seemingly identical meaning.

Humans

On hand stands out as the phrase which is most frequently used about humans, and the fine-grained qualitative corpus analysis gave a rather different picture from the one suggested by the *OED*. The 'in attendance' meaning, marked by *OED* as US, was by far the most common in this British corpus. In no less than 76% of the tokens of *on hand*, it is people who are *on hand*. Frequently the reference is to a 'specialist being available', as in (7).

(7)   If pilots do get in trouble an instructor will be **on hand** to put them right. (BNC CBF)

Other examples are about athletes, footballers and rugby players who happen to be in the right spot to execute a good move, as in (8).

(8)   Paul McGurnaghan's shot came back off the base of the post and David Eddis was **on hand** to hammer the ball into the net. (BNC HJ3)

In a fair number of cases, the reference is to celebrities who are present at some occasion to perform some act, as in (9).

(9)   Believe it or not, Paul Newman is **on hand** to play the President and Susan Sarandon may play the first lady. (BNC CK6)

With *at hand*, human reference is rarer, but it occurs with two main meanings: 'specialist available' as in (10) and 'in the vicinity' (with the word *close*) as in (11).

(10) [. . .] the hard working Mr. Folten who is always **at hand** to offer advice and information on how to get the most out of your short visit. (BNC EBN)
(11) Be prepared for this and ensure that you are close **at hand** with a reverse punch. (BNC A0M)

Of the tokens of *in hand* classified as referring to humans, sixteen are instances of the longer sequence *hand-in-hand*, which can be literal, as in (12), or figurative, as in (13).

(12) People strolled past without giving him a second look – couples **hand-in-hand**, families with pushchairs, groups of friends looking for the right spot for a picnic. (BNC FS8)
(13) Good community care services work best where skilled professionals work comfortably **hand-in-hand** with unskilled staff, families, neighbours and voluntary organizations. (BNC FYW)

Among the eleven tokens of human reference with *to hand*, the 'specialist available' type as in (14) is the most common. However, some tokens refer to people who happen to be present, but are not necessarily experts, as in (15), and there was also one example of the sequence *bring to hand*, which means bring under control (16).

(14) [. . .] she had been severely tempted to just throw in the towel and thumb through the Yellow Pages to find the nearest painter and decorator **to hand**. (BNC JY5)

(15) It was surely an ideal situation for the police, with all the witnesses **to hand**, and even decent interview facilities. (BNC C8D)

(16) "[. . .] introducing some of our ideas on personal training and discipline to ensure bringing the young men of the tribe **to hand** under our guidance in the early stages of their Moranhood." (BNC C90)

Animals

Animals are occasionally referred to, as being experts – or perhaps rather a resource – as in (17), providing an attraction at close distance as in (18) or being put under control as in (19), which is an example of the original equestrian meaning of *take in hand*.

(17) The ferret is, of course, still on the line and remains close **at hand** on the surface near the whole. (BNC BNY)

(18) Obviously I enjoyed to watch any nesting birds so close **at hand** [. . .] (BNC CHE)

(19) She took her mare **in hand** and clicked her tongue authoritatively. (BNC HA2)

Being animate, but still treated by humans more or less as things, Animals make up a small intermediate group between Humans and the next group: Inanimate concrete items.

Inanimate concrete items

In some cases with inanimate concrete items, as in (20)–(22), several of the phrases seem to be synonymous.

(20) Plasticine is useful to have **at hand** for propping up items of icing and marzipan while they are drying. (BNC J11)

(21) Have an emergency tank **on hand**. (BNC FBN)

(22) Have English mustard **to hand**. (BNC CB8)

With concrete reference, the meaning of *in hand* was normally literal, 'with X held in the hand', as in (23) and (24), or a metaphorical extension of that meaning, as in (25) and (26). Note that in (23) and (26), the preposition *with* is present, whereas in (24) and (25), which represent the most common version of the construction by far, *with* is omitted.

(23) As the shadows lengthen, the men can be seen standing around *with a pint of beer* **in hand**, while mothers keep watchful eyes on the kids and catch up on the latest gossip. (BNC A0V)

(24) *Paintbrush* **in hand**, Kylie recalls the beautiful things in life as she creates her own, very individual, landscapes [. . .] (BNC ADR)

Table 4.12 Abstract items referred to by *at hand, in hand, on hand* or *to hand*

Item	at hand	in hand	on hand	to hand	Total
Task/issue/problem	36	28	9	5	78
Information	6	0	1	34	41
Help	28	1	1	2	32
Resources	11	1	3	15	30
Fewer games played in sport etc.	0	22	0	0	22
Action in progress	1	22	0	0	23
Control	0	17	0	0	17
Ongoing activity	11	0	1	1	13
Improvements under way	3	0	2	0	5
Point in time	8	0	0	0	8
Tourist attraction	5	0	1	3	9
Money etc. in possession	0	5	0	2	7
Other	1	0	0	1	2
Total	110	96	18	63	287

(25) [...] they were always prepared to swallow their pride and go, *cap* **in hand**, to the gentry for a few vital coppers. (BNC G39)

(26) Or rather, they're going, but not with *cheque book* **in hand** and buying intentions in mind. (BNC ACR)

Note also that in (23) there is an indefinite article on the held item – *a pint of beer* – whereas in the more eroded versions of the construction the held items – *paintbrush, cap, cheque book* – do not take any form of determiner.

Abstract items

More than one third (39%) of the tokens were abstract, showing the result of a semantic development away from the original meaning of something concrete being situated at, in, on or close to a human hand. This group is more heterogeneous than the others. Table 4.12 gives a breakdown of the various abstract items referred to by *at hand, in hand, on hand* or *to hand*.

There is not space to go into all the subcategories here, but let us just take a look at the first one, 'task/issue/problem'. In this type there is reference to a task that someone has to carry out, an issue which is being discussed, or a problem that needs to be solved. These are common with *at hand* and *in hand* as in (27)–(28), and less common with *on hand* as in (29) and *to hand* as in (30).

(27) Making notes is the best way of keeping your mind on the task **at hand**. (BNC EEB)
(28) However elaborate (indeed, contrived) this theorizing may be, it is not wholly adequate for the task **in hand**. (BNC APH)
(29) Considering the possibly apocalyptic and doom-laden task we have **on hand** [. . .] (BNC CKC)
(30) They just got on with whatever task was **to hand**. (BNC H7E)

The fact that all four phrases are used in the corpus with the same noun, *task*, without any clear difference in meaning, shows that there is variation, probably between different speakers and possibly also in the language of individual speakers. The conclusion must be that the meaning of the individual prepositions adds little to the meaning of the whole sequence. It is rather the sequence "preposition + *hand*" which is meaningful, and this makes it possible to exchange one preposition for the other. The analysis of abstract items shows that there is considerable overlap in use between two or three of the phrases in four of the categories: 'task/issue/problem', 'information', 'resources' and 'tourist attraction'. At the same time, there is clear specialisation in three categories: 'fewer games played, 'action in progress' and 'point in time'.

The phrases *at hand, in hand, on hand* and *to hand* have gone through a change in meaning from the concrete, literal meaning in *at my hand*, to the more abstract prepositional or adverbial meaning in *at hand*. This process can be called lexicalisation. A phrase like *at hand* contains two words which make up one single multi-word unit. However, this is not unlikely to be a stage in a development towards a stage where the phrase becomes a word, like *behind*; the Swedish cognate of *at/in/on/ to hand*, for instance, can be written either as two words or as a single word: *tillhands* (*to*+*hand*+genitive). Whatever the end-point of this process will be, it seems likely that old and new forms and meanings will co-exist. For instance, *in hand* may retain its concrete meaning in *with a glass of beer in hand*, and the preposition *in* may be exclusively used in this phrase in this context, while the meaning of *in hand* in *the task in hand* may develop to become even more general. As far as solid spelling (i.e. spelling as one word) is concerned, a Google search (13 July 2007) threw up the following numbers of hits: *task athand* 241, *task inhand* 122, *task onhand* 51, *task tohand* 0. Some of these tokens are no doubt the result of sloppy typing on discussion forums and technical accidents (see Chapter 10 for a discussion about the quality of web data), but quite a few are from serious, authoritative sources. The fact that there were zero hits for *task tohand* agrees with the results of searches for *athand, inhand*, *onhand* and *tohand* on their own and in various other combinations, in that *tohand* is very much less frequent than the other three. It is not clear why this should be so, but it can perhaps be due to influence from the infinitive *to hand*.

This rather long and detailed study of phrases with *hand* has illustrated a number of points. We have seen that there is much more variation in everyday language use than one would expect from just reading textbooks, grammars and dictionaries, and that corpus methods are ideal to find out about this. The examples where four different prepositions, which in themselves mean very different things, are used with *hand* to mean apparently the same thing show that in communication, sometimes anything goes – people will always try to understand! Still, some collocations are more standard than others, and searches like this can help both learners and native speakers to find out whether a particular construction is acceptable or not, for instance when they are writing in English. Conversely, such searches are useful for teachers, who sometimes have a tendency only to accept the most common variant even if there are several acceptable ones. The exact position of the line between "right" and "wrong" is not always self-evident.

4.4 Colligations

Colligations make up the second type of extended lexical units in Sinclair's system, mentioned in Chapter 3: collocation, colligation, semantic preference and semantic prosody. The term comes from Firth, but was not very clearly defined by him. It is usually taken to refer to the relation between a node word and grammatical categories such as a preposition or a *wh*-clause which co-occur frequently with it, or, expressed differently, the grammatical constructions in which a word frequently occurs. Again, we will use Phrases in English (PIE) to illustrate the phenomenon. Searching for a string consisting of the verb *deny* and two following empty slots, we get the strings listed in Table 4.13. (For more information about PIE, see Chapter 5, section 5.3.)

The term "POS-gram" in Table 4.13 is used in PIE to refer to a string of part-of-speech tags, just as "n-gram" is used generally in linguistics to refer to a string of words (where n can be any number). We can see in the table that in this corpus, *deny* is most frequently followed by a *that*-clause as in (31) or an NP in a transitive construction (i.e. with a direct object) as in (32). Less frequently, we find -*ing* clauses as in (33) and NPs in ditransitive clauses (with a direct and an indirect object) as in (34).

Table 4.13 Colligations of *deny* in the BNC

Phrase	N	POS-gram	Co-occurring grammatical class
deny that the	61	VVI CJT AT0	*that*-clause
deny that there	28	VVI CJT EX0	*that*-clause
deny that it	26	VVI CJT PNP	*that*-clause
deny that they	21	VVI CJT PNP	*that*-clause
deny the existence	20	VVI AT0 NN1	NP (transitive)
deny that he	15	VVI CJT PNP	*that*-clause
deny the charges	15	VVB AT0 NN2	NP (transitive)
deny the importance	13	VVI AT0 NN1	NP (transitive)
deny approval to	12	VVI NN1 PRP	NP (transitive)
deny approval to	11	VVB NN1 PRP	NP (transitive)
deny the reality	11	VVI AT0 NN1	NP (transitive)
deny that she	9	VVI CJT PNP	*that*-clause
deny that the	9	VVB CJT AT0	*that*-clause
deny that they	9	VVB CJT PNP	*that*-clause
deny that a	8	VVI CJT AT0	*that*-clause
deny that i	8	VVI CJT PNP	*that*-clause
deny attempting to	7	VVB VVG TO0	*-ing* clause
deny that some	7	VVI CJT DT0	*that*-clause
deny that we	7	VVI CJT PNP	*that*-clause
deny them the	7	VVI PNP AT0	NP (ditransitive)
deny her the	6	VVI PNP AT0	NP (ditransitive)

Note: See note to Table 2.13.

(31) Raybestos officials **deny that** the move to Ireland was in any way connected with the difficulties faced by producers of asbestos products in the US. (BNC CDD)
(32) Few would **deny the existence** of class differences. (BNC FB1)
(33) They also **deny attempting to** murder two other officers [. . .] (BNC CFC)
(34) How do we encourage membership when you openly **deny them the** right to vote? (BNC HUC)

The idea is that colligations, i.e. co-occurring grammatical categories, just like collocations, are part of the information bound up in a word. When native speakers know the word *deny*, they do not only know its spelling, pronunciation and meaning. They also know the collocations and colligations it occurs in. And when children or foreigners learn English, this is part of what they have to learn.

4.5 Summary

This chapter focused two types of collocations: the statistical type where words co-occur more often than expected within a specified window to the left and right of a keyword, and adjacent collocations, which are more like phrases. We saw that we get a very different picture of the "window collocates" of a word depending on whether the results are presented as absolute frequencies or according to one of the available statistical formulae that measure the collocational strength: mutual information (MI), z-score and log-likelihood. For adjacent collocations, we made a detailed study of collocations with the word *hand*, and in particular *at hand*, *in hand*, *on hand* and *to hand*, finding that these phrases are used sometimes with the same meaning and sometimes with specialised meanings which cannot always be predicted from the meaning of the individual prepositions. We noted that such information, which can easily be got out of corpora, can be of great value for language learners in their language production and for language teachers when they prepare their lessons and mark student papers.

Finally, the notion of colligation was illustrated by the example of the verb *deny* and the different grammatical constructions that it can occur in.

Study questions

1. What are the two main types of collocations mentioned in the chapter and what is the difference between them? Which do you think is most useful for language learners? For linguists?
2. What is meant by a window and how can it be described?
3. How can a word be a collocate of itself?
4. Lists of collocates can be based on absolute frequency or one of a number of statistical measures. What is the difference between the kind of collocates that appear on these lists?
5. What are colligations?

Corpus exercises

Hands-on exercises related to this chapter are available at the following web address:

http://www.euppublishing.com/series/ETOTELAdvanced/Lindquist.

Further reading

Good places to read more about collocations include Sinclair (1991, 1999, 2003), Hunston and Francis (2000) and Stubbs (2001, 2009).

Innovative ways of studying collocations and colligations are described in Stefanowitsch and Gries (2009). For a thorough discussion of the concept 'collocation' and more about collocation statistics, see Evert (2009).

5 Finding phrases

5.1 Phraseology

Corpora and corpus methodology have led to a renewal of the study of phrases, i.e. more or less fixed strings which are used over and over again. Traditionally, researchers concentrated on opaque, "funny" idioms like *kick the bucket, a bee in one's bonnet* and *bark up the wrong tree* (which are in fact very rare in real language use), but more recently the focus has shifted to less striking strings of words which are semantically and grammatically more "normal", but nevertheless seem to be stored and processed as units in the human brain. Such phrases are much more important for the understanding of how the English language works, and for learners who want to learn the language. There is a plethora of terms describing the phenomenon: 'idioms', 'fixed phrases', 'recurring strings' etc., and recently the term 'formulaic sequence' has been introduced for the concept by Wray (2002). In the present book, however, we will use 'phrase' in a non-technical sense.

Phrases are quite close to the second type of collocation that we discussed in the previous chapter, namely adjacent collocations. Phrases are more or less fixed strings of words. Traditionally, people have talked about 'fixed expressions', stressing the fixedness of these expressions, but corpus studies have shown that many of the phrases can actually be varied. For instance, Moon found that around 40% of the large number of phrases she investigated had lexical variations or strongly institutionalised transformations, and around 14% had two or more variations of their canonical (standard) forms (Moon 1998: 120). In her study, Moon investigated 6,776 "fixed expressions and idioms" in a corpus of 18 million words. This was considered reasonably big at the time, but looks rather small by present standards. The corpus was also rather skewed, since 60 per cent of it consisted of newspaper texts. Nevertheless, she got many interesting results. The method she used was to make a list of fixed expressions and idioms based on printed sources like dictionaries

Table 5.1 Conventionalised actions described by formulaic 6-grams containing *hand* in the BNC

Phrase	N
ran a hand through his/her hair	(10 + 12) = 22
put a hand on his/her shoulder	(11 + 6) = 17
put his/her hand in his/her pocket	(16 + 1) = 17
laid a hand on his/her arm	(11 + 3) = 14
put a hand on his/her arm	(6 + 6) = 12

and idiom dictionaries and then search for these in the corpora. The drawback with this method is that it only investigates well-known phrases which have been listed in the dictionaries and other sources, and there is a risk that new phrases and phrases which are less conspicuous will be missed.

In this chapter we will start by investigating some idioms of the "funny" kind and then move on to the less remarkable types. Before we do that, however, we must say a few words about two concepts which were coined by Sinclair (1991: 100): 'the idiom principle' and 'the open choice principle'. Sinclair is one of the strongest proponents of the view that phraseology is central to our understanding of language, and not something belonging in the periphery (cf. Ellis 2008). In short, Sinclair's thesis is that we as language users have at our disposal a very large number of "semi-preconstructed phrases", which are the first options when we speak. Only when we cannot retrieve a suitable phrase or "idiom" from memory do we construct a sentence from scratch by means of the grammar and lexicon of the language. The latter procedure is called open choice. This theory presupposes that we store large numbers of phrases in our brains. We can see indications that this is the case in corpora, which show us that there is a considerable repetitiveness in language. In many situations, there are dozens of ways to express a particular meaning, but we use only the conventional one which we have stored in our brain. This is true for greetings and scores of other phrases used in daily interaction (*good morning, sleep tight, drive safely, here you are*, and so on), but also for the way we describe many routine, everyday actions like the ones listed in Table 5.1.

Most of the tokens in Table 5.1 are from the fiction component of the BNC. The actions could have been described in many other ways, e.g. for the first phrase: *dragged a hand through his/her hair, pulled a hand through his/her hair, moved a hand through his/her hair, passed a hand through his/her hair* or *pushed a hand through his/her hair*. But of these, only *dragged a hand through his/her hair* (three tokens) occurs. Clearly, a conventionalised, ready-made way of describing this action pops up automatically in the writer's mind, so that he or she does not have to construct a sentence by applying grammatical rules to individual lexical items. This of course does not mean that writers cannot decide to use the open choice principle instead, and write *raked a hand through his hair, fiddled a hand through his hair, swept a hand through his hair* or whatever they can come up with. But the thing is, they usually don't.

In passing, we can note that some of these actions are unisex, so to speak – both men and women run their hands through their hair – while some are typically male (putting one's hand in one's pocket) and others typically happen to males (*laid a hand on his arm*). Such who-did-what-to-whom sequences could clearly be used in studies on gender stereotypes in language, which we will come back to in Chapter 8.

How we store phrases in our mental lexicon when we learn a language and how we retrieve these stored phrases in split seconds when we need them are not yet clear, but psycholinguists are devising various experiments to investigate further. Wray (2002) presents an influential model, where lexical items are actually stored several times, both as individual words and as parts of longer sequences, depending on the need of the individual speaker. This double or multiple storage is necessary, since normally we can access not only the complete phrases, but the individual words that make up phrases as well, if we need to – and write things like *he sneaked his hand through his hair*.

5.2 Idioms

There are innumerable intricate definitions of 'idiom' in the literature, but here we will use the following simple version:

> An idiom is a fixed or semi-fixed expression whose meaning cannot be deduced from its parts.

Very few idioms are 100% fixed. Most of them are like *pay through the nose* 'pay an exorbitant sum', where the verb can be inflected for tense (*paid/paying through the nose*); *bend the rules* 'not quite follow the rules', where a different verb can be chosen (*stretch the rules*); or *a tough nut to crack* 'a difficult problem', where one part can be deleted (*a tough nut*). The second part of the definition refers to the fact that most idioms are more or less opaque, i.e. it is hard or impossible to figure out their meaning even if you know the meaning of their parts. In some cases you might be able to guess the general drift of the meaning, as in *to turn the tables* 'to reverse the relation between two people or parties', while in others it is virtually impossible, as in *high and dry* in (1).

(1)   It leaves me **high and dry** as far as the debt's concerned. (BNC H97)

Is it good or bad to be high and dry? Conceivably, it could be either, but in fact the idiom is based on the nautical meaning of being stranded, so it is bad. This idiom is opaque in spite of the fact that it consists of common words combined by simple grammar. Other idioms are opaque because they contain strange words, like *kith and kin* 'friends and relations', or because the grammar is odd, like *by and large* 'in general'. Finally, many idioms are metaphorical, like *a storm in a teacup*, and the extent to which those are opaque has to do with your ability to understand the image used in the metaphor, which, among other things, depends on your cultural background and familiarity with the semantic field from which the image is taken. (We will deal more with metaphors in the next chapter.)

To be fluent in a language you need to know and recognise a large number of idioms. You even have to recognise the idioms when they have been manipulated and distorted for special effect. We will use a very simple method to investigate how this is done with *a storm in a teacup* by searching the web by means of Google. In the advanced search mode of Google, it is possible to choose a particular domain. Choosing uk will give you British pages, edu will give you pages from American educational institutions, gov will give you mainly American government pages, nz will give you New Zealand pages and so on. For each of these, and other similar domain suffixes, there is a good likelihood that a majority of the texts you get will be written by native speakers of that region. But of course not all: there are lots of non-native speakers at all universities in the English-speaking world, there are Americans in the UK etc. But by choosing these suffixes you will avoid much of the non-native English material that you get on pages from non-English-speaking countries like Sweden, Germany or Japan. We will return in more detail to these matters in Chapter 10.

To find variants of *a storm in a teacup*, I typed in the truncated form "*storm in a*" as an exact phrase in the advanced search dialogue box, chose the uk domain, and set the number of hits per screen to 30. (To simplify matters in this illustrative example, I disregard the fact that since this search string ends in *a*, it will only capture variations where the following word begins with a consonant.) As is well known, the results for each hit are given by Google in 3–6 lines in the following form:

> ### *Zoe Williams: Storm in a teen cup | Comment is free | The Guardian-*
> 30 apr 2008 . . . Zoe Williams: Miley Cyrus has no need to apologise for her Vanity Fair pose as it's essentially meaningless.
> www.guardian.co.uk/commentisfree/2008/apr/30/children.usa – 79k –

Table 5.2 Variations in the idiom *storm in a teacup*. From Google search on the uk domain, 20 July 2008: first thirty hits

Idiom	Tokens
storm in a teacup	13
miserable storm in a teacup	1
storm in a British tea cup	1
storm in a D cup	1
storm in a DD cup	1
storm in a dVb cup	1
storm in a Royal D cup	1
storm in a teacake	1
storm in a teasmade	1
storm in a teen cup	1
storm in a test tube	1
storm in a turban	1
storm in a whiskey glass	1
Total	25

Sometimes it is necessary to click on the heading and search the whole web page to find the word or phrase searched for, but in this quick and dirty study we will just count tokens where *storm in a* shows up in these 3–6 lines. The search results for the uk domain are given in Table 5.2.

As can be seen in Table 5.2, only half of the tokens used the so-called canonical complete form of the idiom. The variations are of a few different types. First of all, the nouns in the canonical idiom can be elaborated by modifiers, as in *miserable storm* and *British tea cup*. The most common way to exploit the idiom, however, is to exchange one of the words for one that fits the topic of the text better. The pun on D and DD cups (which are sizes for bras) seems to have been irresistible. Two versions refer to tea: *storm in a teasmade* (which is an automatic device for making tea) and the rather intriguing *storm in a teacake*. And then there are storms in a whiskey glass, a test tube and a turban (!).

A similar search in the New Zealand domain, nz, dredged up the following additional variants among the first thirty hits: *storm in a milk bottle / coffee cup / latte cup / java cup / cappuccino cup / beer cup* and *storm in a six-pack*, which taken together suggest that drinking habits in New Zealand might be different from those in the UK, and that this difference influences language use. (Incidentally, the Swedish variant of this idiom is rather boringly 'storm in a water glass'.) In AmE, the canonical form of the idiom is *a tempest in a teapot*, and a similar search on the edu domain

Table 5.3 Canonical forms of idioms in global Englishes

Idiom	edu	ca	uk	au	nz	za	in	hk	ph
cut a long story short	918	1,710	**46,700**	**11,700**	1,910	2,080	3,170	**151**	113
make a long story short	**8,100**	**12,200**	6,280	4,900	372	1,380	**5,540**	115	**266**
have green fingers	7	9	**1,450**	67	**105**	**30**	5	2	1
have a green thumb	**1,010**	**1,590**	767	**717**	16	16	**6**	**9**	**6**

Note: edu = American academic, ca = Canada, uk = United Kingdom, au = Australia, nz = New Zealand, za = South Africa, in = India, hk = Hong Kong, ph = Philippines. For each regional variety, the figure for the dominating variant is marked in boldface.

Source: From Google searches, 31 July 2008

found the variants *tempest in a teacup* (2) / *washbowl* / *cocktail glass* / *wine glass* / *textbook* / *T-shirt.* It is clear that the authors of all these English variants manipulate the form of the idiom, expecting that the reader will know the canonical form and appreciate the authors' cleverness.

Moon (1998: 133–135) lists several other idioms which have different canonical forms in BrE and AmE. It is a well-known fact that varieties of global English often adhere to either the British or the American norm, both in the lexicon and in grammar. One way to illustrate this is to look at which variant of an idiom is preferred in different geographical varieties. Table 5.3 gives the total number of hits for *cut/make a long story short* 'be brief' and *have green fingers/a green thumb* 'be a good gardener' in a selection of global Englishes.

It has to be pointed out that Google figures are not fully reliable (more about this in Chapter 10). The search was also simplified in that only the infinitive and plural verb forms of *have green fingers/a green thumb* were searched for, but this is not likely to have influenced the relation between the varieties.

Since the total number of words is different in the domains, we cannot compare frequencies between them, but we can compare the ratio between the idiom variants in each domain. For *cut/make a long story short,* we can first note that the *cut* variant is most frequent in the UK and its former colonies Australia, New Zealand, South Africa and Hong Kong, whereas the *make* variant is most popular in the US, Canada and the Philippines (and also India). However, we can also see that the ratio between the variants differs, from 7.4:1 in uk to only 1.3:1 in hk (suggesting that Hong Kong English is almost as much influenced by AmE as by BrE on this point) and from 8.8:1 in edu to 2.4:1 in ph (suggesting that Philippine English is not totally dominated by AmE).

Looking next at *have green fingers/a green thumb*, we find a similar division between the varieties, except that Australia and Hong Kong seem to have defected from their former colonial rulers and switched over to the American *thumb* variant. Another noteworthy thing is that the dispreference for *fingers* is very strong in the US and Canada with ratios well over 100:1, which means that this variant is hardly ever used there.

A larger survey including more idioms and perhaps more English-speaking domains would probably show that the spread of idioms which have different canonical forms in BrE and AmE patterns fairly well with the present and historical spheres of political and cultural influence of Britain and the United States. But as has already been shown by this mini-survey, there will also be individual differences between the idioms, for which the explanations must be sought in detailed studies of the idioms in context. For a language learner who wants to sound natural in any of these English-speaking environments, information of this kind can be very useful.

5.3 Recurrent phrases

A different approach from that of studying the kind of idioms that you find in idiom dictionaries is to study all strings of words that recur in texts with a frequency above a specified limit. This of course has to be done by computer. For instance, Altenberg (1998) investigated recurring phrases in the London-Lund spoken corpus. This is a small corpus (500,000 words), and, defining recurrent phrases as those which were at least two words long and occurred more than once, Altenberg found that there were more than 201,000 recurrent word combinations, making up approximately 80% of the corpus! (With a different methodology and different material, Erman and Warren (2000) arrived at the figure 55%, which is also quite high.) However, Altenberg also points out that many of these have little interest since they consist of fragments of larger structures like *and the* or *in a*. To concentrate on recurring word combinations which were likely to be of greater linguistic interest, he therefore looked at strings of three words or more which occurred at least ten times. He found that such strings could represent a number of different structures, which he called independent and dependent full clauses, single and multiple clause constituents and incomplete phrases. Among the single clause constituents he found the ones presented in Table 5.4, organised according to function.

Table 5.4 Some common types of single clause elements with a length of three words or more in the LLC

Type of element	Example	N
Vagueness tags	and so on	47
	or something like that	16
	and all that	14
	and things like that	14
	something like that	13
	sort of thing	11
	that sort of thing	10
Qualifying expressions	more or less	28
	in a way	15
	in a sense	11
	on the whole	10
Intensifiers/quantifiers	the whole thing	24
	a bit more	17
	a little bit	16
	a lot more	11
	a little more	10
	the whole lot	10
Connectors	first of all	17
	at any rate	15
	in other words	15
	on the other hand	14
	at the same time	10
	as a matter of fact	10
Temporal expressions	at the moment	43
	all the time	26
	in the past	22
	the other day	16
	in the morning	15
	at that time	14
	for the first time	12
	in the afternoon	11
	in the end	11
	at this stage	11
	for a long time	10
	for a moment	10
	in the future	10
	at the time	10
	at the same time	10
Spatial expressions	in this country	22
	at the back	11
	in the country	11
	in the field	11
	in the house	10
	in the world	10

Source: Altenberg (1988: 117)

Table 5.5 Some frequent incomplete phrases with a length of three words or more in the LLC

Example	*N*
out of the	42
a sort of	34
the sort of	30
a lot of	25
because of the	24
a couple of	20
what sort of	19
part of the	19
one of the	19
a kind of	19

Source: Altenberg (1998: 119)

Altenberg observes that the majority of the phrases in Table 5.4 have adverbial function and clearly play important roles in discourse, referring to time, space and the organising of the discourse itself. Many are typical of speech and hardly occur in written language at all.

Altenberg also points out that the phrases are on a cline from the conventionalised and fixed *and so on* to the fully rule-produced compositional *in the house*. An awareness of the conventionalised phrases is of course highly useful to foreign learners who want to sound natural and idiomatic.

While the phrases in Table 5.4 are complete units, a computer search for frequent n-grams (recurring identical sequences of words) will also retrieve a number of strings which are incomplete phrases, like the ones in Table 5.5.

We see in Table 5.5 a number of phrases where at least one word, usually a lexical one, is missing. Since the choice of lexical word depends on the topic of the conversation, the lexical word will vary much more than the rest of the phrase. We will now investigate which words come after these incomplete phrases in a corpus which is approximately 200 times bigger than the LLC, namely the BNC. Before you read the results in Table 5.6, take a look at the phrases in Table 5.5 and see if you can guess which words are most likely to follow the incomplete phrases.

Bearing in mind that Altenberg's incomplete phrases came from a corpus of spoken English, while the collocates in Table 5.6 are from the BNC, which, even if it contains 10 million words of spoken English, a considerable amount of fiction (with dialogue) and newspaper text (with

Table 5.6 Right collocates of some frequent incomplete phrases in the BNC

Incomplete phrase	*Right collocates*
out of the	*window* 750, *way* 652, *room* 385, *house* 378, *car* 333, *question* 277, *water* 197, *door* 189, *country* 165, # (any number) 163
a sort of	*a* 89, *er* 18, *erm* 16, *an* 9, *family* 7, *general* 7, *little* 7, *big* 6, *limbo* 6, *mental* 6
the sort of	*thing* 358, *person* 122, *things* 90, *people* 88, *man* 86, *place* 55, *the* 35, *woman* 32, *questions* 26, *information* 23
a lot of	*people* 1,228, *the* 822, *money* 789, *time* 495, *them* 352, *work* 316, *things* 287, *it* 245, *other* 146, *trouble* 131
because of the	*way* 185, *lack* 89, *nature* 87, *high* 85, *need* 62, *difficulty* 58, *recession* 52, *risk* 51, *large* 48, *presence* 46
a couple of	*years* 598, *days* 498, *weeks* 427, *hours* 373, *times* 301, *months* 233, *minutes* 223, *hundred* 128, *the* 107, *miles* 77
what sort of	*things* 118, *a* 99, *person* 39, *people* 34, *thing* 33, *life* 16, *information* 15, *man* 15, *place* 11, *business* 10
part of the	*world* 295, *country* 223, *process* 187, *same* 135, *reason* 121, *problem* 119, *body* 118, *city* 96, *story* 90, *new* 89
one of the	*most* 4090, *few* 887, *first* 853, *best* 815, *main* 638, *things* 588, *reasons* 508, *major* 476, *great* 475, *world's* 405
a kind of	*a* 29, *er* 15, *erm* 9, *mental* 9, *intellectual* 8, *moral* 8, *cultural* 7, *surrogate* 7, *death* 6, *peace* 6

Source: Incomplete phrases from Altenberg (1998: 119)

quoted speech), still predominantly consists of written English, we can make the following comments.

- Two of the incomplete phrases (*a sort of* and *a kind of*) seem to occur mainly in spoken language, since they have low frequencies in the BNC and occur with typical spoken language hesitation markers like *er* and *erm*.
- The incomplete prepositional phrase *out of the* occurs mainly with concrete nouns, but also with the two abstract nouns *way* and *question* in the phrases *out of the way* and *out of the question*. (*Out of the blue* was number 12, with 146 tokens.)
- The seven most frequent collocates of *a couple of* were time nouns. Few native speakers would probably have guessed this.
- Although most of the collocates are lexical words that complete the phrase, there are also cases where the collocate is a premodifier of the next word, as in *a sort of little* and *one of the major*.
- In some cases the collocate is an article which is part of a following noun phrase, as in *a sort of a* and *a couple of the*.

Table 5.7 The most frequent 5-grams in the BNC

5-gram	N
at the end of the	4,531
by the end of the	1,840
i do n't want to	1,761
i do n't know what	1,751
as a result of the	1,597
in the middle of the	1,516
the secretary of state for	1,365
the other side of the	1,234
at the time of the	1,160
you do n't have to	1,050

As Altenberg notes, these incomplete phrases are "fixed" to a greater or lesser extent, and it is hard or impossible to draw a sharp line between the groups. Instead, there is a cline from quite fixed phrases like *a couple of* on the one hand and phrases that are more likely to have been constructed on the spot by means of the rules of the grammar, like *because of the*, on the other.

The Phrases in English (PIE) database
Recurrent phrases in the BNC can easily be studied by means of the database Phrases in English (PIE), created by William Fletcher (2003/2004). This database contains all n-grams (identical strings of words) with a length between one and eight words which occur three times or more in the BNC. The database is freely available on the net and is very easy to use. We will start by using the "gram" function and type in +++++ to get the most frequent identical strings of five words, 5-grams, in the BNC. The results are given in Table 5.7.

In line with what has been pointed out by Stubbs (2007a: 91), the grammatical construction "Preposion + article + noun + *of* + article" turns up as the most frequent structure among the 5-grams (*at the end of the, by the end of the, as a result of the, in the middle of the, at the time of the*). We also see three 5-grams which are typical of spoken language (which is represented in the 10 million words of transcribed spoken language in the corpus, but also in quotations in newspapers and dialogue in fiction): *I don't want to, I don't know what* and *you don't have to.*

By clicking on the 5-gram in the list presented by the PIE search program we get the concordances and can study the 5-grams in context. The immediate contexts for a random selection of tokens of *at the end of the* are given in Figure 5.1

1. The small resort village of Fluelen **at the end of the** lake was for centuries an important lake port and customs station where goods were trans-shipped from the lake to mule transport for carriage over the Gotthard. (FTU)
2. A working marble quarry is passed **at the end of the** walk. (A65)
3. Sociologically the difference between working and middle classes was that between servant-keepers and potential servants, and was so used in Seebohm Rowntree's pioneer social survey of York **at the end of the** century. (J0P)
4. **At the end of the** discussion the Cabinet: (1) (EEC)
5. But I was so confident I would feel the solidness of either chub or root my reactions are not prepared to stop **at the end of the** strike. (B0P)
6. This figure would have been much smaller in the early 1960s and higher **at the end of the** period. (CDU)
7. Giles Smith CARDIFF'S joy at their 8-6 victory over Heineken League leaders Swansea in this top-of-the-table clash was shattered last night when their inspirational Australian coach Alex Evans announced he may quit the club **at the end of the** season. (CBG)
8. Any gains made are locked in **at the end of the** quarter. Should the market fall, no loss of original capital is incurred: only the cost of the futures and options has to be borne. (CBW)
9. Once the Knights had made their challenges ready for the tourney held **at the end of the** show and the demonstrations of dancing, archery and squire practice had started I wandered off outside the arena to demonstrate spinning with a drop spindle. (HRS)
10. Which put me off gambling for good, because whilst we won every day, it seemed, we'd lost a lot of money **at the end of the** year. (FY4)

Figure 5.1 Extended concordance lines for ten random tokens of *at the end of the* in the BNC.

Even this short list of ten random examples out of the 4,531 tokens in the corpus shows that the phrase occurs in different registers, including spoken language. A first analysis of the right collocates would indicate that the string is used with nouns denoting places (*lake, walk*), time periods (*century, period, season, quarter, year*) and activities (*discussion, strike, show*). Of course more concordance lines would have to be scrutinised before a full picture of the use of *at the end of* could be put together.

The immediate context of ten random tokens of *I don't know what* is given in Figure 5.2.

It seems as if *I don't know what* is frequently part of a construction where it is followed by a clause beginning with a pronoun or a proper name as subject (as in 1, 3, 5, 7, 8, 9) and a lexical verb like *buy, think* and *tell* or a dummy or empty verb like *do*. In 6 it is followed by an object (*book*), and in 4 it seems to function as a complete phrase on its own, expressing confusion: *I don't know what* – full stop.

Looking for the most frequent 5-gram we found that it was *at the end of the* with the structure "PREP + Art + NOUN + *of* + Art". Another way

---

1. **I don't know what** you will buy Saturday. (KDW)
2. To sixty-five thousand. **I don't know what** is now. Then he (KDP)
3. **I don't know what** I am doing. I have a part-time job, but I have been off sick for the last two weeks, because I can't keep my mind on it. (K4L)
4. But ever since the good men started to go down and get married and have families and **I don't know what** . . . well, **I don't know what** . (ASD)
5. I – well, **I don't know what** you must be thinking of me. (BMU)
6. "I swear to you **I don't know what** book you're talking about," he said. (G0P)
7. "**I don't know what** I can tell you," he said. (GW0)
8. "**I don't know what** I'd do without them these days." (HRT)
9. "**I don't know what** Nigel thought, you'll have to ask him that." (CH3)
10. "**I don't know what** progress is, but I don't think that would really have been progress," I said. (H0D)

Figure 5.2 Concordance lines for ten random tokens of *I don't know what* in the BNC.

of using PIE is to look for the most frequent string of tags in the corpus, i.e. the most frequent structure. PIE calls this a POS-gram. The ten most frequent such tag sequences are given in Table 5.8.

Among the ten top tag sequences in Table 5.8, five are noun phrases or fragments of noun phrases (2, 3, 5, 8, 9), four are prepositional phrases or fragments of prepositional phrases (1, 4, 6, 7) and one is part of a verb phrase (10). In this way, a general statistical description of the most frequent structures of the English language might be constructed.

However, sometimes we want to study specific lexical items. For instance, we noted in Chapter 2 that apart from *other*, the most frequent adjectives in the BNC are *good, new* and *old*. It might be interesting to see what nouns these adjectives are used with. This is possible to investigate in PIE by searching for the adjective + the tag for common noun with the search string: *good* + {nn?}. Table 5.9 gives the most frequent combinations.

Most of the phrases in Table 5.9 feel familiar and are almost fixed expressions (*good idea, good news, good time, good thing, good job, good example*). Two are conventionalised greetings (*good evening* and *good morning*), one is most often part of a grammaticalised quantifier (*a good deal*) and one is involved in a set of adverbial expressions including *for a (very) good reason, for no good reason* and *with (very) good reason*. Another observation is that *good* means rather different things in these phrases: 'positive' (*good news*), 'enjoyable' (*good time*), 'well done' (*good job*) etc.

For further illustration we will now use PIE to take a more detailed look at the phraseology surrounding the noun lemma TOE (*toe* and *toes*) (based on Lindquist 2008a). *Toe* occurs 1,616 times in the BNC, which

Table 5.8 The most frequent tag sequences (POS-grams) in the BNC

Rank	Tag sequence	Example	Types	Tokens
1	PRP AT0 NN1 PRF AT0	at the end of the	6,901	105,756
2	AT0 NN1 PRF AT0 NN1	the end of the year	8,485	62,890
3	AT0 AJ0 NN1 PRF AT0	the other side of the	3,677	28,491
4	PRP AT0 AJ0 NN1 PRF	on the far side of	2,908	21,533
5	NN1 PRP AT0 NN1 PRF	increase in the number of	3,285	17,852
6	PRP AT0 NN1 PRF NN1	from the point of view	2,342	16,661
7	PRP AT0 NN1 PRP AT0	on the way to the	2,949	16,581
8	AT0 AJ0 NN1 PRP AT0	the royal society for the	2,563	14,648
9	AT0 NN1 PRF AT0 AJ0	the creation of a new	2,710	14,483
10	VM0 VBI VVN PRP AT0	can be seen in the	2,048	14,337

Table 5.9 *Good* + common noun in the BNC

Phrase	N
good idea	1,851
good news	1,190
good time	876
good thing	822
good deal	783
good job	740
good reason	735
good evening	696
good morning	651
good example	587

makes it a fairly infrequent body noun compared to nouns such as *foot* (frequency 21,339) or *hand* (53,265). To make the investigation complete, we will search for n-grams of all lengths between two and eight words and with the node word (*toe(s)*) in all positions. There are not many recurrent phrases on the 8-, 7- and 6-gram levels but quite a few on the 5-gram level. Figure 5.3 gives the most frequent recurrent strings for each position on the 5-gram level.

The figure illustrates that n-gram is a purely mechanical concept: the n-grams consist of identical strings which may or may not be linguistically structured phrases. There are a few linguistically interesting strings, however. *The toe of his boot* occurs 10 times, and to that we can add *the toe of his shoe* (5) and *the toe of her shoe* (3). This frequent long phrase with *toe* does not refer to a body part at all, but rather to a part of a piece of footwear. (Not actually referring to physical body parts is also

toe + + + +	**toe** on his left foot (3)
+ toe + + +	the **toe** of his boot (10)
+ + toe + +	with the **toe** of his (12)
+ + + toe +	from head to **toe** in (14)
+ + + + toe	covered from head to **toe** (4)

Figure 5.3 The extraction of 5-grams with *toe*.

typical of many other body nouns, like for instance *face* and *hand*.) In all, with various possessive pronouns, there were 15 *the toe of X's boot* and 9 *the toe of X's shoe*. In addition, there were occasional references to the toes of Doc Martens, rubber boots and flip-flops. A typical example is (2).

(2)   Benjamin tapped **the toe of his shoe** on the soft carpet. (BNC HH5)

Another 5-gram with a frequency of 3 is *the toe of the club*, where *toe* refers to a protruding part of a golf club. Such technical meanings of *toe* are not uncommon. The 5-gram *a toe in the water* also occurs three times, but is better seen as the 4-gram *toe in the water*, which occurs 8 times. None of those examples refers to human toes dipped into real water: they are all used figuratively meaning '(make) a careful probe', as in (3)–(4).

(3)   It's always best to dip a **toe in the water** first, rather than plunging in with a programme of hopefully helpful ideas for the improvement of her life and comfort. (C8Y)

(4)   But Nordstrom's catalogue is merely a **toe in the water**. (CR8)

The 4-gram *from head to toe* occurred 74 times and its variant *from top to toe* 19 times. All instances of *from head to toe* refer to the human body covered in clothes or other material or being injured, treated or scrutinised by someone, as in (5)–(7), while *from top to toe* is occasionally also used about other concrete objects, as in (8), or about abstract entities, as in (9).

(5)   The likes of Naomi Campbell and Linda Evangelista were clad **from head to toe** in leather, rubber, latex and PVC. (BNC A7N)

(6)   The King's legs were broken, there were injuries **from head to toe**. (BNC BMN)

(7)   Her glanced raked Polly **from head to toe**. (BNC H7W)

(8)   But John and Veronica Saunders still make time to decorate their home **from top to toe**. (BNC ED4)

(9)   The overwhelming impression left after the debate is of a Tory Party split **from top to toe** over Europe, and a Prime Minister unable to heal the rift. (BNC CEN)

Table 5.10 *On X's toes* in the BNC

	Attention	Posture	Attachment	Attachment	Perception	Other	Total
on his toes	12	21	1	2		2	38
on their toes	31	4	2				37
on your toes	9	9		2	1		21
on the toes		1	7	4	3	1	16
on her toes	3	11	1	1			16
on our toes	14			1			15
on its toes	9	3	1				13
on my toes	6	5		1			12
on yer toes		1					1
Total	84	55	12	11	4	3	169

Source: Lindquist (2008a)

As has been pointed out by Sinclair (2003: 167–172), singular and plural forms of nouns often occur in quite different contexts, and indeed the searches for *toe* and *toes* yielded totally different n-grams. Among the most frequent collocations with *toes* were *on his toes* and *on their toes*. If we add up all the tokens of the 'collocational frame' *on X's toes* we get a frequency of 169 with the five distinct meanings 'attention', 'posture', 'attachment', 'encroachment' and 'perception', as illustrated in (10)–(14).

(10) […] just as black people keep changing the name you are allowed to call them in order to keep whitey **on his toes**. (BNC ECU) [attention]

(11) Culley swung at him, coming up **on his toes** for the blow. (BNC FS8) [posture]

(12) On his legs were hose striped with red and gold, while his feet were hidden in crimson velvet slippers with silver roses **on the toes**. (BNC H9C) [attachment]

(13) It claims it will stick to commercially-led Unix information not treading **on the toes** of existing non-commercial Unix networks […] (BNC CTJ) [encroachment]

(14) […] Briant sat calmly, legs outstretched, […] his eyes fixed **on the toes** of his highly polished shoes as he rocked his crossed ankles in a slow rhythm. (BNC AN8) [perception]

The distribution of these meanings is shown in Table 5.10.

As Table 5.10 shows, the 'attention' meaning as in *keep sb on their toes* or *be on one's toes* is clearly the most common, followed by the 'posture' meaning as in *standing/running/dancing etc. on one's toes*. The 'attachment' meaning, where something is applied or placed on the toes comes next, and then the 'encroachment' meaning as in 'treading on someone's toes'. Finally there are a few cases referring to the fixing of one's gaze etc. on one's toes, and some unclear cases.

Note that the distribution of meanings over phrases with different pronouns is far from even. The phrases with singular pronouns, *on his toes*, *on her toes* and, to some extent, *on my toes*, are mainly about posture. With this meaning there is also a gender difference: about men the reference is especially to fighting contexts, as in (11) above, while about women it is to romantic contexts, as in (15).

(15) She once again burst into tears and, crossing rapidly to George, threw her arm around his neck and stretching up **on her toes**, began to kiss him with a fervour which shocked him. (BNC C98)

The 'attention' meaning predominates clearly in the phrases with plural pronouns like *on their toes* and *on our toes*, and also with *on its toes*. (16) and (17) are typical examples. *On its toes* often refers to groups of people who need to be on the alert, as in (18).

(16) "I also carry out random spot checks with a probe at various points during the week, just to keep everyone **on their toes**," he adds. (BNC HC3)
(17) "A lead of 2–1 guarantees nothing, except the fact that we need to be **on our toes** against a side who will relish the big occasion." (BNC CH3)
(18) The competitive situation keeps the governing party **on its toes** and sensitive to the public's view of policy. (BNC G3L)

It is easy to see how the non-literal, metonymic 'attention' and 'encroaching' meanings have developed from the physical acts of standing on one's toes, ready to move quickly, on the one hand, and accidentally or intentionally stepping on someone else's toes, on the other. The 'attachment' and 'perception' instances are just cases of fully transparent compositional constructions.

This study shows how the PIE database and interface make it possible to look for frequently recurring n-grams of which we are not always consciously aware, but which may nevertheless be stored and retrieved holistically by the brain. We saw that different meanings co-varied with different pronouns and the definite article. This shows that it is not enough to describe the meaning of the phrase frame *on X's toes* as such, since its meaning is influenced by the word that is put into the X slot. Again, this is information which can be highly useful for language learners and language teachers.

Table 5.11 The 8-grams in Dickens that occur five times or more

Rank	Phrase	N	Texts	Google uk
1	with the air of a man who had	15	9	9
2	not to put too fine a point upon	14	1	15,600
3	to put too fine a point upon it	14	1	6,260
4	with his hands in his pockets and his	11	7	101
5	the young man of the name of Guppy	10	1	3
6	what have you got to say to me	9	5	2
7	the waiter who ought to wait upon us	8	1	0
8	what shall I do what shall I do	7	4	48
9	let him remember it that room years	7	1	0
10	him remember it in that room years to	7	1	0
11	remember it in that room years to come	7	1	0
12	monotony of bells and wheels and horses feet	7	1	1
13	it was as much as I could do	6	4	807

Source: Based on Mahlberg (2007: 226); Google figures added

5.4 A literary application: Dickens' recurrent long phrases

We saw in Chapter 3 that keyword analysis could be used for literary purposes. The same goes for recurrent phrases, even if it is perhaps less likely that corpus linguistic methods will find long recurrent phrases that literary scholars have overlooked. Nevertheless, Mahlberg (2007) studied recurrent phrases in a 4.5-million-word corpus containing twenty-three novels by Dickens (although she prefers to talk about 'repeated sequences' or 'clusters'). The novels were downloaded from Project Gutenberg and subjected to analysis by means of WordSmith Tools. Her hypothesis was that repeated clusters would have a literary function in the text, and that eventually she would be able to find out what is characteristic of Dickens's style by comparing her Dickens corpus with another corpus of the same size containing novels by other nineteenth-century authors. In one of her searches, she searched for 8-grams in Dickens. The thirteen most frequent types are given in Table 5.11.

Note in Mahlberg's results that the 9-gram *not to put a too fine point upon it* automatically results in two 8-grams (rank 2 and 3), and that the 10-gram *let him remember it in that room years to come* results in three 8-grams (rank 9–11). In this way, in all n-gram searches, bits of long n-grams will show up as (usually) more frequent shorter n-grams as you go on searching for n-grams down to 2-grams. The table also shows that Dickens recycles some phrases in several of his novels (*with the air of a man who had* occurring in nine texts), while others, such as *the young man of the name of Guppy*, are confined, not surprisingly, to one. Again, as was mentioned in Chapter 3, the frequency data should only be the starting-point for a qualitative analysis of the contexts in which these phrases occur, and Mahlberg does go on to carry out such an analysis in some detail. Out of curiosity about the use of these phrases in present-day English, I searched for them on the uk domain of Google (7 August 2008) and found the figures given in the last column of the table. A few of the hits were actually Dickens texts on the web, but the majority consisted of other uses. As the figures show, most of the n-grams are quite unusual today, except the everyday expression *it was as much as I could do* and the idiomatic saying *not to put too fine a point upon it* 'to express something without unnecessary delicacy'. The latter phrase may in fact have been invented, or at least popularised, by Dickens, since there are no citations of it in the *OED* before Dickens's *Bleak House* in 1853.

This kind of use of corpus methodology for literary and stylistic analysis is relatively new and it is perhaps too early to say whether it is justified to have great expectations of it or not.

5.5 Summary

In this chapter we have continued to study combinations of words, now in the form of phrases of various kinds. The importance of phrases for language processing, both production and reception, was stressed. Investigations showed that language is a mixture of repetition and creative innovation. Further, it was mentioned that many "funny" idioms like *storm in a teacup* are relatively rare, and also that they are often used in non-canonical forms (like *storm in a whiskey glass*). We then moved on to recurrent strings of identical words, so-called n-grams, and noted that these make up a large proportion of all texts. One tool we used for the investigation of such n-grams was PIE, which also offered the possibility of searching for POS-grams, i.e. strings of POS tags, to investigate the most frequent grammatical structures in a corpus. Finally we looked at a literary application using n-gram searches in Dickens's novels.

Study questions

1. What is the difference between idioms like *a red herring* and recurrent phrases like *at the moment*? What is their importance for language learning?
2. Idioms like *A bird in the hand is worth two in the bush* are often used in an abbreviated or manipulated form like *It is a case of the 'bird in the hand'*

(books.google.se/books?isbn=0521589592. . .) and *A fish in the hand is worth two on the Net* (www.uhh.hawaii.edu/academics/hohonu/writing.php?id=115). What does this imply about how these idioms are stored in the mental lexicon? Can you think of other idioms that are manipulated in this way?

3. 'N-gram' is a purely technical term denoting identical strings of words. PIE extracts n-grams (2-grams up to 8-grams) from the BNC. To what extent are such automatically extracted n-grams interesting from a linguistic point of view?

4. What are POS-grams? Why can it be interesting to search for POS strings (tag sequences) as well as strings of words in a corpus?

5. How can searches for recurring n-grams be interesting for the analysis of literary works?

Corpus exercises

Hands-on exercises related to this chapter are available at the following web address:
http://www.euppublishing.com/series/ETOTELAdvanced/Lindquist.

Further reading

The best starting-point if you want to study phraseology is Wray (2002), which has a comprehensive survey of previous work and presents an interesting psycholinguistic perspective. In Wray (2008) she develops her theory further and presents a number of interesting case studies. Her work, however, is not corpus-based to any large extent. Moon (1998) also gives a survey of the field and is an excellent corpus-based study of idioms.

Granger and Meunier (2008) contains a number of interesting up-to-date studies of phraseology, particularly an overview of terms and concepts in the contribution by Granger and Paquot and a survey of the relation between phraseology and linguistic theory in the contribution by Stefan Th. Gries. Similarly, Meunier and Granger (2008) covers the field of phraseology in foreign language learning and teaching. Another useful collection of papers is Schmitt (2004). There are excellent examples of how PIE can be used in Stubbs (2007a, 2007b).

6 Metaphor and metonymy

6.1 Introduction

Traditionally, metaphor was something dealt with by literary scholars and philosophers who were concerned mainly with creative metaphors in fiction. The literature on the topic is enormous, and only a few references can be made here. Metonymy, on the other hand, has not been studied quite to the same extent.

Since the 1980s there has been a huge upsurge of interest in the cognitive aspects of both metaphor and metonymy, i.e. how we use metaphorical and metonymic processes when we think. Much of this is inspired by a book by George Lakoff and Mark Johnson called *Metaphors We Live By* (1980). This chapter will begin with general definitions of metaphor and the related concepts of simile and metonymy, followed by an explanation of Lakoff and Johnson's cognitive theory of metaphor. We will then go on to see how metaphors can be studied by means of corpus linguistic methods.

6.1.1 Metaphor

We will start by establishing what distinguishes metaphors from non-metaphors. Take a look at the phrases *down the drain* in (1) and (2).

(1) On the average, each pound contains about 40% phosphate, which does a fine job of cleaning dishes and clothes. But once flushed **down the drain**, it begins its environmental dirty work. (*Time*)

(2) A fruit cannery was finished before it dawned on its builders that there was no local fruit to can. All in all, $660 million went **down the drain**. (*Time*)

In (1), *down the drain* is used literally, since the text is about something concrete which is actually flushed out in the drainage system. The preposition *down* refers to downwards motion and the noun *drain* refers to a sewage pipe of some sort. In (2), however, the money referred to was clearly not flushed down the toilet – but through the builders' bad planning it was lost as definitely as if it had been. *Went down the drain* in (2) is a metaphor. In a metaphor, language from one semantic sphere is used to describe something in a different sphere – in this case a process in the sphere of waste disposal is used to describe a process in the sphere of business. For a metaphor to work, there must be some aspects of the processes in the two spheres that are similar. In this case it is the fact that something disappears and is lost (although environmentalist have long made us aware that what is flushed down the drain in fact does not disappear at all; it is just transported somewhere else).

A metaphor thus has three parts: the expression (*down the drain*), the meaning ('loss') and the connection between the expression and the meaning (when something is flushed down the drain it is irretrievably lost, at least in a sense). In traditional metaphor theory, these three elements are called 'vehicle' (expression), 'tenor' (meaning) and 'ground' (connection). As we shall see below, however, modern cognitive metaphor theory uses different terms.

The motivation for using a metaphor is usually either to explain something abstract and complicated which is difficult to grasp by means of something concrete and more straightforward, or to express something common and pedestrian in a more colourful and striking way. An example of the former can be seen in (3).

(3)   When something dies, its immune system (along with everything else) **shuts down**. In a matter of hours, the body is **invaded** by all sorts of bacteria, microbes, parasites . . . (http://www.howstuff works.com/immune-system.htm)

In this explanation of the immune system on a webpage for young people, the immune system is metaphorically said to *shut down*, like a business or a shop, and the bacteria, microbes and parasites are metaphorically said to *invade* the body like an enemy army. This way of putting it makes it easier to grasp and remember. In (4) we see an example of how a metaphor is used to create a striking image (and to amuse the reader). A movie reviewer describes the music of the Swedish pop group Abba.

(4)   Those shimmery, layered arrangements, those lyrics in a language uncannily like English, those symmetrical Nordic voices – they all add up to something alarmingly permanent, **a marshmallow monument on the cultural landscape**. (*New York Times*, 2008)

Obviously, the music is not really a monument constructed out of marshmallows in a real landscape, so the reader is forced to find a tenor (meaning) by looking for the ground (the connection between vehicle and the possible meaning). Perhaps the writer wants to say that the music is soft and sweet and easy to consume like a marshmallow? At the same time it is said to be a permanent monument, so maybe it is also rather grand. It is up to the reader to make his or her interpretation.

We now need to make one more distinction: between creative (or novel) metaphors, conventional metaphors and dead metaphors. Creative metaphors are made up by speakers on the spur of the moment, or by skilful writers at their desk who rack their brains for just the right phrase. Creative metaphors are often surprising and striking and they usually demand a certain amount of effort to interpret. *Marshmallow monument* is a creative metaphor. There is not a single instance of this phrase in the 360-million-word COCA, and the only four hits I found on Google led to the same original movie review. *Down the drain*, on the other hand, is a conventional metaphor. In COCA, there are 441 instances of *down the drain* and roughly two thirds of those are metaphorical. Most native speakers and many non-native ones know the metaphor and can easily interpret it when they come across it. The meaning is even given in the *OED*: "Colloq. fig. phr., *to go* (etc.) *down the drain*, to disappear, get lost, vanish; to deteriorate, go to waste" (*OED* s.v. drain, *n*. e). Once upon a time, someone must have used *down the drain* metaphorically for the first time, other people must have liked it and started using it too, and eventually it was 'conventionalised'. The very first citation in the *OED* is (5).

(5)   All his savings are gone **down the drain**. (W. S. MAUGHAM *Breadwinner* i. 52, 1930)

We do not know if Somerset Maugham invented the phrase or perhaps picked it up from current colloquial language at the time.

Dead metaphors, finally, are called dead because they are no longer perceived as metaphors at all. Typical examples are *leg* (of a table) and *hard* (meaning 'difficult'). All dead metaphors were born as creative metaphors and grew up to become conventional metaphors before they ended up as dead metaphors. It could be argued that the term 'dead metaphor' is not ideal since the expressions actually live on in everyday use. It is just the metaphoricity that has worn off, and even that can be revived by will in many cases. The demarcation lines between creative, conventional and dead metaphors are not hard and fast, and individual metaphors can be placed at different points on a cline from creative to conventionalised to dead. Some scholars see dead metaphors as a subtype of conventionalised metaphors. In the rest of this chapter, we will only deal with creative and conventional metaphors. Before we go on with metaphors, however, we need to get similes out of the way.

6.1.2 Simile

Metaphors are sometimes confused with similes, since similes are also based on similarities between two objects or two processes. The classic way to explain the difference is to use examples like (6) and (7).

(6)   He, like you say, **is a lion** in New Jersey politics, incredibly charismatic. (COCA Spoken)

(7)   The visit by a foreigner to their home is a first – a foreigner **is like a lion** to the family, Olga comments. (COCA News)

A metaphor, such as (6), is always untrue (it is not the case that "he" is an animal), and has to be interpreted metaphorically in some way or other (here a clue to the intended meaning is given in the added adjective phrase *incredibly charismatic*). A simile, on the other hand, is always either true or false and has a word that explicitly says that there is a comparison, such as *like* in (7) or *resembles* in (8).

(8)   How do I politely tell her she **resembles a stuffed sausage?** (COCA Magazines)

Most researchers claim that metaphors have greater impact than similes, and it is probably true that it is much worse to be told that you are a stuffed sausage than that you resemble one. In any case, in this chapter we will study only metaphors.

6.1.3 Conceptual metaphors

One of Lakoff and Johnson's fundamental tenets is that metaphors are not limited to "poetic imagination and rhetorical flourish" but rather that "metaphor is pervasive in everyday life, not just in language but in thought and action" (1980: 3). So metaphors are not only a way of putting words on thoughts in an efficient or striking manner; they are also the means by which we are actually able to understand the world. Lakoff and Johnson used the term 'conceptual metaphor' to describe general structures of our cognitive system. Such conceptual metaphors, then, lie behind whole series of more detailed linguistic metaphors. According to Lakoff and Johnson's theory, the conceptual metaphor ARGUMENT IS WAR lies behind metaphorical linguistic expressions like *Your claims are indefensible, He attacked every weak point in my argument* and many more. We think according to the conceptual metaphor, and when we express our thoughts we use metaphorical expressions accordingly. Lakoff and Johnson suggest many more conceptual metaphors. Table 6.1 gives some examples from their book.

Table 6.1 Examples of conceptual metaphors

Conceptual metaphor	Example
IDEAS ARE OBJECTS	I gave you that idea. His words carry little meaning
IDEAS ARE FOOD	That's food for thought. We don't need to spoon-feed our students. That idea has been fermenting for years.
THE MIND IS A MACHINE	My mind just isn't working today. I'm a little rusty today.
LOVE IS MADNESS	I'm crazy about her. She drives me out of my mind.
LOVE IS MAGIC	She cast a spell over me. The magic is gone.
LOVE IS WAR	He is known for many rapid conquests. She fought for him, but his mistress won out.
LIFE IS A CONTAINER	I've had a full life. Get the most out of your life.
LIFE IS A JOURNEY	We've come a long way.

Source: Based on Lakoff and Johnson (1980)

Another set of conceptual metaphors are called orientational metaphors: GOOD IS UP, BAD IS DOWN; MORE IS UP, LESS IS DOWN; CONSCIOUS IS UP, UNCONSCIOUS IS DOWN, and so on. Lakoff and Johnson argue persuasively that these are based on our experiences of the world and not arbitrary. After all, it is usually better to be on top of something than to be under it; when something is added to a pile or poured into a vessel the level goes up; and when we lose consciousness we fall down.

In cognitive metaphor theory, the sphere on which the metaphor is based is called the 'source domain', the sphere which is described by the source domain is called the 'target domain' and the relation between the two is called a 'mapping'. Take, for instance, THE MIND IS A MACHINE. Here MACHINE is the source and MIND is the target. A machine is something that processes raw material to produce some kind of end product, and that feature is mapped onto the mind, which is then seen as something that processes information to produce thoughts, theories etc. In this way, we think about the mind in a certain, perhaps rather mechanical way.

Returning to our example above, to say that money goes *down the drain* could arguably be a reflection of the conceptual metaphor MONEY IS AN OBJECT and a new conceptual metaphor: LOSS IS MOVEMENT IN SPACE. Other linguistic expressions of this new conceptual metaphor are not hard to come up with, as (9)–(12) show.

(9)   Hermione, marrying Walter, had **thrown away** her chance of a university education and a career of her own. (COCA Fiction)

(10) As Jay said, you look at the face of one child, and all your theories **go right out the window**. (COCA Spoken)

(11) What's done is done. My peace of mind **is gone** forever. (COCA Fiction)

(12) The Falcons say the effort and the big hits are there but the victories just keep **slipping away**. (COCA News)

Our example shows that the model provided by Lakoff and Johnson is a powerful tool to analyse and systematise linguistic metaphors. However, there are also complications. The number of conceptual metaphors seems to be endless, and it is unclear how detailed they should be. Another apparent problem is that there are parallel metaphors for the same concept. For instance, LOVE IS MADNESS, but it is also MAGIC and WAR (see Table 6.1). Clearly, we can think about some important concepts in several quite different ways. Deignan (2005), although on the whole favourable to the theory, notes several further weaknesses from a linguist's point of view. One is that Johnson and Lakoff and many other researchers in cognitive metaphor studies use examples that are all based on intuition or impressionistic observation. Research on authentic language in large corpora has shown that some of the linguistic metaphor types discussed by cognitive metaphor scholars are rare or non-existent, while others which are much more frequent in corpora are overlooked. Deignan has also shown that certain important grammatical aspects of metaphors are ignored in cognitive metaphor studies. She notes that the grammar in the target domain tends to be different from that in the source domain and much more restricted (2005: 162). For instance, the metaphorical use of animal nouns as in (6) above (*He is a lion*) is quite rare in real language use, although it exists, as can be seen in (13) and (14).

(13) But **that silly cow** was wrong if she thought she could mess with me! (COCA Fiction)

(14) "You're **a fat pig**. You're disgusting." (COCA Spoken)

Much more common than the nominal use, however, are metaphors with word class shifts. Thus the verbal and adjectival metaphors in Table 6.2 are more frequent than the nominal metaphors.

The cells in the table are filled according to what Deignan found in her corpus. It is not difficult to imagine metaphors in some of the empty cells as well, as for instance in (15)–(17).

(15) It is impossible to imagine him making **piggish** advances towards women – or anyone else – as Arnold has done. (COCA Magazines)

Table 6.2 Part of speech of conventional animal metaphors

Noun	Nominal metaphor	Verbal metaphor	Adjectival metaphor
pig	racist pigs	to pig out ('eat a lot')	–
wolf	lone wolf	to wolf down ('eat hungrily')	–
monkey	she's a little monkey	to monkey around	–
rat	a thieving rat	to rat on ('tell on')	–
horse	–	to horse around	–
weasel	–	weasel out of sth	–
ferret	–	to ferret out sth	–
hound	–	to hound sb out	–
hare	–	to hare ('run')	–
squirrel	–	to squirrel ('collect')	–
ape	–	to ape ('imitate')	–
cat	fat cats ('rich people')	–	catty ('malicious')
kitten	sex kitten	–	kittenish ('playful')
sheep	stupid sheep	–	sheepish ('stupid')
mouse	a timid mouse	–	mousy ('boring')
shrew	a bad-tempered shrew	–	shrewish ('bad-tempered')
fox	old fox ('shrewd person')	to fox ('fool')	foxy ('sexy')
bitch	bitch (about women)	to bitch ('complain')	bitchy ('nagging')
dog	an old dog	to dog ('hunt')	dogged ('persevering')

Source: Adapted from Deignan (2005: 153)

(16) [. . .] Donald Trump surveyed the **wolfish** splendor of his private jet [. . .] (COCA Magazines)

(17) The **weasel** charges us fifteen dollars for a five dollar trip. (BNC HHO)

The fact remains that it is quite hard to find the kind of examples that are often seen in the literature based on introspection (*He is a fox*). One of Deignan's important points is that when such metaphors do occur, they frequently do so in certain collocations: *old fox, little monkey, fat cat*. The conclusion is that there are grammatical and collocational restrictions which limit the way concepts from a source domain can be mapped onto a target domain and that such restrictions are best studied by means of corpora.

Table 6.3 Types of metonymy

Type	Explanation	Examples
Part for whole	The word for a part of something is used to refer to the whole thing	*wheels* 'car' *face* 'person' *the cello* 'the person playing cello'
Whole for part	The word for the whole thing is used to refer to a part or parts of it	*Sweden* 'the Swedish national hockey team' *He ate a dozen oysters* 'he ate the soft parts of 12 oysters'
Association	A word is used to refer to something else with which it is associated	*The White House* 'the US president' *the press* 'newspapers, printed media' *the stage* 'the theatre' *the ham sandwich* 'the customer who ordered a ham sandwich' *the kidney in ward 2* 'the kidney patient in ward 2' *I love Shakespeare* 'I love the works of Shakespeare'

6.1.4 Metonymy

The term 'metonymy' is far less well known than 'metaphor' and is not used in everyday language as 'metaphor' is. The semantic process involved is related, but there is one major difference: in typical metaphors, the mapping is from one domain to a *different* domain, while in metonymy the mapping occurs within the *same* domain. Another way of putting this is to say that metaphor is based on similarity and metonymy is based on association. The most common types of metonymy are shown in Table 6.3.

Some scholars call the part-for-whole and whole-for-part types 'synecdoche' /sɪˈnekdəki/, and only the association type metonymy. It should also be mentioned that the borderline between metaphor and metonymy is not always as clear as has been suggested here: many metaphors have developed out of metonymy. Deignan (2005: 64) gives the example of *turning one's nose up at something*. It can be purely literal, describing the act of turning one's nose upwards; it can be metonymic if a person turns their nose up at something in order to show rejection; and finally it is metaphorical if it used in a context where no nose is actually physically turned up at all, as in (18).

(18) Unless I'm assuming too much, and you're one of these newer couples that **turn their nose up at** matrimony. (COCA Fiction)

Although metonymy thus in some respects is closely related to metaphor, in the rest of this chapter we will focus on metaphors proper.

6.2 Using corpora in the study of metaphor

Traditional metaphor research up to and including much of cognitive metaphor studies has been based on the manual study of text, introspection or a combination of these. More recently, however, researchers have started to use corpora in this field as well, and whole books have been published on the subject (see Further reading below). The problem is how to find the metaphors in a corpus, since metaphor is about meaning and most corpora are not annotated for meaning. But there are some ways around the problem, as has been shown by Deignan (2005: 94–96).

6.2.1 Starting with the source domain

One can take a certain source domain as postulated in cognitive metaphor studies, e.g. MACHINE from THE MIND IS A MACHINE, and see in what kind of metaphors words from that source domain occur. One would then have to think of words that might be used in such metaphors. This is no trivial task. Let us start with *rusty* from Table 6.1. In the COCA there are 2,647 instances of *rusty*. A pilot study of the first 100 concordance lines showed that 25 of these were names of dogs and people, 11 referred to a rusty colour (*rusty hair*) and 12 were metaphors, most of which referred to a rusty voice, not to the mind. Maybe we have to look for certain collocations, as suggested by Deignan, to get closer to metaphors involving THE MIND. What about *a little rusty?* This turned out to be a good context for metaphors: out of 33 tokens, 28 were metaphorical, and many of these referred to mental or physical skills. Searching for *a bit rusty*, finally, I found only the 5 tokens given in the concordance in Figure 6.1, all of which are metaphorical.

Here *a bit rusty* refers to instincts (1), language skills (2, 4), voice quality (3) and horse handling skills (5). The cognitive metaphor THE MIND IS A MACHINE is thus reflected in (1), (2) and (4), although the cognitive metaphor in (2) and (4) could be more narrowly specified as: LANGUAGE IS A MACHINE or perhaps LANGUAGE IS A TOOL, or LANGUAGE IS A WEAPON (cf. Dwight Bolinger's famous book from 1980, *Language: the Loaded Weapon*). Another word that intuitively

1. only once or twice a year, your instincts are bound to be **a bit rusty**. # But it sounded like an interesting problem. (COCA Academic)
2. My Elizabethan English is **a bit rusty**, but (COCA Magazines)
3. And so what poured out of his mouth sounded **a bit rusty**, perhaps a tad hoarse to the casual ear, (COCA Fiction)
4. "Getting **a bit rusty** nowadays," Sam said, "Nowadays she has her hands full." (COCA Fiction)
5. I'm a good horseman, sir. I'm **a bit rusty** now. (COCA Fiction)

Figure 6.1 Concordance for *a bit rusty* in COCA.

1. His glove, a **well-oiled** MacGregor Brooks Robinson autograph, gaped at the window. (COCA Fiction)
2. During the 1980s, when most of Wall Street was humming along like a **well-oiled** money machine, (COCA Magazines)
3. Below us the city glistened like a **well-oiled** body, rippling under the stars. (COCA Magazines)
4. Hetch Hetchy is efficient, Moccasin people say, like a **well-oiled** machine. (COCA News)
5. The realization of **well-oiled** democratic practices and institutions, predictably, will leave individuals still yearning for solitude and (COCA Academic)
6. carrying signs that read Get Out of Vietnam while the rest of us, **well-oiled** and sunning on the rooftops, clutched our bikini tops and peered down curiously at (COCA Fiction)
7. Wendy pulled on the old-fashioned string latch and the door swung open on **well-oiled** hinges. (COCA Fiction)
8. about a million gears were spinning in her head, all meshing perfectly, **well-oiled**, quiet and productive. (COCA Fiction)
9. seat-of-the-pants operation at the International Rescue Committee, this 33-year-old medical-assistance charity is a **well-oiled** machine. (COCA Magazines)
10. That extraordinary technology we brought to the jungles of Southeast Asia, the **well-oiled** firepower, the superbly trained aircraft commander, nervously checking over his shoulder (COCA Magazines)

Figure 6.2 The first ten out of 151 concordance lines for *well-oiled* in COCA.

might be related to the mind-as-machine metaphor is *well-oiled*. The concordance in Figure 6.2 gives the first 10 tokens of *well-oiled* out of 151 in the corpus.

Lines (1), (6), (7) are literal references to the well-oiled status of physical objects. Lines (2)–(4) are similes, two of which use the machine image: *like a well-oiled money machine*, *like a well-oiled body*, *like a well-oiled machine*. Lines (5) and (10) describe well-functioning organisations and institutions as being well-oiled, while (9) in a similar context specifically mentions the word *machine*. Line (8), finally, is the only exponent of the conceptual metaphor THE MIND IS A MACHINE – and it even refers

Table 6.4 Subject complements of *his/her/my mind was X* in COCA

Subject complement	N
a blank	6
an amber, fire-filled jewel	1
a big blank	1
a big blank of love	1
a complete blank	1
a roaring blank	1
a blaze of contradictions	1
a box	1
a bullring, an arena	1
a cacophony of ghostly exhortations	1
a forest	1
a free-for-all of depressing thoughts	1
a jumble	1
a kaleidoscope of scary images	1
a muddle of memories	1
a negative space	1
a slurry of confusion	1
a whirl of thoughts, fantasies and vaporous images	1

to gears spinning in the head. A search through the remaining 141 concordance lines would possibly find a number of further examples. The examples of *rusty* and *well-oiled* show that it is possible to use corpora to get at metaphorical language with the source domains as starting-point, but that the metaphors may be rarer than expected.

6.2.2 Starting with the target domain

Looking for examples of metaphors for a particular target domain is a bit harder. We still have to use linguistic clues to find the meanings we are after. If we stick to THE MIND IS A MACHINE and want to find out what other linguistic metaphors are used to describe the mind, we need to find a way to search for the target domain. One simple solution is to search for patterns containing the word used to describe the domain: *mind*. A search for *his/her/my mind was a/an*, however, did not find a single machine of any sort. The relevant results are given in Table 6.4.

At least in this particular construction, the mind is most frequently depicted as a space (or box) which is either blank or full of a jumble, a cacophony or a whirl of thoughts, fantasies, memories or images. For these uses, the cognitive metaphor seems to be THE MIND IS AN

Table 6.5 Lexical verbs most frequently occurring immediately after *his mind* in COCA

Verb	N
wander, wanders, wandered, wandering	62
raced, racing	45
works, worked, working	37
occupied	14
reeling, reeled	14
turned	13
drift, drifted, drifting	19
filled	7
felt	6
focused	6
spinning	6
cleared	5
knew	5
told	5
whirling	5
held	4
moved	4
playing	4
ran	4

OPEN SPACE or THE MIND IS A CONTAINER. But maybe the search string was not optimal. Next, let us try with *his mind* + LEXICAL VERB. The results are given in Table 6.5.

Some of these verbs fit the MACHINE image: a machine can work, turn and spin. The dominant conceptual metaphor, however, is THE MIND IS A PERSON. This person wanders, races, is occupied, reels, feels, knows things, tells us things, whirls, holds things, moves, plays and runs. A few of the verbs fit the conceptual metaphors THE MIND IS AN OPEN SPACE (*cleared* and perhaps *filled*) and THE MIND IS A CONTAINER (*filled* and perhaps *held*) which we just formulated. The verb *drift* suggests that there is perhaps also a conceptual metaphor THE MIND IS SOMETHING FLOATING ON WATER.

The kind of metaphorical expressions that we have searched for in these examples, where the target domain lemma MIND is included, has been called a 'metaphorical pattern' by Stefanowitsch (2006: 65), who distinguishes these from metaphors where the target domain lemma is not present, as in *My French is a bit rusty*. Stefanowitsch (2006) investigated a random sample from the BNC of 1,000 tokens of the target lexical items of a number of conceptual metaphor sets listed in Kövecses

Table 6.6 Metaphorical mappings for the concept FEAR posited in the literature and the frequency of these in a sample of 1,000 tokens of *fear* in the BNC

Conceptual metaphor FEAR IS . . .	Examples (from Kövecses 1998: 128–129)	Frequency
FLUID IN A CONTAINER	The sight filled her with fear	2
A VICIOUS ENEMY	Fear slowly crept up on him	35
A SUPERNATURAL BEING	He was haunted by fear	4
ILLNESS	Jill was sick with fright	9
INSANITY	Jack was insane with fear	1
AN INCOMPLETE OBJECT	I was beside myself	0
A BURDEN	Fear weighed down heavily on them	0
A NATURAL FORCE	She was engulfed by panic	2
A SUPERIOR	His actions were dictated by fear	13

Source: Adapted from Stefanowitsch (2006: 78–81)

(1998), and then compared his findings with the introspective data presented by Kövecses. Stefanowitsch found that for all the four sets, his method found a majority of the metaphors listed by Kövecses (but in varying frequencies) and in addition a large number of other metaphors which did not figure in the introspective literature. Table 6.6 shows cognitive metaphor mappings for FEAR listed by Kövecses and the number of tokens found for each of these by Stefanowitsch in his sample of 1,000 tokens of the lemma FEAR.

Stefanowitsch thus showed that with this fairly simple corpus method he was able to find most of the metaphorical mappings postulated by cognitive linguistics from introspection and anecdotal evidence. What is more, he also found a number of additional patterns not previously mentioned in the literature. These are given in Table 6.7.

Even if it might be argued that some of the additional metaphors could be subsumed under one or other of the cognitive metaphors in Table 6.6, and that others might be considered metaphors for emotions in general rather than specifically for fear, Stefanowitsch has shown quite convincingly that metaphorical pattern analysis is a viable method to extract metaphors from a corpus. His frequency figures also suggest that the conceptual metaphors discussed in the cognitive literature are not always the ones which are most frequent in authentic corpus material.

Table 6.7 Additional FEAR metaphors found via metaphorical pattern analysis

FEAR/BEING AFRAID IS . . .	Example (abbreviated examples used by Stefanowitsch)	N
[A] LIQUID	trickling/undercurrent of fear	10
A SUBSTANCE IN A CONTAINER (UNDER PRESSURE)	pent up fear	15
[A] MIX	EMOTION be mixed with fear	9
COLD	shiver of fear	14
HEAT	heat of fear	7
LIGHT	flicker of fear	6
DARK	shadow of fear	4
HIGH/LOW (INTENSITY)	fear peak	7
PAIN	ache with fear	8
A SHARP OBJECT	prick/shaft of fear	7
AN ORGANISM	growing fear	9
A WILD/CAPTIVE ANIMAL	fear lurks beneath	6
A BARRIER	barrier of fear	4

Source: Based on Stefanowitsch (2006: 81)

6.2.3 Starting from manual analysis

A third way to extract metaphors from a corpus is to search a small corpus manually to find all metaphors or a certain type of metaphor. This can be a study in itself, or it can serve as a pilot study for a search in a larger corpus for tokens of the metaphors found in the manual pilot study. This adds more data and provides more reliable quantification, but one misses all metaphor types that happened not to show up in the smaller corpus. Charteris-Black (2004) made a manual study of the metaphorical expressions in a corpus of fifty-one inaugural speeches made by US presidents from George Washington to Bill Clinton (33,352 words). He then grouped the metaphors according to their source domains. The results are given in Table 6.8.

I have ordered Charteris-Black's categories according to the number of tokens, i.e. the total number of instances of metaphors from the different source domains. An equally relevant order would be according to the number of types, i.e. the number of *different* metaphors based on each source domain. That figure gives an idea about how productive the source domain is: how easy it is to create new metaphors based on words from the domain.

Table 6.8 Source domains for metaphors in the US Inaugural Corpus

Source domain	Types	Tokens
Conflict	18	116
Journeys	12	76
Body parts	4	76
Religion	6	72
Buildings	12	66
Fire and light	15	51
Physical environment	16	35

Source: Adapted from Charteris-Black (2004: 90)

Table 6.9 Cognitive metaphors based on a number of source domains

Source domain	Cognitive metaphor
Conflict	POLITICS IS CONFLICT
Journeys	PURPOSEFUL SOCIAL ACTIVITY IS TRAVELLING ALONG A PATH TOWARDS A DESTINATION
Body parts	No cognitive metaphor formulated by Charteris-Black
Religion	POLITICS IS RELIGION
Buildings	WORTHWHILE ACTIVITY IS BUILDING; SOCIETY IS A BUILDING
Fire and light	SEEING IS UNDERSTANDING; PURIFICATION IS FIRE
Physical environment including weather	STATES ARE LOCATIONS; A SOCIAL CONDITION IS A WEATHER CONDITION

Source: Metaphors suggested by Charteris-Black (2004: 91–109)

Charteris-Black discusses examples from each of the source domains and tries to find appropriate cognitive metaphors for each of them, as given in Table 6.9.

Again, we see that the formulation of conceptual metaphors to a certain extent is subjective: they can be more or less general, for instance. And it is not always self-evident what tokens belong to what category, as shown by the following text quoted from Charteris-Black (2004: 92), which is meant to illustrate the cognitive metaphor POLITICS IS CONFLICT:

> We are a strong nation, and we will maintain strength so sufficient that it need not be proven in *combat* – a quiet strength based not merely on the size of an *arsenal*, but on the nobility of ideas. We will be ever vigilant and

never *vulnerable*, and we will *fight* our *wars* against poverty, ignorance, and injustice – for those are the *enemies* against which our *forces* can honorably be *marshalled*. (Jimmy Carter) (italics added by Charteris-Black)

As noted by Charteris-Black and many other metaphor scholars, metaphors often occur in clusters, reinforcing each other as they do in this excerpt. But it is not always easy to decide whether a word is used metaphorically or not: *combat* and *arsenal* in the first sentence could also be seen as referring to real war and real arms rather than metaphorical ones, whereas the italicised words in the second sentence are clearly used metaphorically.

We will now use Charteris-Black's findings as a starting-point for a small investigation in a larger corpus of one of these source domains: Buildings. The following words from this domain are cited by Charteris-Black as used in metaphors: *build, cathedral, structure, foundations, threshold, door, house, bridge, pillar* and *barrier*. I looked at 100 tokens of two of these words in the subcorpus 'magazines' in COCA to see if they were used metaphorically, and if so, how. First the verb *build*: it turned out that as many as 43 out of the 100 tokens of this word were used metaphorically; the remaining 57 were used with a literal meaning. Table 6.10 gives an idea of how *build* was used.

Table 6.10 illustrates a fact that strikes many people as surprising: a large number of our most common words are used metaphorically a lot of the time, sometimes more often than they are used with their literal meaning. For *build* in this particular set of examples from the Time corpus, we see that in the concrete, literal uses it refers to the building of various edifices, but also vehicles, machines, systems and objects. The metaphorical uses refer to groups of people, sums of money, businesses, relationships, bodies, collections, actions and various other things. The verb *build* is clearly a very common and versatile vehicle in metaphors, and it is not surprising that it is frequent also in political speeches.

The noun *cathedral* presents a different picture. It is of course much less frequent than *build*, and it turns out that it is also relatively less frequently used in metaphors: in the 100 examples from the Time Corpus 1990–2007 I studied there were 87 literal uses referring to actual cathedrals, 12 metaphorical uses and 1 simile. The uses are described in Table 6.11.

The example of a metaphor with *cathedral* in a political speech given by Charteris-Black is quoted here as (19).

(19) With these, we can *build a great cathedral of the spirit* – each of us raising it one stone at a time. (Nixon) (italics added by Charteris-Black)

Table 6.10 Literal and metaphorical uses of *build* in a selection of 100 tokens from the Time Corpus, 2000s

Kind of use	Kind of object	Object
Literal	Building	aviary, casino, chamber, city, factory, fortress, home (3), hotel, house (6), hut, nursing home, place, plant (2), road, space port, stadium, steak house, temple, the Capitol
	Vehicle	boat, jet, ship, spacecraft, vehicle, warplane
	Machine etc.	engine, generator, machine (4)
	System etc.	circuits, missile shield, network (2), shield, system (2),
	Object	diamond (3), gadget, nanodevice, product, replica, weapon
	Other	anything, body, fire
Metaphorical	Group of people	army, audience, community, country, front, Russia, society
	Money etc.	credit, nest egg, oil stocks, savings, wealth (2)
	Business etc.	brand, enterprise
	Relationship	bridge, economic muscle, economy (2)
	Body etc.	bones, Ian Thorpe, muscle (3)
	Collection	database
	Action	exercise, writing
	Other	critical mass, energy reserve, future, intelligence, opposition (2), presence, protection, reputation, service, skill, solution, stress, success, support (2)

Table 6.11 Literal and metaphorical uses of *cathedral* in a selection of 100 tokens from the Time Corpus, 1990–2007

Literal uses	building (named cathedrals or cathedrals in general)
Metaphorical uses	theatre/movie buildings (3)
	type of ceiling (2)
	stadium
	planetarium
	forest
	Cadillac
	computer
	music
	atom

In using the metaphor, Nixon alludes on the one hand to the grandiose scale, loftiness and spirituality of cathedrals and on the other to the laborious and long-term project it is to build such a structure. The metaphors in *Time* focus on different aspects of cathedrals. The rather conventional use of *cathedral* for entertainment theatres can be seen in (20) and (21).

(20)   The **cathedral** of commercial theater had reopened as a museum and a mausoleum. (*Time*)

(21)   In the dark **cathedral** they giggled, cried, were transported. (*Time*)

Here it is the 'worship' function which is mostly in focus, perhaps combined with the 'grandeur' component. The same goes for (22), which is about the Hayden Planetarium in New York City, and (23), where the concept of catharsis from Greek tragedy is mixed in for good measure.

(22)   A cosmic **cathedral**, was how architect James Polshek proudly described his creation. (*Time*)

(23)   Uptown, in the Bronx, Yankee Stadium had become a **cathedral** of catharsis, the participants emptying their lungs at full volume [. . .] (*Time*)

In other uses, it is the physical similarity rather than the function that is the ground for the metaphor, as in the reference to a type of ceiling in (24) and a forest with exceptionally high trees in (25).

(24)   [. . .] gracious homes with porch decks, two-car garages and **cathedral** ceilings. (*Time*)

(25)   [. . .] the most important thing we can do to save these ancient **cathedral** forests and these 2,000-year-old trees. (*Time*)

In yet other uses, the high-soaring spirit is focused on, as in (26), which describes a musical composition, and (27), which describes the liberated feeling early users of the Macintosh computer are supposed to have experienced.

(26)   The ineffable music, which unfolds seamlessly from small, minimalist melodic motifs, evolves into a soaring Brucknerian **cathedral**. (*Time*)

(27)   The Mac then was a **cathedral** of computing that made mortals suddenly see the beauty and empowering potential of a desktop machine. (*Time*)

The only simile, again, refers to a commercial building; see (28).

(28)   On one hand, I imagine them building the World Trade Center as it was, with no floors, almost like a **cathedral**, but in the spirit of American resilience. (*Time*)

This example shows that starting out from the metaphors found through a detailed manual analysis of a corpus or collection of texts, it is possible to extend the study to a large corpus in order to see to what extent the metaphors in the small investigation are typical of the language as a whole. Looking at *build* and *cathedral*, which were picked up from metaphors in the collection of inaugural speeches, in the much larger Time Corpus we were able to establish that there were both similarities and differences in the way they were used metaphorically there.

6.3 Summary

After the general introduction to the concepts of metaphor, simile and metonymy, much of this chapter concerned studies of metaphor using cognitive metaphor theory, where we saw that the starting-point could be either the source domain or the target. Some criticisms of cognitive metaphor theory were also touched upon, and indeed it should be pointed out that corpus-based metaphor study is in no way bound to this theory. In fact, corpora can be used as data sources for any kind of studies on metaphor, as long as either the source domain or the target can be identified lexically so that searches can be formulated. In the introduction to the chapter I stressed that metaphors are not only interesting for literary scholars: on the contrary, studying metaphor gives us insights into how language works, and probably also into how our brains work when we struggle to make ourselves clear and communicate in a successful way with our fellow human beings.

Study questions

1. What is the difference between metaphor, metonymy and simile? Try to come up with your own examples. Why are metaphors considered to be more powerful than similes?
2. What is the main idea behind conceptual metaphors?
3. What different ways of using corpora in the study of metaphors were introduced in this chapter? Which method do you think seems most viable?
4. It says in the summary that studying metaphors can tell us something about how our minds work. Do you agree? If yes, how? If no, why not?

Corpus exercises

Hands-on exercises related to this chapter are available at the following web address: http://www.euppublishing.com/series/ETOTELAdvanced/Lindquist.

Further reading

A good, accessible introduction to metaphor and metonymy is Knowles and Moon (2006). Semino (2008) relates cognitive metaphor theory to stylistics and discourse analysis and has a substantial chapter on corpus methodology. Deignan (2005) provides an excellent general introduction to the field and in addition gives a critical account of cognitive metaphor theory and discusses corpus methodology in considerable detail. Stefanowitsch and Gries (2006) contains interesting papers on corpus-based approaches to metaphor and metonymy. For those who want to go deeper into metaphor theory there are excellent and up-to-date survey articles in Gibbs (2008).

7 Grammar

7.1 Introduction

So far we have looked at individual words, words in combination and metaphorical uses of words and phrases. These are all areas which can conveniently be studied by means of corpora, since it easy to search for individual words or strings of words, even in untagged corpora. And if the corpora are POS tagged, searches can be made not only for particular word forms, but also for specific word classes, e.g. *light* as a noun, verb or adjective. When it comes to grammar, searches can be more complicated. Grammar is traditionally divided into morphology and syntax. Morphology, i.e. the study of how words are formed and of their parts, such as derivational suffixes and inflectional suffixes, can also be quite straightforward. We will start with such an example in section 7.2. For syntactic structures, however, more ingenuity may be needed in searches. We will look at such examples in section 7.3–7.5.

7.2 *Who* and *whom*

In 1921 the famous American linguist Edward Sapir wrote:

> It is safe to prophesy that within a couple of hundred years from to-day not even the most learned jurist will be saying "Whom did you see". By that time the "whom" will be as delightfully archaic as the Elizabethan "his" for "its". ([1921] 1971: 156)

According to Sapir, since there are no object forms of the interrogative and relative pronouns *which*, *what* and *that*, it feels unnatural and unnecessary (Sapir even uses the word *unesthetic*) to have one for *who*. And indeed, many native speakers feel uncertain about when to use the subject form *who* and when to use the object form *whom*. In questions, instead of the conservative and formally correct *whom* as in (1) it is quite common to hear *who*, as in (2).

Decade	1920s	1930s	1940s	1950s	1960s	1970s	1980s	1990s	2000s
Per million	262.7	264.8	177.4	138.4	154.5	152.6	134.8	153.3	140.3
N	2,006	3,352	2,742	2,323	2,484	2,074	1,533	1,492	902

Figure 7.1 Frequency of *whom* in the Time Corpus: per million words.

(1) [. . .] have you apportioned blame for the deaths of your family? **Whom** do you blame? (BNC HE3)
(2) **Who** do you blame? er Well it's very easy to er blame government [. . .] (BNC KRT)

Similarly, the object relative pronoun *whom* as in (3) is often replaced by *who*, as in (4).

(3) [. . .] and the man **whom** we have called the last Muddletonian, who was a farmer in Matfield in Kent, went out with his lorry [. . .] (BNC KRH)
(4) [. . .] the woman **who** I meet up at you know who works in the coffee shop [. . .] (BNC KDW)

On the whole, *whom* seems to be most secure in the position after a preposition, as in (5), but even here it is often replaced by *who* in spoken English, as in (6).

(5) To **whom** do you report? What sort of budget do you have? (BNC CDK)
(6) To **who**? Everyone. Doesn't matter. (BNC KP1)

Now, let us see if Sapir's predictions hold by looking at the development over time in the Time Corpus, which contains AmE, Sapir's own variety of the language. First we will look at the frequency of the form *whom* through the decades. The figures are given in Figure 7.1.

Figure 7.1 shows that in the 1940s, soon after Sapir's claim at the end of the 1920s, the frequency of *whom* indeed diminished markedly. However, the decrease soon stopped and from the 1950s onwards the situation seems to be totally stable. But *whom* is related to *who*, so we should also look at the frequency of *who*, which is given in Figure 7.2.

Figure 7.2 shows that there is a slow but steady increase of the form

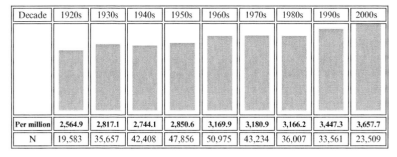

Decade	1920s	1930s	1940s	1950s	1960s	1970s	1980s	1990s	2000s
Per million	2,564.9	2,817.1	2,744.1	2,850.6	3,169.9	3,180.9	3,166.2	3,447.3	3,657.7
N	19,583	35,657	42,408	47,856	50,975	43,234	36,007	33,561	23,509

Figure 7.2 Frequency of *who* in the Time Corpus: per million words.

Table 7.1 Proportion of *whom* out of all *whom* + *who* in the Time Corpus, 1920s–2000s: per million words

Decade	whom	who	Total	Percentage whom
1920s	263	2,565	2,828	9.3
1930s	265	2,817	3,082	8.6
1940s	177	2,744	2,921	6.1
1950s	138	2,851	2,989	4.6
1960s	155	3,170	3,325	4.7
1970s	153	3,181	3,334	4.6
1980s	135	3,166	3,301	4.1
1990s	153	3,447	3,600	4.3
2000s	140	3,658	3,798	3.7

who in *Time* over the decades. It might therefore be interesting to calculate the proportion of *whom* to *who* for each decade. These figures are given as percentages of *whom* out of the total of *who* and *whom* in Table 7.1.

Table 7.1 repeats some of the information from Figures 7.1 and 7.2: the frequency of *whom* goes down around the 1940s and then stays fairly stable, while there is a slow but steady increase in *who* over the decades. The percentage figure for the proportion of *whom* out of all *who* + *whom* does not add much information: the percentage goes down noticeably in the 1950s and then there is possibly a weak trend further downwards, with the lowest figure for the 2000s. It should be noted, however, that these calculations give only a very rough picture of the situation. In order to be certain about the development of the use of *whom* in *Time* one would have to make an analysis of only the cases where there is

Table 7.2 *Get*-passives in LOB, FLOB, Brown and Frown

	1961	*1991/1992*
BrE (LOB, FLOB)	34	53
AmE (Brown, Frown)	35	64

Source: Mair (2006b: 357)

possible variation, i.e. where *who* is used in object position. To make such an investigation automatically one would need a parsed corpus. Still, the figures we have obtained indicate that Sapir's prediction about the future demise of the form *whom* was incorrect: from the 1950s, the frequency of *whom* in written AmE has remained fairly stable.

One further observation can be made about the figures in Table 7.1: the combined total number of *who* + *whom* grows steadily from 2,828 per million in the 1920s to 3,798 per million in the 2000s. This fact is hard to explain without a closer analysis of the actual examples, but most probably it is a matter of either content or writing style. It seems that the use of direct questions about people or relative clauses referring to people has increased during the period, which in turn might be seen as a change in journalistic style, putting a stronger focus on people. The kind of gradual change illustrated by the *who/whom* example would be very difficult to notice without access to a corpus.

7.3 *Get*-passives

In English the passive is normally constructed with the auxiliary *be*, so that *Snoopy kissed Lucy* becomes *Lucy was kissed by Snoopy*. However, there is a more recent construction where the passive is constructed with *get*, as in (7).

(7) Canfield, the man what got the Legion d'honneur hung round his neck and **got kissed** by Marshal Petain besides. (COCA Fiction)

Mair (2006b: 357) has shown that there are signs that the use of *get*-passives is growing in both BrE and AmE, as indicated by the frequency figures in the 1-million-word corpora LOB, FLOB, Brown and Frown, shown in Table 7.2.

These figures are supported by data on AmE from the Time Corpus, given in Figure 7.3.

The Time Corpus figures suggest that there was a moderate rise 1920–1950, then no change for a few decades, followed by a marked rise from the 1990s onward. The rise in per cent between the 1960s and the 1990s in Brown and Frown (82%) is similar to that in the Time Corpus

Decade	1920s	1930s	1940s	1950s	1960s	1970s	1980s	1990s	2000s
Per million	16.4	20.5	28.7	33.2	32.9	32.9	32.9	56.9	89.9
N	125	259	444	558	529	447	374	554	578

Figure 7.3 Frequency of *get*-passives in the Time Corpus: per million words.

(73%) for roughly the same time period, although the whole change in the *Time* figures occurred between the 1980s and 1990s. And then there is a continued strong development in the Time Corpus for the 2000s, which we will not be able to compare with the Brown family until someone compiles a 2020 version of the Brown corpus.

It has been noted that *get*-passives are predominantly used when the verb expresses something negative that has happened to the object, that the object may be partly to blame for this, and that there is personal involvement and stylistic informality on part of the speaker (Mair 2006b: 335–360); compare examples like *get caught, get busted, get sacked, get hurt, get killed* etc. Even a positive word like *kiss* seems to be given a negative interpretation when it is used in the *get*-passive, as in (7) above, where the character Canfield gets kissed by Philippe Petain, who was a French quisling during the Second World War. But the construction is also used with verbs with more positive connotations, such as *pay* in *get paid*. Mair speculates that as the overall frequency of the *get*-passives increases, the negativity may be neutralised. He also notes that the likelihood of verbs occurring in the *get*-passive varies a lot between different verbs. To measure the propensity of a verb to occur in the *get*-passive he uses a 'frequency index', which is calculated by dividing the number of occurrences in *get*-passives by the total number of *be*-passives and *get*-passives and multiplying by 100 (the index then shows the proportion of *get*-passives as a percentage of the total). In Table 7.3 we compare the frequency indices of the twenty verbs which, according to Mair, have the highest indices in the spoken component of the BNC with the indices of the same verbs in the spoken component of COCA. To arrive at these figures, first the frequency for each verb in the *get*-passive was retrieved from the COCA interface by typing the following search string: <[get] caught>, and then the same thing was done with <[be] caught> and similarly with all the other verbs. The square brackets tell

Table 7.3 Frequency indices for selected verbs used in the *get*-passive in the spoken components of the BNC and COCA

Rank in BNC	Verb	BNC Spoken	COCA Spoken	N get/be *in* COCA
		Frequency index		
1	caught	52	39	1,060/1,669
2	paid	40	29	813/1,959
3	smashed	39	18	10/45
4	hit	36	26	506/1,439
5	damaged	33	3	16/447
6	promoted	31	20	44/178
7	fucked	30	0	0/0
8	killed	30	7	472/6,408
9	hurt	30	33	584/1,211
10	shot	29	15	474/2,692
11	beaten	29	11	77/611
12	eaten	26	18	27/121
13	stopped	22	6	56/835
14	sacked	18	13	2/14
15	accused	18	2	33/1,804
16	served	9	2	8/524
17	written	8	1	24/2,279
18	played	7	4	46/1,029
19	invited	7	6	53/779
20	destroyed	6	1	13/1,173

Source: BNC figures from Mair (2006b: 358)

the program to search for all forms of the lemma. For instance, for <[be] caught> it retrieved (in falling frequency order) *was/be/been/were/are/is/being/'re/'s/'m/am caught*. Apart from the frequency for each form, the program also conveniently supplies the total figures, which are given in the right-most column of the table here. The index figures have been rounded to the nearest whole number.

Out of the twenty verbs in the list, only twelve seem to be undeniably negative (at least seen out of context like this): *caught, smashed, hit, damaged, killed, hurt, shot, beaten, stopped, sacked, accused* and *destroyed*. There are six generally positive or neutral words, *paid, promoted, served, written, played* and *invited*, and 2 words which are more uncertain, *fucked* and *eaten*. Although the figures show that most of the negative words appear at the top of the list and most of the positive ones at the bottom, the constraint on using the construction with positive words does not seem to be very strong.

There are some differences between the corpora, but it should be noted that these two spoken subcorpora of BrE and AmE differ considerably in their make-up: the BNC contains many genres of spoken language including a fair amount of spontaneous conversation, also among young people, whereas COCA consists solely of conversation from American television and radio shows, which, however, is approximately 95% unscripted. The fact that all of the American spoken data are from television and radio probably explains why the frequencies for the more informal *get*-passives overall are a bit lower in COCA and why there is less profanity in that corpus. From these figures it is impossible to say whether the difference in the use of *get*-passives for individual words is due to the differences in make-up between the corpora, including the fact that the kind of topics dealt with in the conversations might be different, or to differences between BrE and AmE. To investigate that, more (and, ideally, more comparable) corpora from each variety should be studied. It could be noted in passing, however, that the very low total figures for *get sacked* in COCA (2/14) are explained by the fact that *sack* is mainly a British colloquial term for 'dismiss from employment'. The figures in COCA for the American equivalent, *get fired*, were 204/1506 (12%).

Looking at the *get*-passive in this way we are beginning to get a picture of how this particular construction is used, in particular how the use varies between different verbs and groups of words. Other factors that could be studied in further investigations include age and gender of speaker, genre, level of formality and syntactic context.

7.4 Adjective complementation

Many adjectives in English take either a noun phrase complementation, as in (8), or verbal complementation. The verbal complement can be either infinitival, as in (9), or *to* + *ing*, as in (10).

(8) "[. . .]People are lost because they are not **accustomed to** choice," she says. (COCA Newspapers)
(9) [. . .] U.S. rice millers and shippers, who, in recent years, were **accustomed to** supply much of Iraq's imported rice, [. . .] (COCA Spoken)
(10) In private industry, you're **accustomed to getting** things done very, very quickly. (COCA Spoken)

Rudanko (2006) has shown that in BrE in the eighteenth century, only the types of complement illustrated in (8) and (9) existed – at least in the corpora he investigated. In the nineteenth century, however,

Table 7.4 The form of sentential complements of *accustomed to* in a number of subcorpora in the Bank of English

	London Times	*Spoken BrE*	*US News*	*Spoken AmE*
to infinitive	7	2	2	4
to -*ing*	116	22	90	73

Source: Based on Rudanko (2006)

complements like the one in (10), i.e. *to* + -*ing*, started to appear, although infrequently. One example is given in (11) (from Rudanko 2006: 35).

(11) 'I fancy you Foreign Officials, as well as we Life-Guardsmen, grow **accustomed to swallowing** the dregs of the season,' said Lord Edward, laughing. (1836, Catherine G. F. Gore, Mrs Armytage)

Rudanko found the same for AmE: the first cases of *to* -*ing* occurred in the 1820s, such as (12) from Rudanko (2006: 38).

(12) They soon, like the domestic fowls and animals, became **accustomed to running** abroad unshod. (1829, Timothy Flint, George Mason)

According to Rudanko, the change towards more *to* -*ing* constructions seems to have started at about the same time in BrE and AmE and to have developed at approximately the same speed in the two varieties. The change must have been very quick in the twentieth century, since when Rudanko investigated four large subsets of BrE and AmE in the BoE he found the figures presented here as Table 7.4.

As the figures in Table 7.4 clearly show, by the end of the twentieth century the situation had changed totally: *to* -*ing* was the norm and cases of the older construction with the *to* infinitive had become quite rare. The figures look convincing, but to be even more certain one should replicate the study. I did this by looking at these constructions in two other modern corpora, namely the newspaper and spoken components of the BNC for BrE and the corresponding components of COCA for AmE. After deleting all cases of *accustomed to* + NP, I arrived at the figures presented in Table 7.5.

Neither Rudanko's nor my figures are normalised, which is hardly necessary in this case. It is quite clear that his results from the BoE are supported by mine from the BNC and COCA: the *to* infinitive has become rare after *accustomed*. One instance from COCA was given above as (9) while the two tokens from the BNC are given in (13) and (14).

Table 7.5 The form of sentential complements of *accustomed to* in the BNC
and COCA

	BNC Newspapers	BNC Spoken	COCA Newspapers	COCA Spoken
to infinitive	1	1	0	4
to -*ing*	17	7	37	135

(13) A picture different from those that we are **accustomed to** see, unusual and yet true to nature. (BNC KRH)

(14) Public opinion is growing too large for the channels that it has been **accustomed to** run through. (BNC AAV)

By means of a set of corpora from different periods, it has thus been possible to describe a change in the complementation pattern of one particular adjective, which according to Rudanko is part of a larger system of changes which affects the whole complementation system of English. To investigate this larger change, a number of similar investigations of the complementation of other adjectives would have to be carried out.

7.5 Prepositional gerund or directly linked gerund

Rohdenburg (2002: 80–82) has noted that the prepositional gerund (i.e. preposition + gerund) in examples like (15a) and (16a) is being replaced in Modern English by "directly linked" gerund (i.e. a bare gerund) as in (15b) and (16b).

(15) a. The defence authorities **have had difficulties in finding** researchers to cooperate with them in some fields. (BNC B7C)
b. The defence authorities **have had difficulties finding** researchers to cooperate with them in some fields.

(16) a. When it was time to leave they **had difficulty in getting** off the island. (BNC F9U)
b. When it was time to leave they **had difficulty getting** off the island.

Rohdenburg (2007: 193) argues that the construction with the preposition *in* is more explicit, and hypothesises that the preposition will be retained more often after the plural *difficulties* than after the singular *difficulty*. His reason for this is that the plural is more "cognitively complex" (i.e. contains more semantic components and demands more processing power than the singular) and therefore motivates a more explicit construction which facilitates processing in the brain. He tested his

Table 7.6 Prepositional and directly linked gerunds with the verbs *find* and *get* dependent on and immediately following *he has difficulty/difficulties* on Google, 27 September 2004

	in	*Ø*	*Total*	*Percentage in*
he has difficulty + *finding*	56	220	276	20.2
he has difficulty + *getting*	36	383	419	8.6
Subtotal singular	*92*	*603*	*695*	*13.2*
he has difficulties + *finding*	7	6	13	53.8
he has difficulties + *getting*	9	16	25	36.0
Subtotal plural	*16*	*22*	*38*	*42.1*

Source: Based on Rohdenburg (2007: 194)

hypothesis by means of Google searches, which resulted in the figures in Table 7.6. The symbol 'Ø' means 'zero', in this case 'no preposition'.

Rohdenburg concludes that his hypothesis is supported by these data: the older form with *in* is relatively much more frequent with the plural *difficulties* than with the singular *difficulty*. Another finding is that *in* is retained less often with the frequent and informal *get* than with the less frequent and more neutral *find*. Rohdenburg also reports that he has got similar results in other corpora.

In the following we will replicate Rohdenburg's study in two other corpora: COCA and the BNC, both accessed via the BYU (Brigham Young University) interface. We will study the same words, but also a few others. In order to find other verbs that frequently occur in this construction we start by making searches in COCA and the BNC using the following search strings: <difficulty in *ing> and <difficulty *ing>. The results are given in Tables 7.7 and 7.8.

Table 7.7 shows that with singular *difficulty* in COCA, the Ø variant is generally 2–3 times more frequent than the *in* variant. We also find that the two verbs studied by Rohdenburg, *getting* and *finding*, are the most frequent ones overall. Some other verbs occur frequently in both variants: *making, understanding, keeping* and *reading*. The verbs which occur only in one of the top-ten lists are marked in boldface. It is noteworthy that three of the four boldfaced verbs in the *in* column are rather formal words of Latin origin: *obtaining, identifying* and *determining*. Conversely, three of the four boldfaced words in the Ø column are everyday Germanic words related to the body: *breathing, walking* and *swallowing*. This suggests that the *in* variant is preferred in more formal registers. Next, let us take a look at the BNC results for *difficulty* in Table 7.8.

First of all we should note that in contrast with COCA, the *in* variant

Table 7.7 The most frequent verbs in the construction *difficulty* (*in*) **ing* in COCA

	in		*Ø*	
Rank	Word	N	Word	N
1	getting	65	getting	192
2	finding	49	finding	143
3	**obtaining**	37	**breathing**	130
4	making	36	understanding	83
5	understanding	31	making	73
6	**identifying**	23	**walking**	53
7	**dealing**	21	keeping	48
8	**determining**	18	reading	48
9	keeping	18	**swallowing**	45
10	reading	18	**concentrating**	44

Note: Verbs which occur in only one of the top-ten lists are marked in boldface.

Table 7.8 The most frequent verbs in the construction *difficulty* (*in*) **ing* in the BNC

	in		*Ø*	
Rank	Word	N	Word	N
1	finding	76	getting	53
2	getting	68	finding	43
3	making	33	keeping	19
4	understanding	33	making	19
5	**obtaining**	31	**remembering**	11
6	keeping	22	**coming**	10
7	**persuading**	21	**breathing**	10
8	**accepting**	18	**swallowing**	10
9	seeing	18	seeing	9
10	**establishing**	17	understanding	9

Note: See note to Table 7.7.

is still the more frequent in the BNC. If there is ongoing change from the *in* variant to the *Ø* variant, this change has not gone as far in the BrE of the BNC as it has in the AmE of COCA. We see that again *finding* and *getting* occupy the two first positions (although in different order with and without *in*) and that *making, understanding* and *keeping* are on both lists. *Reading* is missing and has been replaced by *seeing*. Looking at the boldfaced, unique words on the lists, we find that all four in the *in* column are Latinate (*obtaining, persuading, accepting* and *establishing*),

Table 7.9 The most frequent verbs in the construction *difficulties (in) *ing* in COCA

	in		Ø	
Rank	Word	N	Word	N
1	finding	23	facing	38
2	obtaining	23	getting	12
3	getting	18	meeting	11
4	determining	14	confronting	9
5	implementing	13	resulting	9
6	learning	12	understanding	8
7	making	12	dealing	7
8	establishing	11	finding	7
9	achieving	11	surrounding	7
10	recruiting	11	keeping	6

Note: See note to Table 7.7.

Table 7.10 The most frequent verbs in the construction *difficulties (in) *ing* in the BNC

	in		Ø	
Rank	Word	N	Word	N
1	getting	25	facing	48
2	obtaining	24	being	14
3	finding	21	getting	8
4	making	13	confronting	7
5	learning	12	surrounding	6
6	establishing	9	affecting	5
7	trying	9	resulting	4
8	interpreting	8	finding	3
9	applying	7	explaining	3
10	controlling	7	following	3

Note: See note to Table 7.7.

while three of the four verbs in the Ø column are Germanic (*coming, breathing* and *swallowing*). This is further evidence that the change to the Ø variant happens first in more informal registers.

Tables 7.7 and 7.8 give us a fair idea of how the construction is used with singular *difficulty*. However, we should also investigate the plural *difficulties* – after all, one of Rohdenburg's main points was that the plural would favour *in*. The results of similar searches for *difficulties* in COCA and the BNC are shown in Tables 7.9 and 7.10.

Two things are notable in Tables 7.9 and 7.10. The frequencies are rather low and there is relatively little difference in frequency between the *in* variant and the Ø variant. But the most striking result is that only two verbs are the same in the *in* columns and the Ø columns: *getting* and *finding* in both corpora. How can this be? If we look closer at the Ø column, we soon realise that the simple search strings <difficulty in *ing> and <difficulty *ing>, which seemed to work quite well for the singular *difficulty*, did not work for the plural *difficulties*. Remember that we are interested in variation in sentences like *He has difficulties (in) finding a job*, which are OK both with and without the preposition. But the most frequent verb with the plural *difficulties* in both COCA and the BNC, *facing*, does not occur in that kind of context at all. Instead *facing* is part of non-finite postmodifying clauses, as in (17).

(17) Meanwhile, the **difficulties facing** black franchise owners trying to maintain profitable operations in urban areas remain [. . .] (COCA Magazines)

In cases like (17), it is not possible to insert *in* without changing the meaning totally. While in (17) difficulties are facing the black franchise owners, in (18) it is difficult for some unspecified agent to face the black franchise owners.

(18) Meanwhile, the **difficulties in facing** the black franchise owners trying to maintain profitable operations in urban areas remain [. . .]

Clearly, to retrieve only the relevant tokens of the construction under discussion, the search string should be something closer to: < [have] difficulties in *ing>, where [have] stands for all forms of the lemma HAVE. Rohdenburg in fact searched for even more constrained strings: *he has difficulties finding* etc. However, such constrained search strings will also miss a number of cases which arguably are examples of the same construction, as shown by the concordance lines for *difficulties meeting* in Figure 7.4. The constrained search string would have missed some of these instances of HAVE *difficulties *ing* because there is an intervening lexical item between *have* and *difficulties*, as in *had grave difficulties meeting* and *having greater difficulties* meeting. And instances with other verbs than HAVE, which arguably belong to the same construction, will of course be missed as well, like *face difficulties meeting* and *report difficulties meeting*. Such verbs would have to be investigated if we wanted to give a complete picture of the construction. However, searches for FACE *difficulty/ difficulties (in)* returned relatively few tokens, as shown in Table 7.11.

1. As a result, the central government **had grave difficulties meeting** even its current obligations. # It was this financial crisis that helped force
2. associated with being younger t(359) = −2.67, p <.05 and with **having greater difficulties meeting** basic needs? (2, N = 363 = 10.79,
3. transitional governments will inevitably **face enormous difficulties meeting** the basic needs of the people and maintaining stability.
4. Those who **reported difficulties meeting** basic needs, diabetes-related complications, worse subjective health, and dissatisfaction with medical

Figure 7.4 Selected concordance lines for *difficulties meeting* in COCA.

Table 7.11 Frequency of *facing difficulty/ difficulties (in)* *ing* in COCA and the BNC

	COCA (385m words)	BNC (100m words)
FACE *difficulty* *ing*	6	2
FACE *difficulty in* *ing*	6	1
FACE *difficulties* *ing*	8	2
FACE *difficulties in* *ing*	9	5

Examples of the uses with singular *difficulty* are given in (19)–(22).

(19) [...] scholars have **faced difficulty separating** textual interpretation from the social environment [...] (COCA Academic)

(20) Some people with HIV have lost their homes, or **faced difficulty getting** accommodation. (BNC CJ9)

(21) These young women often **face difficulty in acquiring** needed resources [...] (COCA Magazines)

(22) Credit unions perhaps meet most neatly the needs of people who now **face difficulty in getting** value from credit [...] (BNC CCT)

A close look at all the singular instances with the verb FACE showed that a majority were used in academic or newspaper language. Such examples are illustrated in (19)–(22). The same goes for the instances with plural *difficulties*, as illustrated in (23)–(26).

(23) Canada will **face difficulties competing** with the United States in the area of labour costs. (COCA Academic)

(24) [...] they **faced difficulties sustaining** both their solidarity and their ability to build on their new-found strength [...] (BNC FAW)

Table 7.12 Prepositional and directly linked gerunds with a selection of verbs dependent on and immediately following *[have] difficulty/ difficulties* in COCA

	in	*Ø*	*Total*	*Percentage* in
[have] difficulty + finding	8	97	105	8
[have] difficulty + getting	5	111	116	4
[have] difficulty + making	5	48	53	9
[have] difficulty + breathing	1	51	52	2
[have] difficulty + obtaining	3	25	28	11
[have] difficulty + identifying	4	21	25	16
Subtotal singular	**26**	**353**	**379**	**7**
[have] difficulties + finding	1	3	4	25
[have] difficulties + getting	0	4	4	0
[have] difficulties + making	0	1	1	0
[have] difficulties + breathing	0	0	0	–
[have] difficulties + obtaining	1	0	1	100
[have] difficulties + identifying	0	1	1	0
Subtotal plural	**2**	**9**	**11**	**18**

(25) Reading Mastery is used by pupils who **face difficulties in learning** to read. (COCA Academic)

(26) The FMLN itself **faced difficulties in meeting** the initial deadlines [...] (BNC HLT)

The searches reported in Tables 7.7–7.11, Figure 7.4 and examples (17)–(26) are all instances of the kind of small pilot studies that a corpus linguist has to carry out to establish whether a proposed search string gives the desired type of results or not, and to get ideas about new angles from which a certain phenomenon can be approached. The starting-point was that we wanted to replicate Rohdenburg's study in different corpora, and with a few more verbs. On the basis of our exploratory pilot studies, we will now add the following verbs to Rohdenburg's *getting* and *finding: making, breathing, obtaining* and *identifying*. To get a sufficient number of hits, we will not use his search string "he has difficulty/difficulties (in) finding etc.", but rather <[have] difficulty/difficulties (in) finding etc.> in order to get all forms of the lemma HAVE and all possible subjects. The results for COCA are given in Table 7.12 and for the BNC in Table 7.13.

The results presented in Tables 7.12 and 7.13 complement and somewhat modify the picture given by Rohdenburg in Table 7.6. First of all, there is the interesting difference between the American data in COCA and the British data in the BNC mentioned earlier, namely that

Table 7.13 Prepositional and directly linked gerunds with a selection of verbs dependent on and immediately following *[have] difficulty/difficulties* in the BNC

	in	Ø	Total	Percentage of in
[have] difficulty + finding	20	27	47	43
[have] difficulty + getting	13	25	38	34
[have] difficulty + making	8	9	17	47
[have] difficulty + breathing	4	8	12	33
[have] difficulty + obtaining	6	5	11	55
[have] difficulty + identifying	6	4	10	60
Subtotal singular	*57*	*78*	*135*	*42*
[have] difficulties + finding	3	1	4	75
[have] difficulties + getting	3	3	6	50
[have] difficulties + making	0	0	0	–
[have] difficulties + breathing	0	0	0	–
[have] difficulties + obtaining	1	0	1	100
[have] difficulties + identifying	0	0	0	–
Subtotal plural	*7*	*4*	*11*	*64*

there is a clear difference in the frequency of *in* (COCA singular 7 per cent, plural 18 per cent; BNC singular 42 per cent, plural 64 per cent). This difference is of course not visible in Rohdenburg's general Google search. Secondly, the clear difference in frequency of *in* between singular *difficulty* and plural *difficulties* which is seen in Rohdenburg's Google material (singular 13.2 per cent, plural 42.1 per cent) is much less pronounced in our corpora. In COCA the difference is 7–18 per cent and in the BNC 42–64 per cent, but it should be pointed out that the total figures for the plural are so low that percentage figures can be misleading. Still, we could say that our figures do not contradict Rohdenburg's hypothesis that the more complicated plural favours the more explicit construction with *in*.

Looking at the more reliable figures for the singular, we see that the two Latinate words *obtaining* and *identifying* get the highest proportion of *in* in both COCA and the BNC (11% and 16% in COCA and 55% and 60% in the BNC). Formality thus seems to be a factor that influences the choice between *in* and Ø in both geographical varieties, as suggested by Rohdenburg from the differences he found between *finding* and *getting*. It is also noteworthy that the most physical of the verbs studied, *breathing*, has the lowest figures for *in* in both COCA and the BNC (even if the margin to *getting* in the BNC is minimal). This gives some further support to the formality argument, but investigation of more verbs is needed.

Table 7.14 Active and passive clauses in six text categories in ICE-GB

	Active		Passive		
	N	Per cent	N	Per cent	Total
Social letters	4,877	96.4	181	3.6	5,058
Business letters	3,463	87.7	484	12.3	3,947
Academic writing	7,206	78.0	2,043	22.0	9,249
Non-academic writing	8,858	83.0	1,810	17.0	10,668
Press reports	4,716	86.7	727	13.3	5,443
Fiction	6,832	94.2	421	5.8	7,253

Source: Nelson et al. (2002: 251)

Rohdenburg's work and our small investigations here highlight the influence of syntactic complexity on the choice of syntactic construction, but also that the influence of individual lexical items and types of words on grammar is considerable. In addition, we discovered a difference between AmE and BrE.

7.6 Using a parsed corpus: passives revisited

In the study of passives in section 7.3 and the other examples in this chapter, grammatical phenomena had to be investigated by means of searches on strings of lexical items. In a parsed corpus, however, searches can be grammatically specified instead. The advantage of this is that you will get all instances of the grammatical construction you are interested in, rather than just the ones containing the typical lexical items that you use in lexical searches. Nelson et al. (2002: 249–252) were interested in the distribution of passive sentences across a number of different text categories. Since they were using the written part of the parsed version of ICE-GB, they could retrieve all passive clauses from different text categories in the corpus, and then subtract the passives from the total number of clauses in the corpus to get the number of active clauses, in order to calculate the proportion of passives in each category. Trying to get all the passive clauses by means of lexical searches including the lemmas BE and GET would have resulted in a search with low precision, retrieving many irrelevant examples. Nelson et al.'s results are given in Table 7.14.

The authors then go on to study academic and non-academic writing in greater detail, but this short example suffices to show how a rather small corpus (400,000 words) can yield large enough numbers of tokens of grammatical constructions when the corpus is parsed and all relevant tokens can be retrieved. As mentioned in Chapter 2, however, this of course means that you have to trust the grammatical analysis of the people behind the parser and agree with their definition, in this case, of a passive and of a clause.

7.7 Summary

In this chapter we have seen that many areas of grammar can be fruitfully studied in corpora by means of fairly simple search strategies. This is especially true for morphology, as in the case of *who/whom*, but also for grammatical constructions which are distinguished by the use of different lexical items, like *be-* and *get-*passives. And there are many other areas of the interface between the lexicon and grammar where individual lexical items exert a considerable influence over which grammatical constructions are chosen, such as adjective complementation (*accustomed to*) and noun complementation (*difficulty* (*in*) *finding*). In the case of *difficulty* (*in*) *finding* etc. we saw that a number of small case studies had to be carried out in order to find the most suitable search strings, and that one can encounter various surprises before one arrives at reliable results.

In the final example we saw how all instances of a particular construction, in this case passive clauses, could be retrieved from the ICE-GB parsed corpus by searching for the abstract construction rather than particular lexical items.

Study questions

1. The issue of the possible disappearance of the form *whom* is rather complicated, since it is used in several different constructions. In which of these constructions is it most likely to survive? What other factors are relevant if you want to study the distribution of *who* and *whom*?
2. In Table 7.3, two figures are given for COCA: the frequency index (i.e. the proportion of *get-*passives for each verb) and the absolute frequencies. Why is it important to give the absolute figures as well?
3. Why did Rohdenburg hypothesise that the preposition would be used more often after the plural *difficulties* than after the singular *difficulty* in the construction *have difficulty/difficulties* (*in*) *finding*? What did our additional corpus searches find?
4. In the discussion of Tables 7.7 and 7.8, the different usage with Latinate and Germanic words is mentioned. How does the argument go, and can you find any alternative way of interpreting the data?

5. The last example in the chapter made use of a parsed corpus. What are the main advantages and disadvantages of such corpora?

Corpus exercises

Hands-on exercises related to this chapter are available at the following web address:
http://www.euppublishing.com/series/ETOTELAdvanced/Lindquist.

Further reading

A number of classic corpus studies on grammar and other aspects of language are to be found in Aijmer and Altenberg (1991). The proceedings from the ICAME conferences always include interesting short corpus studies on the grammar of English, sometimes with useful methodological comments. Some recent ones are Renouf and Kehoe (2006), Facchinetti (2007) and Pahta et al. (2007). The same goes for the *ICAME Journal*, which is available on the web. Other journals which often publish corpus-based studies on the English language include *English Language and Linguistics* and *Journal of English Linguistics*. Three journals that cover corpus linguistics for all languages and often have articles on English are the *International Journal of Corpus Linguistics*, *Corpus Linguistics and Linguistic Theory* and *Corpora*.

Biber et al. (1999) is the first fully corpus-based grammar of English and presents the results of a large number of mini-studies on aspects of English grammar.

Two handbooks for the BNC, Aston and Burnard (1998) and Hoffman et al. (2008), contain much useful advice on how to search corpora for grammatical phenomena. The latter also has a chapter on advanced searches using regular expressions. Nelson et al. (2002) is a handbook to the parsed version of the ICE-GB corpus.

8 Male and female

8.1 Introduction

In the branch of linguistics called sociolinguistics, the relation of social factors to language use is studied. These factors include the speakers' class membership, education, income, age, gender, sexual preferences etc. The idea is that our language is influenced (or even to some extent determined) by the group we belong to.

In order to be able to use corpora for sociolinguistic studies, the corpora ideally should be marked up with information about the speakers and writers along these lines. Unfortunately, many corpora lack such information and therefore sociolinguistic studies based on general corpora are comparatively rare. However, some corpora do have the information needed to a smaller or larger extent. For instance, the BNC gives the information as far as it is known, which means that for the written component the age of the author is given in 22% of the cases and the sex of the author in 53%. For spoken language, age group is given in 57% of the cases, social class in 27% and sex in 79% (Hoffmann et al. 2008: 31, 35–36). In this chapter we will take a look at one social aspect of language: gender differences.

Language and gender has become a lively field of investigation since the 1970s, inspired by the feminist movement and the feeling that the inequality of men and women in society is mirrored in language and also, conversely, that oppressive societal structures are preserved by language. Some even argue that inequality is created and perpetuated by the language. There are several ways of studying gender roles in language. One prominent direction deals with discourse: how men and women interact by means of language in different situations like everyday conversation or business meetings. Who speaks most? Who interrupts most frequently? Who gives more supportive feedback? Who laughs most often? This is normally studied by close analysis of recorded or transcribed speech but is less amenable to automatic

Table 8.1 Frequency of *firemen* in the Time Corpus: per million words

	1920s	1930s	1940s	1950s	1960s	1970s	1980s	1990s	2000s
firemen	11.4	14.0	12.0	9.3	9.1	8.3	5.9	2.3	0.7

computer searches. Another approach is to look at how men and women are referred to in texts, and this is what the next section will be about.

8.2 Referring to men and women

In English, men are often said to be the "unmarked case". If nothing else is specified, people traditionally think of a man if there is mention of *an American, a doctor, a writer* or *a neighbour*, so that one only has to specify the sex by saying *an American woman, a woman doctor* or *a female writer* if the reference is to a woman, and many people find it more natural to say *the neighbour and his wife* than *the neighbour and her husband*. Other examples are traditional titles, with *Mr* for men and *Mrs* or *Miss* for women, so that the marital status asymmetrically has to be specified for women but not for men. The movement for non-sexist language has tried to introduce the title *Ms* for both married and unmarried women, but with relatively little success. Such active language engineering has been more successful when it comes to avoiding sex-marked professional titles: what used to be called *airline hostesses* are now generally referred to as *flight attendants*, at least in official documents, and *firemen* are often called *firefighters*.

8.2.1 Fires, firemen and firefighters

In order to investigate whether firemen have now become firefighters, I used the Time Corpus, which contains all *Time* issues from 1923 to 2007. The results of a search for *firemen* are given in Table 8.1. The number of words in *Time* differs between decades, with the 1940s, 1950s and 1960s having considerably more words than the other decades. In order to make exact comparisons between the decades possible, the figures have therefore been normalised to tokens per million words (in fact, this is done for you automatically by the search program on the web).

From the peak in the 1930s, the frequency of *firemen* goes down steadily till the 1970s, but this must have some other explanation, since awareness of sexist language was not very strong in those decades. According to prediction, however, the frequency begins to go down more steeply in the 1980s, decreases drastically in the 1990s and seems

Table 8.2 Frequency of *firefighters* in the Time Corpus: per million words

	1920s	1930s	1940s	1950s	1960s	1970s	1980s	1990s	2000s
firefighters	0.24	0.65	0.29	0.21	0.16	0.28	0.25	0.09	2.09

Table 8.3 Frequency of *fire fighters* in the Time Corpus: per million words

	1920s	1930s	1940s	1950s	1960s	1970s	1980s	1990s	2000s
fire fighters	0.00	0.32	1.05	0.83	0.68	1.42	7.50	3.57	8.61

Table 8.4 Frequency of *firemen* and *fire fighters/firefighters* in the Time Corpus: per million words

	1920s	1930s	1940s	1950s	1960s	1970s	1980s	1990s	2000s
firemen	11.4	14.0	12.0	9.3	9.1	8.3	5.9	2.3	0.7
fire fighters/ firefighters	0.24	0.95	1.34	1.04	0.84	1.70	7.75	3.66	10.70

to keep diminishing in the 2000s (although the full figures for that decade were not in when I made my search). The slow decrease all the way from the 1940s may have been caused by *Time* happening to write more about fires in the old days. This uncertainty shows that we need to compare *firemen* with the alternatives to be absolutely sure that there has been a change in favour of the non-sexist terms. My second search was therefore for *firefighters*, as shown in Table 8.2.

Something seems to be wrong here. The figures are very low, and although there is a relatively big rise in the 2000s, there is none in the 1970s, 1980s or 1990s to counterbalance the disappearing *firemen*. What could be the answer to this riddle? Spelling! As we have seen already, lexical computer searches can be skewed by overlooking spelling variants. Another problem sometimes missed by corpus linguists is differences between British and American spelling (*colour/color, towards/toward*) and contractions or lack of contractions in transcribed spoken language (*he'll/he will*). A search for *fire fighters* written as two words solved the mystery, at least partially. The figures are given in Table 8.3. There were no instances of *fire-fighters* written with a hyphen. Table 8.4 combines the figures for comparison.

The results in Table 8.4 are still far from crystal clear. We have established that the term *firemen* is certainly disappearing from the pages of *Time*, and that to some extent it is replaced by *fire fighters*. But there is an

Table 8.5 Adjacent right collocates of *fire* in the Time Corpus

	Word	1920s	1930s	1940s	1950s	1960s	1970s	1980s	1990s	2000s	Total
1	fire department	15	43	55	41	38	26	23	16	11	268
2	fire fighters	0	4	18	16	13	20	90	38	66	265
3	fire chief	4	20	25	28	9	10	15	4	2	117
4	fire engines	6	28	21	26	17	2	5	2	3	110
5	fire bombs	1	1	20	9	20	20	23	7	1	102
6	fire engine	9	24	10	13	14	12	8	1	2	93
7	fire hoses	2	4	11	16	35	5	5	2	2	82
8	fire power	0	1	62	9	6	0	1	0	0	79
9	fire insurance	14	14	14	14	11	11	0	0	0	78
10	fire trucks	4	3	11	19	12	10	9	3	3	74
11	fire storm	0	0	1	0	0	18	17	24	3	63
12	fire escape	1	14	15	15	4	8	1	0	2	60
13	fire hose	3	14	10	11	10	1	2	5	3	59
14	fire fighter	1	0	2	2	3	6	6	9	28	57
15	fire fight	0	0	0	6	14	1	6	9	19	55
16	fire extinguisher	2	7	9	13	2	4	1	5	11	54
17	fire alarm	2	5	10	15	4	3	3	5	3	50
18	fire truck	3	2	6	12	4	9	8	4	2	50
19	fire departments	2	8	9	6	3	7	5	7	2	49
20	fire hazard	5	10	14	3	4	4	3	1	0	44
	Total	74	202	323	274	223	177	231	142	163	1,809

unexplained dip in the use of that word in the 1990s, and there is also a diminishing combined total frequency of the two terms, from 228 in the 1940s to 87 in the 2000s (not shown in the table), which could either be due to *Time* reporting less on fires, or to their use of other terms which I did not think of. In order to check this, I made use of another search feature provided by the corpus webpage to search for the most frequent adjacent right collocates of the noun *fire*. The results are given in Table 8.5.

A cursory look at Table 8.5 shows two things: (1) there is no frequent alternative to *fireman* other than *fire fighter*, at least not one that is written as two words and which begins with *fire*, and (2) many of the words are most frequent roughly in the period between the 1930s and the 1970s, so it seems that the coverage of fires must indeed have gone down after the 1970s for some reason.

8.2.2 Poets, poetesses, actors and actresses

Let us now take a look at a slightly different issue in non-sexist language: the use of feminine suffixes on words denoting occupation. While this is the rule in, for instance, German, it exists only in a small number of

Table 8.6 Frequency of *poet* and *poetess* in the Time Corpus: absolute figures

	1920s	1930s	1940s	1950s	1960s	1970s	1980s	1990s	2000s
poet	537	871	815	1,052	1,147	611	397	335	127
poetess	36	44	54	50	23	6	1	0	0

Table 8.7 Frequency of *actor* and *actress* in the Time Corpus: absolute figures

	1920s	1930s	1940s	1950s	1960s	1970s	1980s	1990s	2000s
actor	463	639	685	1,246	1,122	932	832	732	730
actress	601	697	646	1,077	1,048	726	609	461	387
Total	1,064	1,336	1,331	2,323	2,170	1,658	1,441	1,193	1,117

word pairs in English like *poet–poetess* and *actor–actress*. To call a female poet *poetess* has come to be considered condescending and diminishing. So, is *poetess* used in *Time*, and if not, when did it cease to be used? The figures given in Table 8.6 are quite clear and there is no need to normalise them to see the trend.

As the table indicates, *poetess* is hardly used after the 1970s. This *could* mean that *Time* completely stopped writing about female poets around 1980, but a much likelier conclusion is that from then on they were just called poets (the alternative *woman poet* has only nine occurrences scattered from the 1920s to the 1980s and *female poet* only one, from the 1990s). As with the fire-fighting example above, there is a riddle of diminishing totals. From a maximum 1,170 mentions of poets and poetesses in the 1960s the figure goes down to 335 in the 1990s and looks to be even lower in the 2000s.

What about *actress*: is it disappearing at the same rate? The figures are given in Table 8.7.

Table 8.7 is not quite as easy to interpret right off, even if it seems as if the 1920s and the 2000s figures are mirror images of each other, with *actress* most frequent in the 1920s and *actor* in the 2000s. In cases like this, where we are looking at the relation of two terms, it can be useful to convert the absolute figures to percentages of the total use, as in Table 8.8.

There is an almost uninterrupted downhill development for *actress*, but the word is still alive and kicking and not at all close to disappearance like *poetess*. In fact the decline might be due to *Time* devoting more space to male actors than female ones in the 2000s as compared with the 1920s. In order to investigate the possible decline of *actress* properly we

Table 8.8 Ratio of *actor* and *actress* in the Time Corpus: percentages

	1920s	1930s	1940s	1950s	1960s	1970s	1980s	1990s	2000s
actor	44	48	51	54	52	57	58	61	65
actress	56	52	49	46	48	43	42	39	35

would have to study a representative sample of articles about female actors from the different periods and see which term is used. This, however, is beyond the scope of this book.

8.2.3 Describing males and females

A slightly more subtle phenomenon is the way men and women are described when they are talked and written about. With what adjectives are males and females described, for instance, and with what verbs are they associated? These questions are ones that can relatively easily be answered by means of corpora. Let us take a look at adjectives and verbs associated with men and women in the BNC. First, a search for *a* + adjective + *man/woman* was made by means of PIE. (Note that with this search string only adjectives beginning with a consonant will be retrieved.) The results are shown in Table 8.9.

Eight of the adjectives in the top fifteen are the same for *man* and *woman*, although the rank order differs somewhat: e.g. *good* is no. 2 for *man* and no. 7 for *woman*, and *black* is no. 6 for *man* and no. 10 for *woman*, but on the whole there are no sensational differences. It is more interesting to look at the seven words which are unique for the two lists, shown in rank order in Figure 8.1.

The sets of unique adjectives among the top fifteen give an interesting picture of how men and women are described in the texts in the BNC. Men are *big* (or *great*), *rich* and *nice* (but also frequently *dead*), while women are *beautiful*, *pregnant*, *fat*, *single* and *naked*. Quite often there is also talk about *a real woman*, as in (1) and (2).

(1)   Her eyes swept across his face, and suddenly she had the almost overwhelming desire to tell him that it wasn't important at all, that she was, inside, what he'd called **a real woman**, one who wanted a home and children to fill it, and most of all a husband, a man who would take her in his arms and kiss her until nothing mattered except him [...] (BNC JY7)

(2)   She wore bright clothes, did her hair differently, and she looked taller and thinner. Now she was **a real woman** because someone loved her. (BNC GVM)

Table 8.9 The most frequent adjectives associated with *man* and *woman* in the frame *a* + adjective + *man/woman* in the BNC

Rank	a + *adjective* + man		a + *adjective* + woman	
1	young	873	young	361
2	good	172	married	117
3	#-year-old[a]	133	#-year-old[a]	100
4	married	107	beautiful	67
5	big	100	middle-aged	48
6	black	83	pregnant	42
7	rich	83	good	35
8	tall	77	single	32
9	local	76	real	22
10	great	66	black	21
11	dead	65	fat	21
12	white	62	tall	20
13	nice	61	white	19
14	middle-aged	60	naked	18
15	new	57	different	16

Note: [a] The hash sign # indicates any number, so included here are *2-year-old*, *3-year-old*, *49-year-old* etc.

Man: *big, rich, local, great, dead, nice, new*
Woman: *beautiful, pregnant, single, real, fat, naked, different*

Figure 8.1 Unique adjectives in the top fifteen for *man* and *woman* in the BNC.

But we need to be a bit careful. *A real woman* occurs high up on the rank scale for *woman*, but there are only 22 hits. In fact *a real man* occurs more frequently, with 36 hits, which, however, gives it a lower rank among all the hits with *man*. That a *real man* is something different from a real woman according to the texts in the BNC is illustrated by the examples in (3)–(5).

(3) It's a hunter's paradise, Chuck. It makes a man feel like **a real man**. Makes you remember all men were hunters once and only the fittest of them survived. (BNC FU8)

(4) He's nothing. **A real man** never says sorry! (BNC GVM)

(5) Von Karajan was fine. Well, he was **a real man**, a real general man, he drove fast cars and flew an aeroplane as well as being a fine musician. (BNC ADP)

Our discussion of *man* and *woman* so far has been based on absolute figures, but the case of *real* showed that it is wise to be cautious and take

Table 8.10 Frequency of *man, woman, men* and *women* in the BNC

man	58,243	men	37,079	Total	95,322
woman	22,000	women	38,239	Total	60,239

Table 8.11 Frequency of *single man, single woman, single men* and *single women* in the BNC

single man	53	single men	37	Total	90
single woman	50	single women	98	Total	148

relative figures into account. Looking at the total frequency for *man* and *woman* on their own, so to speak, we get the figures in Table 8.10.

Surprisingly, perhaps, *man* in the singular is two and a half times more frequent than *woman* in the singular. This suggests that individual men are much more frequently talked about in these texts. On the other hand, men and women in the plural are referred to equally often. What about the pronouns *he* and *she*, then? The picture is similar to that of singular *man/woman*, but not as pronounced: *he* 640,620 against *she* 352,846. If we then return to *single*, which was one of the adjectives occurring uniquely with *woman* among the top fifteen adjectives, and combine it with *man/ men* and *woman/women*, we get the figures in Table 8.11.

Looking at the figures in Table 8.11, we get the impression that when we are talking about an individual man or woman, we equally often specify that he or she is single (53–50), whereas it is less common to talk about single men as a group than to talk about single women as a group (37–98). Somehow, single women as a group are more interesting than single men as a group and, moreover, in many texts they are seen as a problem that needs to be addressed, as in (6).

(6)   But as you may expect, unplanned pregnancies were more common in young and **single women**. (BNC EDG)

However, Table 8.11 does not give the whole picture, since we saw in Table 8.10 that on the whole, men are mentioned more often. So it makes sense to calculate how often per mention men and women are specified as being single. This is done by dividing the number of *single* mentions by the total number of mentions of *man/men* and *woman/ women*. We then get the figures in Table 8.12.

It turns out that when men or women are mentioned, regardless of whether it is in the singular or in the plural, women's singlehood is specified about two and a half times more often than men's. Clearly, here is lots of material for a gender study!

Table 8.12 Number of *single man/men* and *single woman/women* per 10,000
mentions of *man/men* and *woman/women* in the BNC

single man	9	single men	10
single woman	23	single women	26

Table 8.13 Most frequent verbs in the frames *she* + verb + *him* and *he* + verb
+ *her* in the BNC

Rank	she + *verb* + him		he + *verb* + her	
1	told	559	told	581
2	gave	219	gave	283
3	saw	201	kissed	162
4	watched	134	took	143
5	heard	134	asked	125
6	loved	132	loved	123
7	wanted	100	wanted	118
8	asked	93	saw	117
9	followed	92	held	100
10	found	73	watched	93
11	let	68	pulled	91
12	reminded	68	left	88
13	felt	60	led	82
14	left	60	handed	75
15	kissed	57	reminded	66

---

she + verb + *him:* *heard, followed, found, let, felt*
he + verb + *her:* *took, held, pulled, led, handed*

Figure 8.2 Unique verbs in the top fifteen in the frames *she* + verb + *him*
and *he* + verb + *her* in the BNC.

8.2.4 What men and women do

In another search, the verb used in the frames *she* + verb + *him* and *he* +
verb + *her* in the BNC was investigated in the same way. The top fifteen
verbs are given in Table 8.13.

In Table 8.13, ten of the verbs occur in both lists. It is interesting to
note that the two (rather passive) verbs of observation *saw* and *watched*
are higher ranked for *she*, while the active verb *kissed* has rank 15 for *she*
and rank 3 for *he*. Let us now turn to the five verbs which are unique for
the two frames, which are given in Figure 8.2.

The verbs used with *she* are more or less passive, while the verbs used with *he* are clearly more active: taking, holding, pulling and leading the female, and handing her things. The roles of women and men as they are conventionally described in the texts in the BNC thus seem to differ clearly, at least as shown by the top fifteen verbs in this frame.

8.3 The way men and women use language

As mentioned in the introduction to this chapter, there are many studies of how males and females interact by means of language in certain contexts, such as in various workplace situations, including job interviews and board meetings, in school and in social life. Such discourse studies can be carried out on corpora as well. However, in this book we will concentrate on some aspects of male and female language which are somewhat easier to study. One popular belief about the difference between men's and women's language is that women know and use more colour terms, because they are more interested in fashion, home decoration etc.

8.3.1 Colour terms

To investigate men's and women's use of colour terms, we will make searches in the written component of the BNC. This consists of approximately 90 million words, but we will only be able to use the approximately 45 million words in texts which have been marked up with the gender of the author. The frequency figures for a selection of colour terms are given in Table 8.14.

A number of comments can be made on the basis of the figures presented in Table 8.14. First of all, it is clear that in these texts, female writers do use more colour terms than men. For every single term, the frequency per million words is higher for the female authors. The relation between the figures has been calculated as a quota by dividing the female frequency figure by the male frequency figure. This quota varies from the colour term with the least difference, *cerise* (quota 1.17, or 17% more female uses) to the colour term with the biggest difference, *beige* (quota 5.08, or 408% more female uses). The frequency of these terms is quite low, however (especially for *cerise*), so the figures are not very reliable. But it seems quite clear that many of the most frequent colour terms are used approximately 50% more often by the female writers, and that many of the terms in the medium frequency range are used twice or three times as often. One can only speculate about the reasons for this. One possible explanation is that female writers deal with

Table 8.14 Male and female authors' use of colour terms in the BNC

| | Male authors | | | Female authors | | | Female/ male quota |
	Rank	N	Per million	Rank	N	Per million	
black	1	7,527	247.32	2	4,815	332.30	1.34
white	2	6,713	220.57	1	5,101	352.04	1.59
red	3	4,250	139.65	3	3,061	211.25	1.51
green	4	3,927	129.03	5	2,560	176.68	1.40
blue	5	2,770	91.02	4	2,787	192.34	2.11
brown	6	2,279	74.88	6	1,828	126.16	1.68
yellow	7	1,299	42.68	8	890	61.42	1.44
pink	8	653	21.46	7	963	66.46	3.10
purple	9	339	11.14	9	335	23.12	2.08
crimson	10	118	3.88	10	159	10.97	2.83
mauve	11	44[a]	1.44	12	56	3.86	2.68
beige	12	38	1.25	11	92	6.35	5.08
indigo	13	25	0.82	13	40	2.76	3.37
cerise	14	9	0.30	14	5	0.35	1.17

Note: [a] The total number of hits for *mauve* in the texts written by male authors was 89, but 45 of these were from the same text, referring to Vincent van Gogh's cousin, the Dutch painter Anton Mauve; these have been deducted from the total.

different topics, where the description of colours is more relevant, and where "specialist" colour terms like *purple, crimson, mauve, beige* and *indigo* are used. The everyday word *pink* is also used considerably more often by female writers, while, surprisingly, there is little difference with *cerise* (again, the total frequency was so low that the lack of difference may be due to chance).

As for rank, the order is quite similar between the genders, with some exceptions: *white* is more frequent than *black* among the females, and *blue* more frequent than *green*. *Pink* and *beige* also come higher on the female list than on the male list, but there is never more than one rank's difference, which goes to show that the relative order of cultural importance of these colours is fairly fixed, at least in the contexts which are described in the BNC.

The facts in Table 8.14 can be related to issues in, for instance, politics or sociology. But how they should be interpreted is a matter of opinion depending on whether you think it is good or bad or neither good nor bad that men and women use language differently in this respect.

Table 8.15 Frequency of hedging *kind of / sort of* in different disciplines in MICASE

Discipline	N per 1,000 words
Physical sciences/Engineering	1.36
Biology/Health sciences	2.56
Social sciences/Education	2.66
Humanities/Arts	3.73

Source: Based on Poos and Simpson (2002: 11, fig. 2b)

8.3.2 Hedging

In an article in 1973, George Lakoff introduced the term 'hedging', which has become widely used to describe the way speakers mark tentativeness or uncertainty about what they are saying. For instance, researchers are taught to be careful about their claims, to hedge, and to say, for instance, *the results seem to indicate that* rather than *the results prove that.* In 1975, in her book *Language and Woman's Place,* Robin Lakoff suggested that one of the things that characterise the speech of women is that they hedge more, i.e. that they show greater tentativeness and insecurity due to their role in a male-dominated culture. Later, however, Holmes (1986) showed that the situation is much more complex than this, and that a greater use of hedges does not necessarily need to be a sign of submissiveness but can rather be a sign of politeness and a will to mitigate.

One way of hedging is to use phrases like *sort of* and *kind of,* as in (7) and (8), which are from spoken BrE in the BNC.

(7) They were **sort of** equally distributed in those ages. (BNC G4V)

(8) [...] but of course, it had **kind of** stirred up a hornets' nest! (BNC KB9)

By using *sort of* in (7), the speaker is not making a strong claim about the distribution of whatever it was that was distributed: he or she is making a hedged claim. In (8), the function of *kind of* is to introduce a metaphor, which is down-played a bit and made less strong by the hedge.

As already mentioned, academic English is one area where hedging is particularly prominent. Poos and Simpson (2002) investigated the use of hedges by male and female speakers in different academic disciplines in MICASE. One of their findings was that the use of *kind of / sort of* differed between disciplines, as can be seen in Table 8.15.

Table 8.15 shows interestingly that the more "exact" in a traditional

Table 8.16 Distribution of *you know* by function and by sex of speaker in a corpus of spoken New Zealand English

Function	Number of occurrences	
	Female	Male
Speaker certain		
Conjoint knowledge signal	12	13
Emphatic	22	10
Attributive	29	20
Subtotal	*63*	*43*
Speaker uncertain		
Appealing	16	18
Linguistic impression signal, lexical	17	22
Linguistic impression signal, qualifying	1	10
Linguistic impression signal, false start	8	9
Subtotal	*42*	*59*
Grand total	105	102

Source: Based on Holmes (1986: 14)

sense the discipline is, the fewer *kind of / sort of* hedges does it use, with the lowest figure for physical sciences/engineering and the highest for humanities/art. However, Poos and Simpson found no clear correlation between gender and frequency of using these particular hedges. The overall hedging frequency for males was 2.26 per 1,000 words and for females 2.01 per 1,000 words, so if anything the males used a slightly higher number of hedges. This squares very well with what Holmes (1986: 13) found when she studied men's and women's total use of the hedge *you know* in a corpus of spoken New Zealand English. In 50,000 words the females used 105 *you know* and the males 102. However, Holmes points out that it is important to analyse the specific *function* of *you know* in each token. When she did that, she found some differences, as shown in Table 8.16.

Holmes comments that the figures show that "women use *you know* significantly more frequently to convey speaker certainty, while men use it more to convey uncertainty" (1986: 13). Her study shows that to get to the bottom of male and female language, the function of different expressions has to be taken into account, which means that quantitative studies must be accompanied by qualitative analysis.

Let us now investigate the use of *kind of* and *sort of* in a considerably bigger corpus, the spoken component of the BNC. Poos and Simpson rightly pointed out that all tokens of *kind of* and *sort of* are not used as hedges, as shown by (9) and (10).

Table 8.17 *Kind of* in the spoken components of the BNC

Subcorpus	N	Per million words
Demographic, female	245	108
Demographic, male	136	94
Context-governed, female	331	322
Context-governed, male	1,312	375

Table 8.18 *Sort of* in the spoken components of the BNC

Subcorpus	N	Per million words
Demographic, female	2,159	954
Demographic, male	1,330	915
Context-governed, female	1,359	1,324
Context-governed, male	4,399	1,258

(9)   What **kind of** weapons? (BNC KB3)
(10) No I shouldn't think the Chinese have got much time for **that sort of** approach to life. (BNC KC0)

If you just search on the untagged string you will even get examples like (11), where *kind* is an adjective.

(11) It's very **kind of** you all [. . .] (BNC KB0)

Poos and Simpson therefore weeded out all irrelevant tokens manually, so that their figures only include bona fide hedging instances of *sort of* and *kind of.* The larger a corpus you use, the more daunting such manual editing gets. One way of getting around the problem is to analyse a random set of, say, 100 concordance lines to see what proportion of tokens are relevant. I did this for *sort of* in the spoken subcorpora of the BNC and found that for *sort of*, approximately 94% of the tokens could be considered to be hedges, while for *kind of* the proportion was somewhat lower. Nevertheless, for the rather rough pilot study reported here, I decided to include all instances of *sort of* and *kind of.* The BNC spoken component is divided into a demographic component, which contains mainly conversation, and a context-governed component, which contains a greater variety of spoken texts including lectures, sermons, panel discussions etc. The frequency figures for *kind of* and *sort of* are given in Tables 8.17 and 8.18.

Note the important fact that the figures given in the right-most column in Tables 8.17 and 8.18 state the number of occurrences per million words of female and male speech, respectively. The main conclusion that can be drawn from the figures in the tables is that the phrases *kind of* and *sort of* are used equally frequently by men and women in spoken BrE, and also that *sort of* is much more frequent than *kind of*, especially in the demographic, more conversational subcorpus, where it is about ten time more frequent. In the context-governed subcorpus it is about four times as frequent. These rough figures, then, do not answer the question whether females hedge more than males. There could still be a difference, but to find out about that, a detailed analysis of the function of the tokens would have to be carried out.

The searches for Tables 8.17 and 8.18 were only made for the forms *kind of* and *sort of*, but of course both phrases are often pronounced with a reduced *of* and are sometimes spelt *kinda* and *sorta*. There were no instances of *sorta* in the corpus, but 24 instances of *kinda*, as in (12).

(12) Yeah, I, I <pause> **kinda** like that one. (BNC HM2)

Such examples should of course also be included in a detailed study of these phrases. The fact that no examples of *sorta* turned up in the transcriptions is probably due to the conventions adopted by the transcribers, either subconsciously or by decision, since there are fifteen tokens of *sorta* in the written component of the BNC, usually from the dialogue in novels, as in (13).

(13) Bus seems **sorta** empty somehow. (BNC HWM)

To conclude, my quick study in the BNC gave some support to Poos and Simpson's and Holmes's conclusion that there do not seem to be any major differences in the extent to which men and women hedge by means of *sort of* and *kind of*. However, there are many more hedging devices that could be investigated, and as Holmes pointed out, closer attention should be given to their different functions. As for *sort of* and *kind of*, there are many other interesting things to investigate about these particular phrases, for instance differences in use between genres, and which different adjectives, nouns, verbs, adverbs and prepositions are modified by the phrases (cf. Gries and David 2007).

8.4 Summary

In this chapter we related corpus results to conditions in society, specifically to the relation between the genders. We started out by looking at examples of changes in how men and women were referred to in *Time* during the last century, changes which may be the result of conscious reforms. We then went on to investigate with what adjectives men and women are described in the BNC. The differences can be seen as reflections of men's and women's roles in society. The same thing can be said about the picture given of men and women by the verbs they are associated with in the corpus. A different approach is to look at differences in how men and women themselves use the language. Our study of colour terms supported the common view that women know and use more colour terms than men, while the studies reported on regarding the use of hedges (*sort of, kind of, you know*) were more inconclusive and showed that with complex discourse issues detailed qualitative analyses are called for.

A general conclusion to the chapter is that many things regarding men's and women's language can be described by means of corpora, and ongoing changes can be documented, but how this knowledge should be related to the situation of males and females in society and possible reforms in that area are a matter of opinion.

Study questions

1. What kind of information is crucial if you want to use corpora for sociolinguistic studies? What corpora and text archives can be useful for corpus-based gender studies?
2. The chapter describes how some occupational terms have become less sexist over the years. Can you think of other occupational terms which have changed in the same way? Do you think there is a difference in these changes between different genres and between spoken and written English?
3. The results in Table 8.13 are based on search strings which retrieve examples of what men are reported as doing to women in the corpus and vice versa, which perhaps says something about the relation between the sexes. Do you think there would be similar results if the search strings had been *he* + *verb* + *him* and *she* + *verb* + *her*?
4. Have you yourself noticed differences in male and female speech among your friends at school or work? If you have, what do you think is the reason for the differences?

Corpus exercises

Hands-on exercises related to this chapter are available at the following web address:
http://www.euppublishing.com/series/ETOTELAdvanced/Lindquist.

Further reading

There are many recent books on language and gender, but most of them are based on sociolinguistic and discourse studies rather than corpus-based. An accessible starting-point is Litosseliti (2006), which covers many aspects of gender and language and suggests further reading and further research. Goddard and Meân ([2000] 2009) is a good source of ideas for small projects. Another good starting-point is Holmes and Meyerhoff (2003), which contains overview articles by many of the leading researchers in the field. Research methodologies are described in Harrington et al. (2008). Most textbooks in sociolinguists take up gender differences. Tagliamonte (2006) is a hands-on introduction to the sociolinguistic study of variation, and Romaine (2008) outlines the relationship between corpus linguistics and sociolinguistics.

9 Language change

9.1 Introduction

Throughout this book we have come across phenomena in language that have changed over time – which is not strange, since in fact *all* aspects of language change over time. It is, however, possible to adopt a 'synchronic' perspective and describe the language at one particular point in time, to take a freeze-frame picture. But even if we do that, we have to be aware that the language was different before and will be different afterwards. Looking at the pre-history of today's linguistic phenomena often helps explain why their structure is the way it is. This is taking a 'diachronic' view. For instance, in the course of our corpus-based studies in this book we have already seen that in COCA, the use of *but* rose between the early 1990s and the early 2000s, while the use of *however* went down (Chapter 2), that the term *global warming* replaced *greenhouse effect* in *Time* magazine between the 1980s and the 2000s (Chapter 3), that the share of *whom* out of all *who* and *whom* went down from 9.3% in the 1920s to 3.7% in the 2000s in the Time Corpus (Chapter 7), that *get*-passives increased in the same corpus in the same period (Chapter 7), and finally that gender-marked nouns like *fireman*, *poetess* and *actress* were being replaced by gender-neutral words over the same period, but at very different rates (Chapter 8).

In fact, one of the most rewarding things you can study in corpora is language change. There are two major ways to do this: studying 'change in real time' and studying 'change in apparent time'. In the first kind you need to have a diachronic corpus, i.e. a corpus which contains texts from different time periods and where the texts have been marked up for year of production. The Time corpus which we have used throughout the book is such a corpus with almost a century's perspective. Alternatively, you can use similar corpora from different time periods. The LOB/FLOB and Brown/Frown corpora from 1961 and 1991/1992, giving a 30-year perspective, are examples of this. Then there are a number of

167

dedicated historical corpora, which either have a longer time span in themselves, or contain material from a limited period in the past.

In sociolinguistic studies, the method called 'change in apparent time' is often used. The idea is that if you have a number of people of different ages, and there are marked differences between the way different age groups speak, you can assume that language change is going on and that the language is moving in the direction of the way the younger speakers are talking. When the older generation dies out, their way of talking will die with them. However, you can never be absolutely sure that this is what is going to happen. There is always a possibility that the younger people will change their way of talking as they grow older, so that there is a stable situation where the youngsters always speak in their particular way, and the old people in theirs. This phenomenon is called 'age grading' (cf., e.g., Nevalainen and Raumolin-Brunberg 2003).

Finally, you can study language change by looking at different varieties of a language, such sa AmE and BrE. By comparing the state of certain constructions in the two varieties, you can make the assumption that one is changing in the direction of the other. But again, these are just assumptions.

It is one thing to show that change has taken place and quite another to explain *why* change occurred. In historical linguistics it is common to talk about internal and external causes of change. Internal causes can be sought in the language itself: that the phrase *got you* is often pronounced /gɒtʃə/ (sometimes informally spelt *gotcha*) is due to the fact that when we pronounce the sounds /t/ and /j/ in quick succession they automatically come out as /tʃ/. In this way the language changes because of the way we pronounce the sounds of the language – and ultimately because of the way our vocal tract, tongue and other parts of our speech apparatus interact. Similarly, when some irregular verbs become regular over time it is seen as a result of the language system's own "drift" to become more regular, since presumably it is better to have a system with as few exceptions as possible. But humans also seem to like the exceptions and irregularities – we are not robots or computers, after all!

External causes, on the other hand, are due to factors outside language, such as fashion or language contact, when speakers of different languages mix and interact. For instance, many Scandinavian words were borrowed into English during the Viking settlements around the year 1000, when *window* (from Old Norse *vindauga* 'wind-eye') was borrowed and finally ousted the Old English *eyethurl* 'eye-hole'. *Window* then met competition from the Old French *fenester* (based on Latin *fenestra*) up till the sixteenth century before it finally (?) won out. With historical changes, only time can tell what the end result will be:

in Modern Norwegian *window* is *vindu*, while in Modern German it is *Fenster* and in Modern Swedish *fönster*.

Since the 1990s, corpora have become very important tools for historical linguists, helping them to find examples and see patterns much more efficiently than they were able to do before, when they had to collect all examples from texts by hand. Still, even more than when you study corpora of contemporary language, historical linguists need to go back and scrutinise the original texts, which if you go really far back may exist only in a number of manuscript copies in different hands and often in different dialect forms. This makes this kind of historical corpus linguistics very different from studies on the language of the last few hundred years, and if as a student you want to make a historical corpus investigation of English from earlier periods, it is recommended to do it in the context of a course in the history of the English language. In this chapter we will start with studies of change that is going on right now, and then go on to look at studies of longer time periods based on historical corpora.

9.2 What is likely happening with *likely*

In English, *likely* can either be an adjective meaning 'probable', as in (1), or an adverb meaning 'probably', as in (2).

(1)   Still, it is **likely** that Gorbachev and Bush will sign a full treaty by year's end. (*Time* 1990s)
(2)   Clinton's Framework will **likely** suggest that cyberspace remain "a duty-free zone," [. . .] (*Time* 1990s)

Both the adjective and the adverb use are listed in dictionaries, but the *OED* says about the adverb: "Now chiefly *most likely, very likely*, otherwise rare exc. *Sc. dial.*, or (freq.) *N. Amer.*" (*OED* s.v. likely B adv. 2). In other words, the *OED* thinks that the bare adverbial use in (2) (without *most* or *very*) has become rare except in Scottish dialect and in AmE. The adverbial use has been around a long time in BrE: the earliest citation in the *OED* is from Wycliffe's translation of the Bible c. 1380. However, all the citations in the dictionary after 1900 are from North American sources, the latest being the prediction about future information technology in (3).

(3)   It is possible to predict that within a few years the microfiche **likely** will move from the library into the study and home. **1971** *Publisher's Weekly* 22 Nov. 14/1

In order to investigate the present-day use of adverbial *likely* in AmE and BrE we will first look at its distribution in a number of frequent contexts in COCA and the BNC. The results are given in Table 9.1.

Table 9.1 Frequency of adverbial *likely* in different contexts in COCA and
the BNC: per 100m words

	COCA	BNC
will likely	992	53
likely will	275	10
will most likely	103	39
will very likely	17	9
will more likely	14	7
will quite likely	1	3

Table 9.1 shows that adverbial *likely* is indeed more frequent in the
American corpus – from 27.5 times more frequent in the phrase *likely
will* and 18 times more frequent in the phrase *will likely* to twice as
common in the phrase *will more likely*. The phrase with *quite* is the exception – here the frequency is higher in BrE, but this is probably due to
the fact that the overall frequency of the word *quite* is more than twice
as high in the BNC as in COCA (39,898 tokens per 100 million words
against 17,640 per 100 million words). British people like the word *quite*
more than Americans.

The large difference between the two varieties makes one wonder
whether there is ongoing change in one or both of them. Let us therefore first look at the short time perspective given by COCA, where
it is possible to see the distribution over five-year periods from 1990
onwards. This is shown in Figures 9.1 and 9.2 for the two phrases *will
likely* and *likely will*.

Figures 9.1 and 9.2 show that adverbial *likely* seems to be on the
increase in AmE, with 50 per cent more instances per million words
in the period 2005–2008 than in 1990–1994. There is unfortunately no
similar, easily accessible corpus that would give us the data for BrE.
Instead I searched *The Independent* on CD-ROM for 1990, 1995, 2000
and 2005 to see if there is a similar trend there. The string *likely will* did
not occur at all (except for one irrelevant token in 2005); the figures for
will likely are given in Table 9.2.

In spite of the fact that there were fifty-three tokens of *will likely* in
the BNC, the major part of which is from around 1990, there was not
a single token in *The Independent* of that year. From then on, however,
there is a small but growing trickle of examples: a doubling between
1995 and 2000, and another 27% added between 2000 and 2005. These
figures suggest that adverbial *likely* is being reintroduced into BrE, probably through influence from AmE. Ten of the twenty-two tokens from
2000 are given in Figure 9.3.

Period	1990–1994	1995–1999	2000–2004	2005–2008
Per million	**5.7**	**7.3**	**7.5**	**9.1**
N	588	752	768	713

Figure 9.1 Distribution of *will likely* in COCA: per million words.

Period	1990–1994	1995–1999	2000–2004	2005–2008
Per million	**2.2**	**2.8**	**2.7**	**3.3**
N	232	292	277	259

Figure 9.2 Distribution of *likely will* in COCA: per million words.

Table 9.2 Distribution of *will likely* in *The Independent*, 1990–2005: absolute figures

Year	N
1990	0
1995	11
2000	22
2005	28

Among the concordance lines, there are several dealing with business, politics, sports and the arts, which implies that *will likely* is used in a variety of fairly serious registers. To check the distribution over different registers, we will use the division into subcorpora in COCA and the BNC. Figure 9.4 shows the results for COCA.

Figure 9.4 confirms the impression given by the concordance lines from *The Independent* in Figure 9.3. In AmE, *will likely* is used frequently in magazines, newspapers and academic texts, but rarely in spoken language and in fiction. Next, in Figure 9.5, we will see whether this holds for the BNC as well.

The low number of examples in the BNC makes it difficult to draw

1. he says. "Now they occur about every three years. By 2010 they **will likely** be an annual event." The most damaging recent burst o
2. h Gibson's kinetic screen presence . . . This is an inspiring epic that **will likely** bring a new era of Revolutionary action heroes." We mig
3. lise, glamorise, dehumanise, make a spectacle of, anaesthetise – **will likely** come into play. And with a Holocaust exhibition there is
4. ada lost more than their unbeaten run. A mistake by team officials **will likely** cost the team a medal. The Americans routed New Zeal
5. uter-maker Hewlett-Packard. As with Cisco last week, the market **will likely** get fretful in the run-up, and bored in the aftermath. In L
6. ll is not well in the food sector, as both AB Foods and Tate & Lyle **will likely** demonstrate. The former has seen its forecasts signific
7. ependent publisher, but any other author considering following suit **will likely** be faced with a number of commercial and legal proble
8. make it, and the attrition rate is likely to be high. Any serious fault **will likely** manifest itself on the way down the Atlantic and before t
9. a result. When the case concludes tomorrow, the House of Lords **will likely** reserve judgment until the autumn. Their final decision w
10. ed. Analysts believe that the latest spin in the genetics revolution **will likely** shape the next 20 years, not only for the biotechs, but f

Figure 9.3 Concordance lines for *will likely* in *The Independent*, 2000.

Section	Spoken	Fiction	Magazine	Newspaper	Academic
Per million	**4.5**	**0.6**	**11.6**	**9.7**	**9.8**
N	358	43	936	738	746

Figure 9.4 Distribution of *will likely* over subcorpora in COCA.

any safe conclusions. But here, too, there are very few tokens in spoken language and fiction, and the same holds also for academic text. The newspaper category has a fairly high frequency just as in COCA, but *will likely* is clearly most frequent in the miscellaneous category. This large category (making up half of the written part of the corpus) includes non-academic prose, biography and other published materials of various

Section	Spoken	Fiction	Newspaper	Academic	Misc.
Per million	0.0	0.3	0.5	0.1	1.0
N	0	4	5	1	43

Figure 9.5 Distribution of *will likely* over subcorpora in the BNC: per million words.

kinds. In the early 1990s, apparently, adverbial *likely* had started being used in non-fiction books, but was used less in newspapers and hardly at all in academic English and the spoken language. If indeed the use of adverbial *likely* is being reintroduced into BrE, both the concordance lines in Figure 9.3 and the statistics in Figures 9.4 and 9.5 suggest that it is happening in non-fiction prose.

9.3 Grammaticalisation: The history of *beside(s)*

Many grammatical function words in modern English are the results of a historical process in which words with more lexical content over time developed into more grammatical words. The term for this is 'grammaticalisation'. The standard textbook example is the development of *going to* from a phrase meaning that somebody is moving from one place to another to a pure marker of futurity, as illustrated in the present-day examples in (4)–(9).

(4) I'm **going to the** shopping center, I say, starting for the door. (COCA Fiction)

(5) Wednesday finished her drawing and showed it to me. Goatee, annoyed expression, three hoops in the ear and one in the nose – a perfect caricature of the waiter. She eyed him as he moved behind the bar. "I'm **going to** buy cigarettes from that man and I'm going to give him this as a tip." "You devil you," I murmured. She was already gone. I leaned on a fist and watched her on her way to the bar, working the crowd like a hostess. (COCA Fiction)

(6) [. . .] I'm going away for the summer. I'm **going to the** University of Wisconsin. (COCA Fiction)

(7) If you didn't like 1988, you're **going to hate** 1992. (COCA Newspapers)

(8)   It's **going to** snow!" they shouted. (COCA Fiction)
(9)   Well, I guess I was **gonna** – I was **gonna** ask you whether the facts back up your findings in this poll. (COCA Spoken)

Example (4) illustrates the original state where *going to* meant 'movement towards a point in space'. Then it developed the meaning 'movement towards a point in space with the intention of doing X', as in (5), where the person called Wednesday is moving across the room towards the bar with the intention of buying cigarettes. In (6) we see that *going to* can be used about a movement which is not happening at the moment of speaking, but planned for the future. In (7) the meaning is pure future, with no intention on the part of the participants, and in (8) even more so since there is no animate subject. In (9), finally, *going to* has been phonetically reduced to *gonna*, which is a pure marker of the future, as is shown by the fact that you cannot say **I'm gonna New York tomorrow*, but you can say *I'm going to go to New York tomorrow* or *I'm gonna go to New York tomorrow*. That it was possible to show the different stages in the grammaticalisation of *gonna* with contemporary examples illustrates the fact that the old meanings do not always disappear – it is actually quite common that they linger on in parallel with the new meanings, a phenomenon called 'layering'. It is not always possible to draw a sharp line between such layered meanings.

Rissanen (2004) studied the development and grammaticalisation of the preposition and conjunct *beside(s)* in English, using a number of corpora including the Helsinki Corpus of English Texts (HC). The origin of *beside* according to the *OED* is *be* + *sidan* (prep. + dative singular of *side*) in Old English (OE), but Rissanen found only one example of this construction in the OE corpora he searched, which led him to conclude that even if the grammaticalisation may have its roots in OE, the story really began in the Middle English (ME) period (1100–1500). In Old English, *side* usually referred to the side of the human body or an animal, or, by extension, to the side of a building, a ship or a mountain. In the ME period, there was first of all a more general shift from animate referents, such as humans or animals, to inanimate referents, such as ships and walls, as indicated by the figures in Table 9.3.

Table 9.3 shows that there is a shift from predominantly animate meaning in the earliest parts of the corpus to a more even distribution between animate and inanimate meaning in the later parts. The extremely high figures for inanimate in ME3 are due to the skewing effect of a few individual texts in that subcorpus. Even so, the trend is clear.

Rissanen then goes on to discuss a number of abstract meanings of

Table 9.3 The noun *side* with animate and inanimate referents in the ME part of the HC: absolute figures

Subcorpus	Period	Animate	Inanimate
ME1	1150–1250	8	2
ME2	1250–1350	17	13
ME3	1350–1420	19	71
ME4	1420–1500	43	38

Source: Rissanen (2004: 157)

side that develop during the ME period, including the following listed by the *MED*, (somewhat abbreviated here):

- Interest, concern; regard, point of view
- One of two parties to a dispute
- One or two of contrasting abstractions, positions etc.
- To the side, aside, away

Rissanen shows that similar semantic developments occurred with the grammaticalised construction *be* + *side* (spelt variously *bi side, biside, besides* and *bisiden*). The variant spellings highlight a problem which historical researchers especially have to be aware of: to be certain of finding all tokens of a particular item, a large variety of spellings, likely and unlikely ones, must be searched for. Spelling in the old days was pretty wild! This should not be forgotten by linguists working on modern corpora either, as we saw with the compound *firefighters/fire fighters* (Chapter 8), which could be written solidly as one word or separately as two words.

Rissanen found examples of *beside* as a preposition (*bi side þe buregh* 'beside the city/fort') and as an adverb (*gære haueð bisiden* 'had a spear at the side') as early as the thirteenth century. There was a development from concrete to abstract meanings with these grammaticalised forms as well (senses from the *MED*, abbreviated):

Adverb
1. at the side
2. nearby
3. to one side
4. in addition
5. (a) of time: near; of rank: equal

Preposition
1. at, next to; alongside; with
2. near; (at a certain distance) from

Table 9.4 *Beside(s)* in the Early Modern English part of the HC

	Preposition				Adverb			
	beside		besides		beside		besides	
	Local	Abstract	Local	Abstract	Local	Abstract	Local	Abstract
EModE1	6	17	4	18	1	3	0	4
EModE2	1	3	2	21	1	9	1	13
EModE3	1	3	0	24	0	0	0	24

Note: EModE1 = 1500–1570); EModE2 = (1570–1640); EModE3 = 1640–1710).
Source: From Rissanen (2004: 165)

> 3. to one side of
> 4. in addition to
> 5. outside (a place); outside (the bounds of reason etc.); without

It is interesting to see that the meaning of the preposition especially has developed from 'nearby' to 'outside', from nearness to distancing. Rissanen explains this by the process of 'subjectification', where the point of view 'moves inside' the speaker:

> As long as the point of view is an outsider's or neutral, the idea of 'side' most naturally refers to somebody or something in the immediate vicinity of the person or object governed by *beside(s)*. But when the relation is defined from the point of view of this referent, distancing, movement away, becomes a natural extension of meaning. With this development the way is paved for the emergence of abstract meanings – not only 'in addition to' but also 'outside', 'except', etc. (Rissanen 2004: 162).

After having covered ME, Rissanen also investigates the Early Modern Period (1500–1700), where he finds that the development continues, with the development of further abstract meanings and an increase in the proportion of abstract uses, as shown in Table 9.4.

We can see in Table 9.4 that at the end of the Early Modern English (EModE) period, i.e. around 1700, both the preposition and the adverb are mostly written *besides* (with an *s*) and have abstract meaning. However, there is a new change ahead. Rissanen made further searches in ARCHER (A Representative Corpus of Historical English Registers), which partly overlaps with the HC but includes material up to 1990. Even if this corpus contains different kinds of text (including American English) from the HC, the results are quite striking, as shown in Table 9.5.

Although there are some differences in details, Table 9.5 shows that

Table 9.5 *Beside* and *besides* in the ARCHER Corpus

| | Preposition | | | | Adverb | | | |
| | *beside* | | *besides* | | *beside* | | *besides* | |
	Local	Abstract	Local	Abstract	Local	Abstract	Local	Abstract
1650–1699	0	2	0	29	0	2	0	20
1700–1799	3	11	0	47	1	6	0	54
1800–1899	11	2	1	34	0	0	1	29
1900–1990	23	3	0	9	0	0	0	18

Source: Rissanen (2004: 166)

for the first three centuries in ARCHER, the pattern is the same as for the two last portions of EModE in the HC: *besides* is the most frequent form and it is primarily used with abstract meaning. In the 1900s, however, something quite remarkable has happened. *Beside* has grown in frequency as a preposition with local (concrete) meaning, while the adverb function is now only fulfilled by the form *besides*, always with abstract meaning. The situation is still a bit messy in the left-hand (preposition) half of Table 9.5, but on the whole the situation has been clarified and the two forms have specialised in different ways, both semantically and grammatically.

Finally, Rissanen investigated these forms in FLOB (1991 BrE), Frown (1992 AmE) and the BNC, and found that *beside* is now the most frequent form overall (approximately 2:1 in FLOB and the BNC, but with a more even distribution in Frown) and that it is only used as a preposition, while *besides* is still used both as a preposition and an adverb.

Since we now have access to further diachronic data from the Time Corpus, I decided to investigate how *beside* and *besides* were used in *Time* from the 1920s to the 2000s. Figure 9.6 shows the occurrences of *beside* as an adverb.

Figure 9.6 shows that *beside* is occasionally used as an adverb, as in (10), but there are extremely few cases, so Rissanen's observation that *beside* now has specialised as a preposition is supported. In addition, there are more cases at the beginning of the century than at the end.

(10) They started marching up Main Street. The State Police fell in **beside**. (*Time*, 1920s)

Decade	1920s	1930s	1940s	1950s	1960s	1970s	1980s	1990s	2000s
Per million	0.7	0.4	0.2	0.0	0.1	0.1	0.2	0.1	0.0
N	5	5	3	0	2	1	2	1	0

Figure 9.6 Frequency of *beside* (adverb) in the Time Corpus: per million words.

Decade	1920s	1930s	1940s	1950s	1960s	1970s	1980s	1990s	2000s
Per million	50.3	48.0	43.3	35.0	26.5	20.8	18.8	16.5	15.2
N	384	607	669	588	426	283	214	161	98

Figure 9.7 Frequency of *beside* (preposition) in the Time Corpus: per million words.

I also looked at the distribution of *beside* as a preposition, as in (11), and found the surprising picture shown in Figure 9.7.

(11) This is left untouched in the center of the table **beside** the lamb. (*Time*, 1920s)

Beside as a preposition is indeed much more frequent than *beside* as an adverb, but for some reason the frequency per million words goes down drastically from 50.3 in the 1920s to a mere 15.2 in the 2000s. It is hard to say why this is so. Looking at the concordance lines from the 1920s and the 2000s, I can see no immediate difference in the type of phrases that *beside* is used in. Searching on a number of other prepositions (*below, behind, in front of*) I found no similar decrease in numbers, so this seems to be a specific phenomenon related to *beside*, which needs to be investigated in more detailed qualitative investigations.

Let us now turn to *besides*. The frequencies for *besides* as an adverb, as in (12), are given in Figure 9.8.

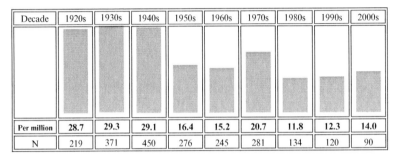

Decade	1920s	1930s	1940s	1950s	1960s	1970s	1980s	1990s	2000s
Per million	22.8	24.2	32.4	24.4	31.2	33.8	24.0	26.4	24.0
N	174	306	500	409	502	460	273	257	154

Figure 9.8 Frequency of *besides* (adverb) in the Time Corpus: per million words.

Decade	1920s	1930s	1940s	1950s	1960s	1970s	1980s	1990s	2000s
Per million	28.7	29.3	29.1	16.4	15.2	20.7	11.8	12.3	14.0
N	219	371	450	276	245	281	134	120	90

Figure 9.9 Frequency of *besides* (preposition) in the Time Corpus: per million words.

(12) **Besides**, fruits and vegetables seem to have other, hidden health benefits. (*Time*, 2000s)

Figure 9.8 demonstrates that *besides* as an adverb has a fairly even frequency all through the period. There are some minor fluctuations, but no signs of change. The situation with *besides* as a preposition, as in (13), is different, however, as can be seen in Figure 9.9.

(13) Every hit **besides** the bull's eye is irretrievably lost. (*Time* 2000s)

Figure 9.9 shows that the prepositional use of *besides* decreased rather sharply in the 1950s to a level at about half the frequency of before, and then stayed at that level.

In this rather long example we first followed Rissanen on his quest for the history of *beside* and *besides* from the beginnings more than a thousand years ago up to the 1990s, through a succession of increasingly large corpora. For the early stages in the history of the language the

amount of extant text is small, and the historical linguist usually finds
rather few tokens, which have to be examined carefully one by one.
Very much of the work for those periods still has to be qualitative, just
as in the pre-electronic-corpus days of historical linguistics. The difference made by corpora is that it is now easier to find examples of the
words or constructions you are looking for, even if spelling conventions
(or the lack of them) certainly create obstacles.

As we get closer to our own time the corpora get bigger. Providing
that we formulate our search strings well and that the corpora have sufficient mark-up for the task at hand so that we can achieve both high
precision and high recall, we get more reliable statistics. The story of
beside(s) told here was based on a number of overlapping corpora with
different characteristics. This is a quite common situation – Lindquist
and Levin (2000) called this the necessity to compare apples and
oranges in corpus linguistics. In the next section, however, we will stick
to one single source.

9.4 The *OED* as Corpus: Starting to say *start to* and *start* V-*ing*

We saw in section 9.3 that it was possible to make a long-term diachronic study of grammatical features by combining several different
historical and modern corpora. There is, however, one other source of
historical linguistic data which is relatively easy to access through most
university libraries: the *OED* online. The *OED* contains a large number
of authentic (although sometimes slightly abbreviated) quotations from
the last 1,000 years. The distribution of quotations (also called citations)
is given in Table 9.6.

The new edition (2000–) is continuously added to, so these figures
will keep growing. As Mair points out, one has to be aware of the particular characteristics of this "corpus". It contains sentence fragments
rather than stretches of text, the coverage is uneven and there is a
certain Victorian bias towards the socially acceptable, although, according to Mair, the latter problem was redressed to some extent in the
second edition, so that, for instance, four-letter words (i.e. obscenities)
were included for the first time.

In an investigation of the grammaticalisation of *start to* and *start* V-*ing*
(i.e. *start* + gerund) into a semi-auxiliary of inception ('beginning'), as in
my examples in (14) and (15), Mair (2004) demonstrated how the *OED*
can be fruitfully used for diachronic studies. ('Semi-auxiliary' means
that the construction shares some features with the auxiliaries; for
instance, it is constructed with another verb just like the auxiliaries *may*
and *can: may turn, can turn, starts to turn.*)

Table 9.6 The *OED* quotation base: chronological breakdown

Period	Number of quotations	Estimated number of words
−1000	19,769	198,000
1001–1100	2,324	23,000
1101-1200	11,582	116,000
1201-1300	46,205	462,000
1301–1400	97,150	972,000
1401–1500	96,411	964,000
1501–1600	253,528	2,535,000
1601–1700	383,208	3,832,000
1701–1800	273,676	2,737,000
1801–1900	763,987	7,670,000
1901–2000	481,376	4,814,000
2001–2008	33,636	336,000
Total	2,462,852	24,659,000

Source: Based on Mair (2004: 124): figures for 2001–2008 added

(14) If you come forward and angulate slightly with the knees, the skis will **start to** turn gradually out of the fall line. 1973 C. FOWLER *Skiing Techniques* 20/1 (*OED* s.v. angulate)

(15) Whenever I'm cheesed off I just open it and **start** reading. 1948 A. BARON *From City, from Plough* 161 (*OED* s.v. cheesed)

This development had happened by about 1800, so that at that time *start* competed with *begin* in these contexts.

In grammaticalisation studies, frequency is an important concept. First of all, the phrases that grammaticalise normally have to be fairly frequent for the grammaticalisation process to commence through repeated use. Then, when the grammaticalisation has occurred, the meaning of the grammaticalised item becomes more general and fits more contexts, which in turn usually leads to increased frequency. For instance, when *beside* stopped referring only to an actual part (the *side*) of the body of a human or an animal and could be used first about inanimate things and then abstractly in phrases like *That's beside point!*, obviously there was a great chance that the frequency would go up.

Mair had seen with other cases of grammaticalisation that this increase in frequency often came considerably later than the first instances of the new construction, and wanted to see whether there was such a delay with *start to/start V-ing* as well. He therefore divided the centuries from 1600 to 2000 into 25-year periods, and searched each

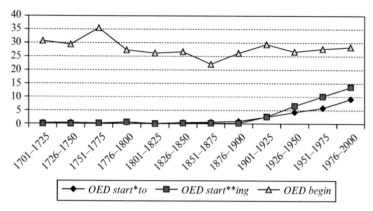

Figure 9.10 Frequency of *begin/start* + gerund and infinitive, 1700–2000 in the *OED*: per 10,000 citations.
Source: Based on Mair (2004: 130)

period in the *OED* for instances of *start* to, *start* *ing*, *begin* to and *begin* *ing*. The results are shown in Figure 9.10 (The years 1600–1699 have been left out here.)

Figure 9.10 clearly demonstrates that it took about one hundred years after the new grammaticalised forms *start to* and *start V-ing* were introduced c. 1800 before they started to increase in frequency, which happened around 1900. From then on, the increase is steady and rather steep, with the -*ing* construction taking the lead. At the same time, constructions with *begin* remain fairly stable. Mair mentions that manual analysis and post-editing showed that there is a problem with precision in these figures: they include quite a few irrelevant examples, such as instances of the expression *from start to finish* (where *to* is a preposition) and several others, especially in the early centuries. In the twentieth century, however, most of the hits are relevant, and since it is in this century that the rise in frequency occurs, the precision can be seen as acceptable.

Mair's study clearly demonstrates that in certain cases, in spite of the drawbacks, the *OED* can be used for diachronic investigations where other historical corpora may be too small or too limited in diachronic scope.

9.5 Sociolinguistic explanations of language change: The rise of third person singular -*s*

One of the several corpora of historical texts that have been compiled at Helsinki University is the Corpus of Early English Correspondence

Table 9.7 Third person singular indicative suffix *-s* vs. *-th*: percentage of *-s*

	1520–1559			1640–1681		
	-th	-s	% -s	-th	-s	% -s
Royalty	17	0	0	0	55	100
Nobility	58	13	18	10	158	94
Gentry	274	25	8	45	635	93
Clergy	86	4	4	35	217	86
Social aspirers	177	5	3	23	170	88
Professionals	56	1	2	36	200	85
Merchants	304	33	10	8	107	93
Other non-gentry	30	42	58	3	39	93
Total	1,002	123	11	160	1,581	91

Note: HAVE and DO excluded. Male informants.
Source: Based on Nevalainen and Raumolin-Brunberg (2003: 140)

(CEEC). It consists of 6,000 personal letters written by nearly 800 different writers between 1410 and 1681. There is a fair balance between different social groups, although of course only literate people are represented. Personal letters are an excellent data source for sociolinguistic research on earlier periods, since they are usually closer to the spoken language than are printed texts. Since the letter writers in this corpus are known, it is possible to relate language changes to age, gender and social class. We will look at one investigation made by Nevalainen and Raumolin-Brunberg (2003: 139–141).

In EModE, the old third person singular suffix *-th*, as in (16), was replaced by the new *-s*, as in (17) (my examples).

(16)   This day my lord knowe**th** not whether he goe**th** home afore this tyme, or noo. (CEEC)

(17)   The King goe**s** on Weddensday next to More Park, whear he staye**s** till Friday, hunts and feasts. (CEEC)

Such changes often start in one social group and spread to others. This can be seen in Table 9.7 from Nevalainen and Raumolin-Brunberg (slightly simplified here).

As Nevalainen and Raumolin-Brunberg point out, what we see in the left-hand part of Table 9.7, referring to 1520–1559, is so-called social stratification in the choice of *-s*. The term 'social stratification' is based on the idea that society consists of 'strata' or layers like the layers of rock or soil in geology. Your language depends on which stratum of society

you belong to, and in this particular case the choice of third person singular indicative suffix is correlated with the writers' place in the social
hierarchy. In the mid-sixteenth century, more than half of the people in
the lowest stratum, 'other non-gentry', had already switched to -*s*, while
none of the royalty at the top had done so. The relatively high figures
for the nobility and gentry are explained by the fact that several of these
writers came from the north, where -*s* had spread earlier.

The right-hand part of Table 9.7 shows what had happened a century
later. Now most people used -*s* most of the time (the royalty always did
so), and there was no major difference between the top and bottom of
society in this respect. Nevalainen and Raumolin-Brunberg speculate
that the slightly lower figures for the clergy and the professionals may
be caused by their dealing professionally with linguistically conservative religious and legal documents.

Looking at language and language change through a sociolinguistic
lens, as Nevalainen and Raumolin-Brunberg have done here, tells us
something about how language and social circumstances interacted in
the past, and makes it possible to compare with what is going on today
and achieve a better understanding of current developments.

9.6 Summary

In this chapter we started out by looking at changes in the use of adverbial *likely* which seem to be going on right now. We then went back
1,000 years to follow the grammaticalisation of *beside(s)* through the
centuries right up to the present day by means of a number of different
corpora. We also saw how the *OED* online could be used as a corpus, and
how a corpus of medieval letters could give insights into the influence of
social stratification on language use and language change.

In some of these studies data from different corpora were compared,
and it is important to point out that the composition of corpora from
different time periods must always be carefully considered: do they
contain the same or different genres, the same or different varieties,
etc.? Old genres may develop, change and disappear over time, while
new genres are born. For instance, since people are writing fewer and
fewer personal letters, what should the letters in the CEEC be compared with today? Perhaps e-mail messages would be an option, but
they have their own characteristics, which would have to be taken into
account.

In many chapters in this book, development over time was part of
the investigations discussed. In fact, many corpora and text databases,
like newspaper CD-ROMs and collections of literature, are eminently

suitable for diachronic studies, both for discovering and documenting change and for finding its internal and external causes.

Study questions

1. The introduction to this chapter claims that language changes constantly. Can you think of any further examples of this, in English or any other language? What consequences does this have for synchronic language studies?
2. What does 'change in apparent time' mean? Why are results showing change in apparent time more uncertain than results showing change in real time?
3. Some changes originate in informal spoken language ('change from below') and other changes are initiated in more formal, written language ('change from above'). What kind of change is the spread of adverbial *likely* in the word order *will likely* in BrE, according to the data presented in this chapter?
4. In what ways do corpus linguists, and especially historical corpus linguists, take spelling variants into account?
5. What are the advantages and disadvantages of using the *OED* as a corpus?
6. What is social stratification, and how does it influence language and language change?

Corpus exercises

Hands-on exercises related to this chapter are available at the following web address:
http://www.euppublishing.com/series/ETOTELAdvanced/Lindquist.

Further reading

Hogg and Denison (2006) is an authoritative general introduction to the history of the English language. Rissanen (2000, 2008), Kohnen (2007) and Claridge (2008) provide good surveys of historical corpora. Nevalainen (2006) is an accessible guide to the EmodE period (1500–1700) and includes a section on corpus resources. Curzan (2009) is a brief introduction to using corpus methodology in the study of language change. A number of interesting corpus-based studies on nineteenth-century English are published in Kytö et al. (2006). Mair (2006a, 2009) covers twentieth-century English and is good on general corpus methodology. Bauer (1994) is also a good introduction to ongoing change in English.

A sociolinguistic approach to historical linguistics is taken by Nevalainen and Raumolin-Brunberg (2003), who discuss a number of key concepts, such as change in real time, change in apparent time and age grading, in a very pedagogical manner. The standard textbook on grammaticalisation is Hopper and Traugott ([1993] 2003); papers on corpus approaches to grammaticalisation can be found in Lindquist and Mair (2004).

10 Corpus linguistics in cyberspace

10.1 Introduction

There are a number of areas of linguistic research where standard corpora, even if they contain 100 million words or more, do not provide enough data. One such area is lexical studies, where studies on morphological productivity (e.g. the creation of new words by means of affixes), collocations and formulaic sequences containing infrequent words especially demand very large databases. For instance, in an investigation of constructions consisting of a body part noun + the preposition *to* + the same body noun again (such as *face to face*), Lindquist and Levin (2009) used a newspaper corpus of 300+ million words and still were only able to find sporadic examples of phrases like *belly to belly* (2) and *chest to chest* (6). The same holds for studies on rare grammatical constructions and the relation between grammar and individual lexical items or groups of lexical items. Furthermore, the fact that the standard corpora are usually fixed or closed, containing data from a specific time period, means that they quickly become dated and unsuitable for studies of the most recent developments in language. Moreover, there are regional varieties of English for which no or only very small corpora have been compiled. And finally there are text types which have not been put into corpora yet. Some of these text types only exist on the web, such as discussion forums, chats and blogs.

The cost of compiling very large corpora of the standard type is prohibitive, and making smaller, specialised corpora is also time-consuming, so the incentive to look for simpler and less expensive alternatives is strong. It is therefore not surprising that linguists have looked to the web for solutions. In this chapter we will look at a number of ways in which the web can be used for linguistic research and discuss some of the drawbacks and remaining problems. First of all, the web as a whole can be used as a giant corpus which is searched by means of various search engines and interfaces – this has been called "web *as* corpus". Second, the web can be a source for creating new corpora – this is "web *for* corpus". We will begin by discussing some general aspects of using the web as a corpus and as a source for corpus compilation, and then look at some illustrative examples of how the web has been used in research.

10.2 The web as corpus

The web is enormous, but nobody knows exactly how big it is. According to Fletcher (2007: 25), in 2005 it consisted of 10 billion (thousand million) to 20 billion publicly available webpages, and the figure is growing at a phenomenal speed. In July 2008, Google announced that their processing systems had come across 1 trillion (1,000,000,000,000) unique URLs on the web (*http://googleblog.blogspot.com/2008/07/we-knew-web-was-big.html*). In addition to this, there are an even greater number of pages that are not publicly available and which are not reached by the so-called web-crawlers or robots (computer programs) which constantly roam the web to index pages and make them searchable for commercial search engines like Google and Yahoo. The web is not only growing but also constantly changing, since many pages are updated regularly and others are disappearing. This instability of the web means that you cannot be certain that you can return the next day and find the examples that you have used in your research in order to check them, and that investigations based on the web cannot be replicated by other researchers. Since the web is constantly changing, researchers often state the date on which they made their search. In April 2005, Hoffmann (2007: 82), retrieved 15,800 webpages containing the phrase *so not true*, as in my example (1), in a Google search on the web.

(1)   And by the way, the myth that says you lose all this weight when you breastfeed? *That is **so not true**!* (www.femalefirst.co.uk/celebrity/Salma+Hayek-23503.html)

This could be compared with the meagre ten instances of the same construction he found in a reasonably big corpus of CNN transcripts containing 172 million words. When I replicated Hoffmann's Google search on 30 May 2008 I retrieved more than ten times as many hits, 182,000 pages. And only six months later, on 13 December 2008, the figure was 1,160,000 pages! This example illustrates one of the problems with using the whole web as a corpus. We do not know how much of the increased figures for *so not true* is due to the mind-boggling growth of the Internet, and how much is due to an increase in this new use of *so*. In this case it is probably a combination of the two. Another example is Mair (2007),

Table 10.1 Prepositions following *different*. From Google searches

	10 April 2002	30 May 2004	13 December 2008	Growth 2004–2008
from	2,790,000	8,160,000	63,500,000	+678%
than	1,110,000	2,500,000	19,000,000	+660%
to	410,000	825,000	8,070,000	+773%
Total	4,310,000	11,485,000	90,570,000	+689%

Source: Based on Mair (2007: 238–239): figures for 2008 and growth rate added

who reports on a study on the choice of preposition after the adjective *different* in a number of web domains on the basis of Google searches in April 2002 and May 2004. His total figures together with the figures resulting from a corresponding search made by me on 13 December 2008 are given in Table 10.1.

Mair was interested in the variable use of prepositions in different regional varieties of English, but here we are only looking at the total figures for all web domains. Since *different from/than/to* are not expressions that are likely to change very much with fashion (as might have been the case with the fad phrase *make a difference*, for instance), the increases in number must be due to the growth of the English-speaking web, or rather a growth in the number of webpages that are indexed and searched by Google, between 2002 and 2008. As can be seen in the right-most column, the increase in four and a half years is around +700%. Note that Google gives only rounded frequency figures when the numbers are high. These figures are the result of behind-the-scene calculations and not of an exact counting of, for instance, sixty-three million five-hundred thousand pages containing the string *different from*. In addition, Google will never let you inspect more than 1,000 pages. This means that Google frequency figures should always be taken with a pinch of salt.

A further complication with using the web as corpus is the way the commercial search engines work. They are all set up to facilitate the retrieval from the web of information, not linguistic data. While successful searching on earlier search engines, such as Alta Vista, depended on carefully formulated search strings which enabled linguists to specify their searches in interesting ways, more recent search engine generations have limited some of the search options. Instead they make use of information about the user's search history and geographical location, so that now an identical search in Sweden and New Zealand will get different results, with different pages listed as the most relevant. Furthermore, so-called page ranking is based on the number of pages that are linked to a particular page and its popularity with users. The search engines are continually developed and can be changed overnight without notice, so search results can vary greatly from one day to the next.

The lack of linguistic annotation on the web is an additional complication. Since there is no POS tagging or any other linguistic mark-up, all searches will have to be formulated as strings of words or combinations of words, with or without wildcards. This makes precision a problem while recall is not: searches usually retrieve far too much. Furthermore, the meta-information about the texts on the web is extremely limited (often restricted to language, domain and latest update). This means that we usually do not know much about the authors' age, social class or gender; most of the time we do not even know if they are native speakers of English, or, if they are, what variety of English they speak. Finally, the quality of the data is influenced not only by the large proportion of texts produced by non-natives but also by the informal, unedited nature of much of the material in discussion forums, blogs and so on. Nevertheless, in spite of all these reservations, web searches by means of the Advanced Search mode of Google and other commercial search engines can be a useful and sometimes necessary complement to searches made in other corpora, as we shall see in some of the examples below.

10.3 Using commercial search engines for linguistic research

In this section we will take a closer look at how searches for linguistic purposes can be made on the web by means of commercial search engines. Although there are several alternative search engines, we will use Google as an example. Choosing the option Advanced Search, we are presented with the form in Figure 10.1.

If you are looking for a string of words like *storm in a teacup*, you can type it in within quotation marks, "storm in a teacup", in the Simple Search form, but it is easier to do it on the second line of the Advanced Search form, where no quotation marks are needed. The same goes for phrases with a variable slot, i.e. where there is variation in one of the positions. For instance, if you think that there might be variation in the verb in the phrase *to outstay one's welcome*, you type in *to * one's welcome*. The kind of results this type of search can give is illustrated by the first ten hits for this search string, in Figure 10.2.

The concordance lines in Figure 10.2 have been cleaned up from the way they are represented on Google. Remember that the hits are not given in random order, but according to Google's underlying page ranking. This means that popular webpages like online dictionaries

Figure 10.1 Advanced Search form on Google, 14 December 2008.

1. overstay [əuvə'steɪ] vt *to overstay one's welcome* → trattenersi troppo a lungo (come
2. outstay [aut'steɪ] vt *to outstay one's welcome* → quedarse más de la cuenta.
3. It is almost impossible *to outlive one's welcome* in the Catskill Mountains,
4. In recent times, it usually refers *to overstaying one's welcome* at a party.
5. Just as there is an art **to not overstaying one's welcome**, there's something to admire in lawmakers who know when to stop making laws.
6. in excess of, over and above: **to stay beyond one's welcome**
7. outstay transitive verb **to ~ one's welcome** s'éterniser. . . .
8. Deutsch-Englisch-Übersetzung für **to overstay one's welcome** im Online-Wörterbuch dict.cc
9. Moreover Air One Carnet tickets give you access **to Air One's Welcome** Lounge at Rome
10. It takes time, efforts **to create one's welcome** page

Figure 10.2 The first ten hits for the search string "to * one's welcome" on Google, 13 December 2008.

(lines 1, 2, 6, 7 and 8) will occur near the top, while it is more unclear how some of the other pages ended up there. Note that there were four different verbs in the relevant construction among the first ten hits: *overstay, outstay, stay beyond* and *outlive*. While the first two are well-known alternatives (with 1,130 and 3,540 tokens respectively in the infinitive on the entire web), the third and fourth were more surprising and should be investigated further. A new search for the exact phrase *stay beyond one's welcome* yielded only five hits, all of them from online bilingual word lists, which is a strong warning that this may not be a real English expression at all! The fourth example, *outlive one's welcome*, was similarly suspect, with only two hits on the whole web, showing that this is not an established variant of the expression either. Lines 9 and 10, finally, are clearly irrelevant: by chance the prepositional phrase *to Air*

One's Welcome Lounge fits the search string in spite of the fact that *to* here is a preposition rather than an infinitive marker, *Air One's* a proper name in the genitive rather than a verb + possessive pronoun, and *welcome* part of another proper name, *Welcome Lounge.* Similarly, in line 10, *welcome* is not a noun functioning on its own as the object of the verb, but part of a noun compound, which gives the phrase a totally different meaning. The results of this trial search may be disappointing, but they go to show that you always have to analyse the output from Google searches carefully and go on with follow-up searches when needed.

Further down in the Advanced Search form in Figure 10.1 there are two important fields: "Language" and "Search within a site or domain". It is useful to be able to specify language if the word you are searching for exists in many languages. Specifying "English" when you search for the word *but*, for instance, you will avoid having your results contaminated by a lot of German *Hut* 'hat' or Swedish *hut* 'shame, respect'. Even more useful is the domain/site field. Here you can specify which domain or site you want your search to be made in. Typing in uk you will get pages from the UK, nz will give you pages from New Zealand, bbc.co.uk will give you hits only from BBC webpages and bbc.co.uk/ sport will give you hits from BBC's sport pages, etc. Obviously you cannot be certain that the texts on pages from specific national domains are written by native speakers from these countries, or even that they are written by native speakers at all, but investigations have shown that features which have been established independently as being typically British are dominant in webpages from the UK, and so on. Table 10.2 lists the domain suffixes for some countries where English is spoken as a first or second language.

Note, however, that there are also so-called generic top domains, such as *.com*, *.edu*, *.gov*, *.mil* and *.org.* These are open for everyone but especially used in the US, where the suffix .us is less frequently used. There is also a certain commercial and vanity use of some suffixes based on the accidental meaning of the abbreviation, so that for instance *.nu*, which is the suffix for *Niue*, a small island in the South Pacific, is used in Sweden because it means 'now' in Swedish. We will make use of the domain feature in section 10.5 below. Before we do that, however, we will look at efforts to avoid some of the problems caused by the nature of the commercial search engines.

10.4 Piggybacking: WebCorp

One way of solving some of the problems mentioned above is to add pre- and post-processing facilities to the commercial web engines.

Table 10.2 Domain suffixes for selected countries where English is spoken as a first or second language

Australia	.au
Bahamas	.bs
Barbados	.bb
Belize	.bz
Bermuda	.bm
Botswana	.bw
British Indian Ocean Territory	.io
British Virgin Islands	.vg
Cameroon	.cm
Canada	.ca
Cayman Islands	.ky
Cook Islands	.ck
Fiji	.fj
Gambia	.gm
Ghana	.gh
Gibraltar	.gi
Guernsey	.gg
Hong Kong	.hk
India	.in
Ireland	.ie
Isle of Man	.im
Jamaica	.jm
Jersey	.je
Kenya	.ke
Liberia	.lr
Malta	.mt
Namibia	.na
New Zealand	.nz
Nigeria	.ng
Norfolk Island	.nf
Pakistan	.pk
Philippines	.ph
Puerto Rico	.pr
Sierra Leone	.sl
Singapore	.sg
Solomon Islands	.sb
South Africa	.za
Sri Lanka	.lk
Uganda	.ug
United Kingdom	.uk
United States	.us
Zambia	.zm
Zimbabwe	.zw

This has been done in several web concordancer projects, for instance KWiCFinder, developed by William Fletcher, and WebCorp and its successor WebCorp Linguistic Search Engine, developed by Antoinette Renouf and associates. We will take a closer look at WebCorp, which in principle is a linguist's interface to the web accessed via a chosen commercial search engine. The user is presented with forms for Simple or Advanced Search. The Advanced Search form is given in Figure 10.3.

Note that WebCorp makes use of the results from online searches through one of the commercial search engines (there is a choice of a number of them). This means that several of the options available on the WebCorp search page are actually features of the underlying search engine (in the default mode, Google): searching for a word or a pattern, choosing domain or URL (but WebCorp conveniently supplies clickable favourite domains and groups of URLs, such as "UK Broadsheet newspapers", which includes *The Times, The Telegraph, The Guardian, The Observer* and *The Independent*), textual domain, and a word filter where you can specify words that must or must not occur on the same webpage. But there are also some additional post-editing features. One of these is quite useful: under "Output format" it is possible to choose "Plain text (KWIC)" and get a concordance nicely centred on the search word instead of the usual messy Google list. Unfortunately, in the version available at the time of writing, the concordance lines are not numbered and the source (URL) is not given in this format. Another feature is a collocates table and a list of "key phrases" based on the "HTML tables (KWIC)" output option. However, this mostly yields relatively uninteresting results, since it is based only on the maximum 500 webpages that WebCorp allows you to search, and the collocates are listed according to raw frequency rather than strength of collocation. There has been some disappointed criticism of WebCorp for its slowness and low recall, but in the WebCorp Live version the speed has improved considerably, and for some simple investigations the post-editing resources and the user-friendly interface can be of use as an alternative to Advanced Searches on e.g. Google.

To solve the remaining speed problems and the low recall, the WebCorp team has proposed a new approach: to download a huge representative portion of the web into a mega-corpus which can then be processed by means of various corpus tools. This seems to be a more viable solution, and at the time of writing a very promising beta-version called the WebCorp Linguist's Search Engine was available.

WebCorp Live

An improved version of the original WebCorp, designed to search the web for concordances in real time

Search term:

Enter a word, phrase (no quotes necessary) or *pattern*

See the Guide for an explanation of the options

Search Engine: Google

Case Options: Case Sensitive

Output Format: HTML

Web Addresses (URLs): Show for concordance lines

Concordance Span: 5 word(s) to left and right
OR
Full sentences?

Number of Pages to Retrieve: 100
One concordance line per web site

Site Domain / Country:
(Works with Google, AltaVista, Ask and Live Search)
Leave blank to search the whole web.

Clear

For a specific domain search enter a URL (without the http://) - e.g. www.nytimes.com
or *part* of a URL - e.g. ac.uk for all UK academic institutions.
Seperate multiple domains with spaces.

Add popular domains:

UK Broadsheet Newspapers   BBC News   Argentina   France   New Zealand
UK Tabloid Newspapers   Wikipedia   Australia   Germany   Spain
French Newspapers   Brazil   Italy   UK
US Newspapers   US Academic   Canada   Japan
UK Academic   China   Netherlands

Textual Domain:
All
Select Open Directory category

Word Filter:

Include extra words which must or must not appear on the same web page as the search term.
Use the minus sign (-) to exclude words
e.g. for the search term 'plant' you may specify leaf -nuclear as a filter, to restrict the range of senses retrieved

Didn't there used to be more options here?

Collocation and Date options are now available after retrieving the concordances.

Exclude link text   Exclude e-mail address from match

Submit

By using the WebCorp tools you are agreeing to be bound by the Terms of Use.

Figure 10.3 Advanced Search form on WebCorp Live, 14 December 2008.

10.5 Regional variation: agreement with collective nouns

In Chapter 5 we saw that the web could be used for investigations of regional differences in the use of idiomatic phrases like *cut/make a long story short*, through consecutive searches in the relevant top domains of the web. Here we will investigate regional variation in an area of grammar: subject–verb agreement with collective nouns like *family*, *company*, *group* and so on. Levin (2001) studied in detail how usage in British and American differs, finding that on the whole AmE prefers so-called grammatical agreement (*the team is*) while there is greater variation in BrE depending on the context, so that both grammatical agreement and so-called notional agreement (*the team are*) are used and accepted. In the following investigation we will study this in a number of domains on the web representing English from the UK, the US, Canada, Australia, New Zealand, India, South Africa, the Philippines and Hong Kong, first to see whether we find the claimed difference between BrE and AmE and, second, to see whether the other countries are closer to one or the other of these varieties. Since there is no tagging on the web that would enable a search on collective nouns as a group, the search has to be on individual nouns. After some experimenting, I decided to look at just one collective noun, using the following search string: "my OR your OR his OR her OR our OR their family is" to capture all instances of a personal possessive pronoun + *family is*. Then I searched for the corresponding string with *are*. The results are presented in Table 10.3, where the regional varieties have been ordered from left to right according to the frequency of singular agreement. For AmE, I searched the .edu domain, and for BrE, the academic subdomain. ac.uk.

First of all, we have to be aware that this is a rather quick and dirty investigation, in that the hits include not only relevant tokens as in (2) and (3) but also some irrelevant cases as in (4), where the head of the subject with which the verb agrees is not *family* but *learning*, and (5), where the head of the subject noun phrase is *my feelings* and not *family*.

(2)   **Your family is** awesome. But spending time with them isn't. (orlando.
      metromix.com/tv/photogallery/family-shmamily/745897/
      content)

(3)   **My family are** awesome, I love them very much. (jimiminar.blog-
      spot.com/2008/09/you-cant-change-your-family.html)

(4)   No matter what position in life they held, they are important to
      you and learning about **your family is** an opportunity to preserve
      your Family History [. . .] *www.timelessgen.com/*

Table 10.3 Regional distribution of singular and plural agreement with *my/ your/his/her/our/their + family +* BE

	ph	*in*	*hk*	*edu*	*za*	*au*	*nz*	*ac.uk*	*ca*
Poss. pronoun + *family* + *is*	8,040	16,500	614	44,700	6,540	33,100	6,260	1,470	32,200
Poss. pronoun + *family* + *are*	2,330	5,350	203	17,100	3,360	22,900	4,600	1,940	53,500
Total	10,370	21,850	817	61,800	9,900	56,000	10,860	3,419	85,700
Per cent singular	78	76	75	72	66	59	58	43	38

Note: Poss. Possessive; ph = Philippines, in = India, hk = Hong Kong, edu = American academic, za = South Africa, au = Australia, nz = New Zealand, ac.uk = UK academic, ca = Canada.
Source: Google searches, 14 December 2008

(5)   *Brad Pitt: My Feelings For* **My Family Are** *Indescribable | Celebrity*
       . . . www.celebrity-babies.com/2008/12/brad-pitt-today.html

However, there is no reason to suspect that there is any major difference in the proportion of irrelevant examples between the domains, so the results should be relatively reliable in a rough and ready way. If we trust the figures, Table 10.3 shows that both singular and plural agreement occurs in all varieties, although to a varying extent. There is a clear difference between AmE and BrE, with 72 per cent singular agreement in the US material and 43% in the UK material. Even if these figures give a fair picture of the relation between the two varieties, it is likely that the extent to which singular agreement is used in the US is somewhat exaggerated due to the irrelevant tokens.

As for the other varieties, it is hard to see a clear pattern in the results. Possibly there is a "single agreement group" with the US and Hong Kong, India and the Philippines, a "plural agreement group" with the UK and Canada, and an "undecided group" in between with South Africa, Australia and New Zealand.

Levin (2001) showed in his study that one should not see collectives as one monolithic group of nouns which behaves/behave in the same manner; individual nouns or subgroups of nouns display their own patterns. In order to get a more complete picture of verb agreement with collective nouns in these varieties, further studies would have be made with other nouns.

It is also interesting to compare the geographical clustering concerning agreement with clustering based on other phenomena, such as the choice of variant in phrases like *to cut/make a long story short* which we studied in Chapter 5. The results presented in Table 5.3 showed that the US, Canada, India and the Philippines preferred *make*, whereas the UK, Australia, New Zealand, South Africa and Hong Kong preferred *cut*. Those results match fairly well with the agreement results, except for Canada, which is at the far "British end" for collectives but far to the "US end" with *cut/make a long story short*, and Hong Kong, which is at the US end for collectives and slightly towards the British end with *cut/make a long story short*. Further investigations of a large number of features would answer the question whether there is a discernible pattern of "families" of different Englishes.

10.6 Grammar: adjective comparison

We have seen throughout this book that the web can be used to study all kinds of grammatical phenomena, but due to the web's messiness it is always advisable to compare web results with data from more controlled corpora. One case where it is particularly well motivated to use the web is when you are looking for something that is extremely rare and therefore hardly occurs in even the largest standard corpora. It may be that information about such rare and perhaps peripheral constructions is not very useful for second language learning, but it can be highly interesting for linguists, since it tells us something about how language works and about how innovations are created.

In English, adjectives can be compared either synthetically (*livelier, liveliest*) or analytically (*more lively, most lively*). Monosyllabic adjectives are almost always compared synthetically (*bigger, biggest*) and adjectives with three syllables or more almost always analytically (*more intelligent, most intelligent*), while for disyllabic adjectives there is some competition between the two methods. Mondorf (2007) set out to investigate semantic and pragmatic factors which constrain the choice between synthetic and analytic adjective comparison. She had at her disposal the BNC plus a set of newspaper CD-ROMs amounting in all to 599 million words, but found that even this size was not enough for the kind of searches she wanted to make. She therefore turned to Google searches. One of her theoretical assumptions was that analytical comparison is easier to process, i.e. that it takes less time and effort for the listener to understand *more lively* than to understand *livelier*, among other things because *more* signals early on that a compared form will follow. A further assumption was that concrete nouns are easier to process than abstract

a blunt nose/approach
a clear river/thought
a cold summer/look
a dark colo(u)r/character
a fresh taste/approach
a tight grip/estimate
a round face/number

Figure 10.4 Search combinations for an investigation of adjective comparison with concrete/abstract nouns.
Source: Based on Mondorf (2007: 219)

ones, and therefore concrete nouns would occur more often with synthetic comparison. Her hypothesis was thus:

> The analytic comparative variant is more likely to occur with nouns with abstract meanings than with nouns with concrete meanings.

In spite of the fact that monosyllabic adjectives are usually said to take synthetic comparison, Mondorf decided to investigate monosyllabic adjectives to see whether their mode of comparison was influenced by the kind of noun they modified. A sufficiently large sample could be drawn from the web, but since the queries had to be made for lexical items, only a limited number of adjectives (seven) were searched for, and for each adjective only two following nouns (one concrete and one abstract) were investigated. Her search combinations are listed in Figure 10.4.

The results supported the hypothesis that analytic comparison is more frequent with abstract than with concrete nouns. All of the investigated adjectives were more often compared analytically when they modified the abstract noun of the noun pair, as in (6) and (7), than when they modified the concrete noun, although this also occurred, as in (8) and (9) (my examples).

(6) Last November, however, at the United Nations, Canada took a **more blunt** approach at challenging countries like Iran on their human rights [. . .] (www.thehilltimes.ca/html/cover_index. php?display=story&full_path=/2007/january/22/rubin/)

(7) Personally I don't see why there are 8 in a package as 10 seems like a **more round** number. (www.epinions.com/review/ Hallmark_Disney_Cars_Invitations_8_Count_1INV2364/ content_450864320132)

(8) The aircraft had a **more blunt** *nose* as opposed to the pointed nose in other Gnat models. (www.bharat-rakshak.com/IAF/Images/ Vintage/Fighters/Gnat/IE1059B.jpg.html)

(9)   The patient's who have a **more round** face, may experience more
       sagging around the jaw line as gravity begins to pull the skin down.
       (www.optimalhealthtoday.com/blog/2007/03/aging-and-black-
       skin.html)

Since the large standard corpora are not tagged for categories like
abstract and concrete noun, an investigation such as Mondorf's had to
be based on combinations of selected lexical items which would have
extremely few occurrences in a standard corpus of 100 million words.
Even on the web, she found only 21 tokens of *a more blunt nose* and 51
tokens of *a more blunt approach*, 0 tokens of *a more tight grip* and 5 tokens
of *a more tight estimate.*

In a second part of her study, Mondorf investigated cases of gradual
increase, which is normally expressed either by a pair of synthetically
compared adjectives, as in (10), or by two analytically compared adjectives, as in (11) (my examples).

(10)   And with each smile I put on I became **happier and happier.**
       This was one of my favorite days working ever. (blog.lib.umn.edu/
       rufx0006/anthem/2004_08.html)
(11)   And as I was watching, I became **more and more happy.** (mailman.
       mit.edu/pipermail/lebanon-articles/2004-November/000004.
       html)

Occasionally, however, there is a mix of the two kinds of comparison,
as in (12) and (13).

(12)   [. . .] the very earth itself, as it grew greener and greener, seemed
       also to grow **happier and more happy.** (www.archive.org/stream/
       noctesambrosiana01wilsuoft/noctesambrosiana01wilsuoft_djvu.
       txt)
(13)   The sims [name of a computer game] was good, until the 15th
       expansion pack, it just got **more silly and sillier.** (news.gameplay.
       co.uk/forum/viewtopic.php?t=20384&view=next)

Mondorf found suggestions in the literature that the order in (12), with
synthetic first and analytic last, would be the more common in these
rare mixed cases, since the "heavier" two-word combination expresses a
stronger degree of intensity and thus should come last in an expression
of gradual increase. She first searched a set of text databases of English
fiction from 1460 to 1894 consisting of 98 million words, and found five
tokens of mixed constructions of gradual increase, all with the order
synthetic–analytic as in (12). She then searched the web and found
another fifteen tokens, also of the synthetic-before-analytic order. Since

Table 10.4 Standard and non-standard past tense forms in FRED

	Non-standard	Standard	Total	% non-standard
sink	24	14	38	63.2
drink	18	18	36	50.0
sing	15	15	30	50.0
ring	13	16	29	44.8
begin	6	13	19	31.6
Total	76	76	152	50.0

Source: Based on Anderwald (2007: 274)

there was not a single instance of the reversed order with the verbs she investigated, the hypothesis about the preferred synthetic–analytic order was strongly supported. A further finding was that fourteen out of the fifteen web tokens were from historical texts and only one represented present-day language use. My example in (13) seems to contradict this, but you can usually find one or two occasional counter-examples to any hypothesis in a big corpus, and especially on the web. The odd counter-example is thus not a strong objection to the results.

10.7 Dialect and non-standard language

There are specialist corpora of dialects, like the Freiburg English Dialect Corpus (FRED), which are of course ideal for studying English dialects, but surprisingly enough you can also study dialects on the web. We have already touched on the fact that much of the text on discussion forums and blogs is informal and sometimes non-standard. People write quickly without editing, and the result sometimes looks almost like spoken language – it may even be intended to look like spoken language.

Anderwald (2007) studied non-standard past tense forms like *he rung the bell* and *she drunk ale* in traditional dialects. She searched for non-standard past tense forms of the verbs *begin, sing, drink, ring* and *sink* in FRED as well as on the web. The results from FRED are given in Table 10.4.

As Table 10.4 shows, in the traditional dialect texts in FRED, half of the instances of past tense forms of these verbs are non-standard.

Anderwald then searched for the same verbs plus *stink, shrink* and *spring* in the uk domain of the web. Due to the fact that the web is untagged, the web searches were restricted to personal pronouns + the standard and non-standard past tense forms. She first used WebCorp,

Table 10.5 Standard and non-standard past tense forms on the web. From Google searches for pronoun + past tense verb forms in the UK domain

	Non-standard	Standard	Total	% non-standard
sink	3,299	16,133	19,432	17.0
sing	6,027	83,712	89,739	6.7
drink	3,854	60,299	64,153	6.0
ring	2,085	69,329	71,414	2.9
begin	2,349	665,225	667,574	0.4
Total	17,614	894,698	912,312	1.9

Source: Based on Anderwald (2007: 274)

but found that she could not use the WebCorp results to compare the infrequent non-standard forms with the very frequent standard forms, since WebCorp retrieves only a limited number of pages (in Anderwald's case 200 pages; the maximum was later increased to 500). The frequency of the standard forms will be drastically reduced by the page limitation, while 200 or 500 pages may be enough to retrieve *all* instances of a rare non-standard form from the web. All instances of the rare form are thus compared to a very much reduced number of the common form, which skews the results.

Due to these problems, Anderwald decided to use Google Advanced Searches instead. To compensate for the rather low precision, she went through a random sample of the hits manually, excluded irrelevant items and then extrapolated the results to the whole material. With this method, Anderwald arrived at the results displayed in Table 10.5. *Stink*, *shrink* and *spring* have been left out here.

As Anderwald points out, the figures for *begin*, which is very frequent and predominantly standard, skew the results somewhat. With *begin* left out, the proportion of non-standard forms rises to 6.2%. This means that 6.2% of the past tense forms of these verbs look like the verb forms in (14)–(18) (my examples).

(14) As he tried to heave himself free **he sunk** further so in the end Mrs Vitiello, 55, was forced to summon help. (www.dailymail.co.uk/news/article-513447/Walker-trapped-muddy-bog-freed-40-strong-rescue-team.html)

(15) I was lost as **she sung** her song: "Take me down to Mexico City, Where the boys are fine n' the gals are pretty, Their hands are grubby and faces are gritty [. . .] (www.route57.group.shef.ac.uk/experimental-01-homage.html)

(16) **I drunk** that 3rd glass of wine (still on an empty stomach) and headed to the pub where I was meeting my bosses and the people working at that company. (www.therapyinthemaking.co)

(17) I forgot to send them my proof of no claims, so **they rung** me. (www.dooyoo.co.uk/motor-insurance/diamond-car-insurance)

(18) **She begun** her career as a youth worker in the London boroughs of Hackney and Newham [. . .]. (www.artscouncil.org.uk/aboutus/ council_for_region.php?rid=10)

The almost randomly picked examples in (14)–(18) show that the non-standard dialect past tense forms are still used in a variety of registers: tabloid news-reporting in (14), a fan website in (15), a blog in (16), a webpage on insurance in (17) and an official arts council page in (18). Anderwald's study convincingly shows that the web can be used for the study of some aspects of present-day dialects as well as standard language.

10.8 Web genres and compiling corpora from the web

With the development of electronic communication or computer-mediated communication (CMC), a number of new text types have been born. For instance, mobile phone text messages have been compiled into corpora, where researchers have studied how the limited format and cumbersome inputting technology have encouraged short sentences, abbreviations and graphic symbols (emoticons, a.k.a. smileys). On the web, too, new genres and text types have developed, for instance discussion forums, chat, personal homepages and blogs. Most of these are more or less interactive, and the language in them therefore has some features of the spoken language. On the other hand, the language is of course still written; perhaps one could argue that this is a hybrid mode. Accessing these new modes, however, is not trivial. Some researchers have compiled their own corpora by joining forums as lurkers (inactive members), manually downloading discussion threads and converting them into searchable database form. This is very time-consuming and involves copy-and-paste operations, post-editing (e.g. deleting all quoted material) and mark-up. Hopefully there will be automatic methods in the near future. For instance, WebCorp Linguist's Search Engine has "blogs" as a search option, which promises to give access to that particular genre. Since most of the CMC genres that have been investigated are interactive, many studies focus on interactive language features such as emotional language and politeness.

Downloading more traditional text genres from the web is somewhat more straightforward. Two successful examples on a large scale are Mark Davies's Time Corpus and COCA, which we have used throughout this book. Davies "simply" automatically downloads text databases which are freely available on the web, indexes them, tags them and makes them searchable with a custom-built concordancing program through a web interface. While this is relatively uncomplicated with the Time Corpus, which is just from one source, COCA is a much larger undertaking, since it has the ambition of being a balanced corpus of contemporary AmE.

It is also possible to extract your own specialised corpus from the web. Hundt and Biewer (2007) report on such an undertaking. They compiled a corpus, the South Pacific and East Asian Corpus (SPEAC), by downloading articles from a number of newspapers in the area, in all 1.52 million words. The downloading took place during two one-month periods, when they aimed to download 4,000 words per day from each newspaper, half of it from front-page news and half from editorials. They mention a number of complications, which are listed here in abbreviated form:

1. Sample size and stylistic variation. It turned out that there was not enough material of these types in all the papers on all days, so that the data from the different varieties were not fully comparable.
2. Availability. Some of the papers were not available on all the days.
3. Conversion of data. The conversion from the HTML documents to the web turned out to cause some problems.
4. Authorship. Although the researchers tried to choose articles that seemed to be written by local reporters, they could not be sure that some of the material was not written by British or American journalists or based on international press agency material.

In their conclusion, Hundt and Biewer note that although their corpus was downloaded manually, in the future such downloading should ideally be made automatically, taking into account the problems that the manual download had made apparent.

10.9 Summary

In this chapter we have tried to grasp the enormous size of the web and to see how it can be harnessed for linguistic research. We saw the motivations for using it: it is large, it contains many geographical varieties and genres that may be hard to get at elsewhere, it is up to date, it is available and it is free. We also saw the drawbacks: it is messy, it contains lots of dubious material, it is unstable, it can be hard to search with sufficient precision. Nevertheless, more and more linguistic research is carried out on the web.

We have illustrated how web investigations can fruitfully be carried out in the areas of phraseology (*outstay/overstay one's welcome*), grammar (*blunter/more blunt*), regional variation (*my family is/are*) and dialect/ non-standard English (past tense forms of *sink, ring* etc.). We also noted that the web is a very useful source for compiling new corpora, both on a large scale (the Time Corpus and COCA) and on a smaller scale (SPEAC), although there are a number of pitfalls, and automatic down-loading is far from trivial: programming skills are recommended.

Much more work is needed before web-based corpus linguistics reaches the relative maturity of "old" corpus linguistics based on stand-ard corpora. For instance, many of the basic facts about the workings of the commercial search engines are not known (and may never be fully disclosed, since they are business secrets), and the metalinguistic information about the texts is patchy or non-existent. Nevertheless, it is quite clear that an important part of corpus linguistics in the future will be web-based in one way or another.

Study questions

1. What are the main reasons why linguists use the web as corpus? Can you think of reasons other than those mentioned in this chapter?
2. What are the main problems connected with using the web as corpus?
3. How do interfaces like WebCorp work? What are the advantages and what are the drawbacks?
4. How can regional variation be studied on the web? What are the complications?
5. What kind of corpora can be compiled by means of the web? Do you think that traditional corpus-making will be made obsolete by the web?

Corpus exercises

Hands-on exercises related to this chapter are available at the following web address:
http://www.euppublishing.com/series/ETOTELAdvanced/Lindquist.

Further reading

Much of the information and discussion on corpus linguistics and the web and many of the examples in this chapter are from Hundt et al.

(2007) and Lindquist (2008b) These questions are also dealt with in Bergh and Zanchetta (2008). Crystal ([2001] 2006) is the best guide to language on the Internet. Schmied (2006) is an illustration of how one can study world Englishes on the web. For examples of studies of web discourse see, for example, Herring (1996) and Maricic (2005). Sharoff (2006) is a technical paper on how to compile corpora from the web. If you plan to create your own corpus, Wynne (2005) is a good source.

References

Adolphs, Svenja (2006), *Introducing Electronic Text Analysis: A Practical Guide for Language and Literary Studies*, London: Routledge.

Aijmer, Karin (2008), 'Parallel and comparable corpora', in Anke Lüdeling and Merja Kytö (eds), *Corpus Linguistics: An International Handbook. Vol. I*, Berlin: de Gruyter, 275–291.

Aijmer, Karin and Bengt Altenberg (eds) (1991), *English Corpus Linguistics: Studies in Honour of Jan Svartvik*, London: Longman.

Altenberg, Bengt (1998), 'On the phraseology of spoken English: The evidence of recurrent word combinations', in A. P. Cowie (ed.), *Phraseology: Theory, Analysis and Applications*, Oxford: Oxford University Press, 101–122.

Anderwald, Lieselotte (2007), '"He rung the bell" and "she drunk ale": Non-standard past tense forms in traditional British dialects on the Internet', in Marianne Hundt, Nadja Nesselhauf and Carolin Biever (eds), *Corpus Linguistics and the Web*, Amsterdam: Rodopi, 271–285.

Aston, Guy and Lou Burnard (1998), *The BNC Handbook: Exploring the British National Corpus with SARA*, Edinburgh: Edinburgh University Press.

Atkins, B. T. Sue and Michael Rundell (2008), *The Oxford Guide to Practical Lexicography*, Oxford: Oxford University Press.

Baker, Paul, Andrew Hardie and Tony McEnery (2006), *A Glossary of Corpus Linguistics*, Edinburgh: Edinburgh University Press.

Baroni, Marco and Stefan Evert (2009), 'Statistical methods for corpus exploitation', in Anke Lüdeling and Merja Kytö (eds), *Corpus Linguistics: An International Handbook. Vol. II*. Berlin: de Gruyter, 777–803.

Bauer, Laurie (1994), *Watching English Change: An Introduction to the Study of Linguistic Change in Standard Englishes on the Twentieth Century*, London: Longman.

Bergh, Gunnar and Eros Zanchetta (2008), 'Web linguistics', in Anke Lüdeling and Merja Kytö (eds), *Corpus Linguistics: An International Handbook. Vol. I*, Berlin: de Gruyter, 309–327.

Biber, Douglas (1993), 'Representativeness in corpus design', *Literary and Linguistic Computing* 8 (4), 243–257.

Biber, Douglas, Susan Conrad and Randi Reppen (1998), *Corpus Linguistics: Investigating Language Structure and Use*, Cambridge: Cambridge University Press.

Biber, Douglas, Stig Johansson, Geoffrey Leech, Susan Conrad and Edward Finegan (1999), *Longman Grammar of Spoken and Written English*, London: Longman.

Channell, Joanna (1999), 'Corpus-based analysis of evaluative lexis', in Susan Hunston and Geoff Thompson (eds), *Evaluation in Text: Authorial Stance and the Construction of Discourse*, Oxford: Oxford University Press, 38–55.

Charteris-Black, Jonathan (2004), *Corpus Approaches to Critical Metaphor Analysis*, Basingstoke: Palgrave.

Claridge, Claudia (2008), 'Historical corpora', in Anke Lüdeling and Merja Kytö (eds), *Corpus Linguistics: An International Handbook. Vol. I*, Berlin: de Gruyter, 242–258.

Crystal, David [2001] (2006), *Language and the Internet*, second edition, Cambridge: Cambridge University Press.

Culpeper, Jonathan (2002), 'Computers, language and characterisation: An analysis of six characters in *Romeo and Juliet*', in Ulla Marttala Melander, Carin Östman and Merja Kytö (eds), *Conversation in Life and Literature. Papers from the ASLA Symposium, Uppsala, 8–9 November 2001*, Uppsala: ASLA, 11–30.

Curzan, Anne (2009), 'Historical corpus linguistics and evidence of language change', in Anke Lüdeling and Merja Kytö (eds), *Corpus Linguistics: An International Handbook. Vol. II*, Berlin: de Gruyter, 1091–1090.

Deignan, Alice (2005), *Metaphor and Corpus Linguistics*, Amsterdam: Benjamins.

De Smet, Hendrik (2005), 'A corpus of Late Modern English', *ICAME Journal* 29, 69–82.

Ellis, Nick C. (2008), 'Phraseology: The periphery and the heart of language', in Fanny Meunier and Sylviane Granger (eds), *Phraseology in Foreign Language Learning and Teaching*, Amsterdam: Benjamins, 1–13.

Erman, Britt and Beatrice Warren (2000), 'The idiom principle and the open choice principle', *Text* 20 (1), 29–62.

Estling, Maria (1998), *A Preposition Thrown out (of) the Window? On British and American Use of out of and out*, Report from Växjö University – Humanities No. 5, Växjö: Växjö University.

Estling, Maria (1999), 'Going out (of) the window? A corpus-based study of competing constructions', *English Today* 15, 22–27.

Evert, Stefan (2009), 'Corpora and collocations', in Anke Lüdeling and Merja Kytö (eds), *Corpus Linguistics: An International Handbook. Vol. II*, Berlin: de Gruyter, 1212–1248.

Facchinetti, Roberta (ed.) (2007), *Corpus Linguistics 25 Years On*, Amsterdam: Rodopi.

Fillmore, Charles (1992), '"Corpus linguistics" or "computer-aided armchair linguistics"', in Jan Svartvik (ed.), *Directions in Corpus Linguistics*, Berlin: de Gruyter, 35–60.

Firth, J. R. (1957), 'A synopsis of linguistic theory, 1930–1955', in *Studies in Linguistic Analysis*, special volume, Philological Society, Oxford: Blackwell, 1–32. Reprinted in F. R. Palmer (ed.), *Selected Papers of J. R. Firth 1952–59*, London: Longman, 168–205.

Fletcher, William (2003/2004), *PIE: Phrases in English*, http://pie.usna.edu.

Fletcher, William (2007), 'Concordancing the web: Promise and problems, tools and techniques', in Marianne Hundt, Nadja Nesselhauf and Carolin Biewer (eds), *Corpus Linguistics and the Web*, Amsterdam: Rodopi, 25–45.

Francis, W. Nelson and Henry Kučera (1964), *Manual of Information to Accompany a Standard Sample of Present-day Edited American English, for Use with Digital Computers*, Providence, RI: Brown University.

Garside, Roger, Geoffrey Leech and Tony McEnery (eds) (1997), *Corpus Annotation*, London: Longman.

Gibbs, Raymond W., Jr (2008), *The Cambridge Handbook of Metaphor and Thought*, Cambridge: Cambridge University Press.

Goddard, Angela and Lindsey Meân [2000] (2009), *Language and Gender*, London: Routledge.

Granger, Sylviane (ed.) (1998), *Learner English on Computer*, London: Addison-Wesley Longman.

Granger, Sylviane (2008), 'Learner corpora', in Anke Lüdeling and Merja Kytö (eds), *Corpus Linguistics: An International Handbook. Vol. I*, Berlin: de Gruyter, 259–274.

Granger, Sylviane and Fanny Meunier (2008), *Phraseology: An Interdisciplinary Perspective*, Amsterdam: Benjamins.

Granger, Sylviane and Magali Paquot (2008), 'Disentangling the phraseological web', in Sylviane Granger and Fanny Meunier (eds), *Phraseology: An Interdisciplinary Perspective*, Amsterdam: Benjamins, 27–49.

Gries, Stephan Th. (2006), 'Some proposals towards a more rigorous corpus linguistics', *Zeitschrift für Anglistik und Amerikanistik* 54 (2), 191–202.

Gries, Stefan Th. (2008), 'Phraseology and linguistic theory: A brief survey', in Sylviane Granger and Fanny Meunier (eds), *Phraseology: An Interdisciplinary Perspective*, Amsterdam: Benjamins, 3–25.

Gries, Stephan Th. and Caroline David (2007), 'This is kind of/sort of interesting: Variation and hedging in English', in Päivi Pahta, Irma Tavitsainen, Terttu Nevalainen and Jukka Tyrkkö (eds), *Studies in Variation, Contacts and Change in English. Vol. 2: Towards Multimedia in Corpus Studies*, available at http://www.helsinki.fi/varieng/journal/volumes/02/gries_david.

Gries, Stefan Th. and Anatol Stefanowitsch (eds) (2006), *Corpora in Cognitive Linguistics: Corpus-Based Approaches to Syntax and Lexis*, Berlin: de Gruyter.

Halliday, M. A. K. (1991), 'Corpus studies and probabilistic grammar', in Karin Aijmer and Bengt Altenberg (eds), *English Corpus Linguistics: Studies in Honour of Jan Svartvik*, London: Longman, 30–43.

Harrington, Kate, Lia Litosseliti, Helen Sauntson and Jane Sunderland (eds) (2008), *Gender and Language Research Methodologies*, Basingstoke: Palgrave Macmillan.

Heid, Ulrich (2008), 'Corpus linguistics and lexicography', in Anke Lüdeling and Merja Kytö (eds), *Corpus Linguistics: An International Handbook. Vol. I*, Berlin: Walter de Gruyter, 131–153.

Herring, Susan (ed.) (1996), *Computer-Mediated Communication: Linguistic, Social and Cross-Cultural Perspectives*, Amsterdam: Benjamins.

Hoffmann, Sebastian (2004), 'Using the *OED* quotations database as a corpus: A linguistic appraisal', *ICAME Journal* 28, 17–30.

Hoffmann, Sebastian (2007), 'From webpage to mega-corpus: The CNN transcripts', in Marianne Hundt, Nadja Nesselhauf and Carolin Biever (eds), *Corpus Linguistics and the Web*, Amsterdam: Rodopi, 69–85.

Hoffmann, Sebastian, Stefan Evert, Nicholas Smith, David Lee and Ylva Berglund Prytz (2008), *Corpus Linguistics with BNCweb: A Practical Guide*, Frankfurt: Peter Lang.

Hogg, Richard and David Denison (eds) (2006), *A History of the English Language*, Cambridge: Cambridge University Press.

Holmes, Janet (1986), 'Functions of *you know* in women's and men's speech', *Language in Society* 15 (1), 1–22.

Holmes, Janet (1995), *Women, Men and Politeness*, London: Longman.

Holmes, Janet and Miriam Meyerhoff (2003), *The Handbook of Language and Gender*, Oxford: Blackwell.

Hopper, Paul J. and Elizabeth Closs Traugott [1993] (2003), *Grammaticalization*, second edition, Cambridge: Cambridge University Press.

Huddleston, Rodney and Geoffrey Pullum (2002), *The Cambridge Grammar of the English Language*, Cambridge: Cambridge University Press.

Hundt, Marianne (2008), 'Text corpora', in Anke Lüdeling and Merja Kytö (eds), *Corpus Linguistics: An International Handbook. Vol. I*, Berlin: de Gruyter, 168–186.

Hundt, Marianne and Carolin Biewer (2007), 'The dynamics of inner and outer circle varieties in the South Pacific and East Asia', in Marianne Hundt, Nadja Nesselhauf and Carolin Biever (eds), *Corpus Linguistics and the Web*, Amsterdam: Rodopi, 249–269.

Hundt, Marianne, Nadja Nesselhauf and Carolin Biewer (eds) (2007), *Corpus Linguistics and the Web*, Amsterdam: Rodopi.

Hunston, Susan and Gill Francis (2000), *Pattern Grammar*, Amsterdam: Benjamins.

Jespersen, Otto (1909–1949), *A Modern English Grammar on Historical Principles*, Copenhagen: Ejnar Munksgaard.

Jespersen, Otto (1938), *En sprogmands levned*, Copenhagen: Gyldendal. English translation (1995), *A Linguist's Life*, ed. and trans. Arne Juul, Odense: Odense University Press.

Johansson, Stig (2003), 'Contrastive linguistics and corpora', in Sylviane Granger, Jacques Lerot and Stephanie Petch-Tyson (eds), *Corpus-Based Approaches to Contrastive Linguistics and Translation Studies*, Amsterdam: Rodopi, 31–44.

Johansson, Stig (2007), *Seeing through Multilingual Corpora: On the Use of Corpora in Contrastive Studies*, Amsterdam: Benjamins.

Johansson, Stig (2008), 'Some aspects of the development of corpus linguistics in the 1970s and 1980s', in Anke Lüdeling and Merja Kytö (eds), *Corpus Linguistics: An International Handbook. Vol. I*, Berlin: de Gruyter, 33–52.

Johansson, Stig and Signe Oksefjell (eds) (1998), *Corpora and Cross-Linguistic Research: Theory, Method and Case Studies*, Amsterdam: Rodopi.

Kennedy, Graeme (1998), *An Introduction to Corpus Linguistics*, London: Longman.

Knowles, Murray and Rosamund Moon (2006), *Introducing Metaphor*, London: Routledge.

Kohnen, Thomas (2007), 'From Helsinki through the centuries: The design and development of English diachronic corpora', in Päivi Pahta, Irma Taavitsainen, Terttu Nevalainen and Jukka Tyrkkö (eds), *Towards Multimedia in Corpus Studies*, Helsinki: University of Helsinki, available at http://www.helsinki.fi/varieng/journal/volumes/02/kohnen.

Kövecses, Zoltán (1998), 'Are there any emotion-specific metaphors?', in Angeliki Athanasiadou and Elzbieta Tabakowska (eds), *Speaking of Emotions: Conceptualization and Expression*, Berlin: de Gruyter, 127–151.

Kytö, Merja, Mats Rydén and Erik Smitterberg (eds) (2006), *Nineteenth Century English: Stability and Change*, Cambridge: Cambridge University Press.

Lakoff, George (1973), 'Hedges: A study of meaning criteria and the logic of fuzzy concepts', *Journal of Philosophical Logic* 2, 458–508.

Lakoff, George and Mark Johnson (1980), *Metaphors We Live by*, Chicago: Chicago University Press.

Lakoff, Robin (1975), *Language and Woman's Place*, New York: Harper and Row.

Leech, Geoffrey, Greg Myers and Jenny Thomas (eds) (1995), *Spoken English on Computer: Transcription, Mark-up, and Application*, London: Longman.

Leech, Geoffrey, Paul Rayson and Andrew Wilson (2001), *Word Frequencies in Written and Spoken English: Based on the British National Corpus*, London: Longman.

Levin, Magnus (2001), *Agreement with Collective Nouns in English*, Lund: Liber.

Lindquist, Hans (2008a), 'Stubbing your toe against a hard mass of facts: Corpus data and the phraseology of STUB and TOE', in Andrea Gerbig and Oliver Mason (eds), *Language, People, Numbers: Corpus Linguistics and Society*, Amsterdam: Rodopi, 217–229.

Lindquist, Hans (2008b), 'Corpus linguistics in cyberspace', review of Marianne Hundt, Nadja Nesselhauf and Carolin Biewer (eds), *Corpus Linguistics and the Web*, *International Journal of Corpus Linguistics* 13 (4), 551–563.

Lindquist, Hans (2009), 'A corpus study of lexicalized formulaic sequences with preposition + *hand*', in Bobbi Corrigan, Edith Moravcsik, Hamid Ouali and Kathy Wheatley (eds), *Formulaic Language. Vol. I: Structure, Distribution, Historical Change*, Amsterdam: Benjamins, 239–256.

Lindquist, Hans and Maria Estling Vannestål (2005), '*Fatigue* fatigue: The spread and development of a vogue word in British and American English', in Solveig Granath, June Miliander and Elisabeth Wennö (eds), *The Power of Words: Studies in Honour of Moira Linnarud*, Karlstad: Karlstad University, 103–113.

Lindquist, Hans and Magnus Levin [2000] (2007), 'Apples and oranges: On comparing data from different corpora', in Christian Mair and Marianne Hundt (eds), *Corpus Linguistics and Linguistic Theory*, Amsterdam: Rodopi, 201–213. Reprinted in Wolfgang Teubert and Ramesh Krishnamurthy (eds), *Corpus Linguistics: Critical Concepts in Linguistics. Vol. I*, London: Routledge, 160–172.

Lindquist, Hans and Magnus Levin (2009), 'The grammatical properties of recurrent phrases with body part nouns: The N_1 *to* N_1 pattern', in Ute Römer and Rainer Schulze (eds), *Exploring the Lexis-Grammar Interface*, Amsterdam: Benjamins, 171–188.

Lindquist, Hans and Christian Mair (eds) (2004), *Corpus Approaches to Grammaticalization in English*, Amsterdam: Benjamins.

Litosseliti, Lia (2006), *Gender and Language: Theory and Practice*, London: Hodder Arnold.

Longman Dictionary of Contemporary English [1978] (2003), fourth edition, London: Longman.

Lüdeling, Anke and Merja Kytö (2008), *Corpus Linguistics: An International Handbook. Vol. I*, Berlin: de Gruyter.

Lüdeling, Anke and Merja Kytö (2009), *Corpus Linguistics: An International Handbook. Vol. II*, Berlin: de Gruyter.

Mahlberg, Michaela (2007), 'Corpus stylistics: Bridging the gap between linguistics and literary studies', in Michael Hoey, Michaela Mahlberg, Michael Stubbs and Wolfgang Teubert, *Text, Discourse and Corpora*, London: Continuum, 219–246.

Mair, Christian (1998), 'Corpora and the study of the major varieties of English: Issues and results', in Hans Lindquist, Staffan Klintborg, Magnus Levin and Maria Estling (eds), *The Major Varieties of English: Papers from MAVEN 97*, Växjö: Acta Wexionensia, 139–157.

Mair, Christian (2004), 'Corpus linguistics and grammaticalization theory: Statistics, frequencies, and beyond', in Hans Lindquist and Christian Mair (eds), *Corpus Approaches to Grammaticalization in English*, Amsterdam: Benjamins, 121–150.

Mair, Christian (2006a), *Twentieth-Century English: History, Variation and Standardization*, Cambridge: Cambridge University Press.

Mair, Christian (2006b), 'Tracking ongoing grammatical change and recent diversification in present-day standard English: The complementary role of small and large corpora', in Antoinette Renouf and Andrew Kehoe (eds), *The Changing Face of Corpus Linguistics*, Amsterdam: Rodopi, 355–376.

Mair, Christian (2007), 'Change and variation in present-day English: Integrating the analysis of closed corpora and web-based monitoring', in Marianne Hundt, Nadja Nesselhauf and Carolin Biewer (eds), *Corpus Linguistics and the Web*, Amsterdam: Rodopi, 233–247.

Mair, Christian (2009), 'Corpora and the study of recent change in language', in Anke Lüdeling and Merja Kytö (eds), *Corpus Linguistics: An International Handbook. Vol. II*, Berlin: de Gruyter, 1109–1125.

Mair, Christian and Marianne Hundt (1999), '"Agile" and "uptight" genres: The corpus-based approach to language change in progress', *International Journal of Corpus Linguistics* 4 (2), 221–241.

Maricic, Ibolya (2005), *Face in Cyberspace: Facework, Impoliteness and Conflict in English Discussion Groups*, Växjö: Växjö University Press.

McEnery, Tony and Andrew Wilson [1996] (2001), *Corpus Linguistics*, second edition, Edinburgh: Edinburgh University Press.

Meunier, Fanny and Sylviane Granger (2008), *Phraseology in Foreign Language Learning and Teaching*, Amsterdam: Benjamins.

Meyer, Charles F. (2002), *English Corpus Linguistics: An Introduction*, Cambridge: Cambridge University Press.

Meyer, Charles F. (2008), 'Pre-electronic corpora', in Anke Lüdeling and Merja Kytö (eds), *Corpus Linguistics: An International Handbook. Vol. I*, Berlin: de Gruyter, 1–13.

Minugh, David (2000), '*You people use such weird expressions*: The frequency of idioms in newspaper CDs as corpora', in John M. Kirk (ed.), *Corpora Galore: Analyses and Techniques in Describing English*, Amsterdam: Rodopi, 57–71.

Mondorf, Britta (2007), 'Recalcitrant problems of comparative alternation and new insights emerging from Internet data', in Marianne Hundt, Nadja Nesselhauf and Carolin Biever (eds), *Corpus Linguistics and the Web*, Amsterdam: Rodopi, 211–232.

Moon, Rosamund (1998), *Fixed Expressions and Idioms in English: A Corpus-Based Approach*, Oxford: Clarendon.

Mukherjee, Joybrato (2004), 'Corpus data in a usage-based cognitive grammar', in Karin Aijmer and Bengt Altenberg (eds), *The Theory and Use of Corpora*, Amsterdam: Rodopi, 85–100.

Murray, K. M. Elisabeth (1977), *Caught in the Web of Words*, New Haven: Yale University Press.

Nelson, Gerald, Sean Wallis and Bas Aarts (2002), *Exploring Natural Language: Working with the British Component of the International Corpus of English*, Amsterdam: Benjamins.

Nevalainen, Terttu (2006), *An Introduction to Early Modern English*, Edinburgh: Edinburgh University Press.

Nevalainen, Terttu and Helena Raumolin-Brunberg (2003), *Historical Sociolinguistics*, London: Longman.

Oakes, Michael P. (1998), *Statistics for Corpus Linguistics*, Edinburgh: Edinburgh University Press.

Oxford English Dictionary online. www.oed.com.

Pahta, Päivi, Irma Taavitsainen, Terttu Nevalainen and Jukka Tyrkkö (eds) (2007), *Towards Multimedia in Corpus Studies*, Helsinki: University of Helsinki, available at http://www.helsinki.fi/varieng/journal/volumes/02/kohnen.

Palmer, Harold E. [1933] (1966), *Second Interim Report on English Collocations*, Tokyo: Kaitakusha.

Poos, Deanna and Rita Simpson (2002), 'Cross-disciplinary comparisons of hedging: Some findings from the Michigan Corpus of Academic Spoken English', in Randi Reppen, Suzanne Fitzmaurice and Douglas Biber (eds), *Using Corpora to Explore Linguistic Variation*, Amsterdam: Benjamins, 3–23.

Renouf, Antoinette and Andrew Kehoe (eds) (2006), *The Changing Face of Corpus Linguistics*, Amsterdam: Rodopi.

Rissanen, Matti (2000), 'The world of English historical corpora: From Cædmon to the computer age', *Journal of English Linguistics* 28, 7–20.

Rissanen, Matti (2004), 'Grammaticalisation from side to side: On the development of *beside(s)*', in Hans Lindquist and Christian Mair (eds), *Corpus Approaches to Grammaticalization in English*, Amsterdam: Benjamins, 151–170.

Rissanen, Matti (2008) 'Corpus linguistics and historical linguistics', in Anke Lüdeling and Merja Kytö (eds), *Corpus Linguistics: An International Handbook. Vol. I*, Berlin: de Gruyter, 53–67.

Rohdenburg, Günter (2002), 'Processing complexity and the variable use of prepositions in English', in Hubert Cuykens and Günter Radden (eds), *Perspectives on Prepositions*, Tübingen: Niemeyer, 79–100.

Rohdenburg, Günter (2007), 'Determinants of grammatical variation in English and the formation/confirmation of linguistic hypotheses by means of Internet data', in Marianne Hundt, Nadja Nesselhauf and Carolin Biewer (eds), *Corpus Linguistics and the Web*, Amsterdam: Rodopi, 191–209.

Romaine, Suzanne (2008), 'Corpus linguistics and sociolinguistics', in Anke Lüdeling and Merja Kytö (eds), *Corpus Linguistics: An International Handbook. Vol .I*, Berlin: de Gruyter, 96–111.

Rudanko, Juhani (2006), 'Watching English change: A case study on complement selection in British and American English', *English Language and Linguistics* 10 (1), 31–48.

Sapir, Edward [1921] (1971), *Language: An Introduction to the Study of Speech*, London: Rupert Hart-Davis.

Schmied, Josef (2006), 'New ways of analysing ESL on the WWW with WebCorp and WebPhraseCount', in Antoinette Renouf and Andrew Kehoe (eds), *The Changing Face of Corpus Linguistics*, Amsterdam: Rodopi, 309–324.

Schmitt, Norbert (ed.) (2004), *Formulaic Sequences: Acquisition, Processing and Use*, Amsterdam: Benjamins.

Scott, Mike (2004), *WordSmith Tools*, Version 4.0, Oxford: Oxford University Press.

Scott, Mike and Chris Tribble (2006), *Textual Patterns, Key Words and Corpus Analysis in Language Education*, Amsterdam: Benjamins.

Semino, Elena (2008), *Metaphor in Discourse*, Cambridge: Cambridge University Press.

Sharoff, Serge (2006), 'Creating general-purpose corpora using automated search engine queries', in Marco Baroni and Silvia Bernardini (eds), *WaCky! Working Papers on the Web as Corpus*, Bologna: Gedit, available at http://corpus. leeds.ac.uk/serge/publications/wacky-paper.pdf.

Sinclair, John (1991), *Corpus Concordance Collocation*, Oxford: Oxford University Press.

Sinclair, John [1998] (2004), 'The lexical item', in Edda Weigand (ed.), *Contrastive Lexical Semantics*, Amsterdam: Benjamins, 1–24. Reprinted in John Sinclair and Ronald Carter (eds), *Trust the Text: Language, Corpus and Discourse*, London: Routledge, 131–148.

Sinclair, John (1999), 'A way with common words', in Hilde Hasselgård and Signe Oksefjell (eds), *Out of Corpora*, Amsterdam: Rodopi, 157–179.

Sinclair, John (2003), *Reading Concordances: An Introduction*, London: Longman.

Sinclair, John, Susan Jones and Robert Daley (2004), *English Collocation Studies: The OSTI Report*, ed. by Ramesh Krishnamurthy, London: Continuum.

Starcke, Bettina (2006), 'The phraseology of Jane Austen's *Persuasion*: Phraseological units as carriers of meaning', *ICAME Journal* 30, 87–104.

Stefanowitsch, Anatol (2006), 'Words and their metaphors: A corpus-based approach', in Anatol Stefanowitsch and Stefan Th. Gries (eds), *Corpus-Based Approaches to Metaphor and Metonymy*, Berlin: de Gruyter, 63–105.

Stefanowitsch, Anatol and Stefan Th. Gries (eds) (2006), *Corpus-Based Approaches to Metaphor and Metonymy*, Berlin: de Gruyter.

Stefanowitsch, Anatol and Stephan Th. Gries (2009), 'Corpora and grammar', in Anke Lüdeling and Merja Kytö (eds), *Corpus Linguistics: An International Handbook. Vol. II.* Berlin: de Gruyter, 993–952.

Stenström, Anna-Brita, Gisle Andersen and Ingrid Kristine Hasund (2002), *Trends in Teenage Talk: Corpus Compilation, Analysis and Findings*, Amsterdam: Benjamins.

Stubbs, Michael (2001), *Words and Phrases: Corpus Studies of Lexical Semantics*, Oxford: Blackwell.

Stubbs, Michael (2005), 'Conrad in the computer: Examples of quantitative stylistic methods', *Language and Literature* 14 (1), 5–24.

Stubbs, Michael (2007a), 'An example of frequent English phraseology: Distributions, structures and functions' in Roberta Facchinetti (ed.), *Corpus Linguistics 25 Years On*, Amsterdam: Rodopi, 89–105.

Stubbs, Michael (2007b), 'Quantitative data on multi-word sequences in English: The case of the word *world*', in Michael Hoey, Michaela Mahlberg, Michael Stubbs and Wolfgang Teubert, *Text, Discourse and Corpora*, London: Continuum, 163–189.

Stubbs, Michael (2009), 'Technology and phraseology: With notes on the history of corpus linguistics', in Ute Römer and Rainer Schulze (eds), *Exploring the Lexis–Grammar Interface*, Amsterdam: Benjamins, 15–31.

Svartvik, Jan (1992), 'Corpus linguistics comes of age', in Jan Svartvik (ed.), *Directions in Corpus Linguistics*, Proceedings of Nobel Symposium 82, Stockholm, 4–8 August 1991, Berlin: de Gruyter, 7–13.

Svartvik, Jan (2007), 'Corpus linguistics 25+ years on', in Roberta Facchinetti (ed.), *Corpus Linguistics 25 Years On*, Amsterdam: Rodopi, 11–25.

Svartvik, Jan and Randolph Quirk (1980), *A Corpus of Spoken English Conversation*, Lund: Gleerups.

Tagliamonte, Sali A. (2006), *Analysing Sociolinguistic Variation*, Cambridge: Cambridge University Press.

Thompson, Geoff and Susan Hunston (eds) (2006), *System and Corpus: Exploring Connections*, London: Equinox.

Tognini-Bonelli, Elena (2001), *Corpus Linguistics at Work*, Amsterdam: Benjamins.

Wallis, Sean (2008), 'Searching treebanks and other structured corpora', in Anke Lüdeling and Merja Kytö (eds), *Corpus Linguistics: An International Handbook. Vol. I*, Berlin: de Gruyter, 738–758.

Wasow, Thomas (2002), *Postverbal Behavior,* Stanford: CSLI.

Winchester, Simon (1998), *The Professor and the Madman,* New York: HarperCollins.

Winchester, Simon (2003), *The Meaning of Everything,* Oxford: Oxford University Press.

Wray, Alison (2002), *Formulaic Language and the Lexicon,* Cambridge: Cambridge University Press.

Wray, Alison (2008), *Formulaic Language: Pushing the Boundaries,* Oxford: Oxford University Press.

Wynne, Martin (ed.) (2005), *Developing Linguistic Corpora: A Guide to Good Practice,* Oxford: Oxbow Books, available at http://ahds.ac.uk/linguistic-corpora.

Wynne, Martin (2008), 'Searching and concordancing', in Anke Lüdeling and Merja Kytö (eds), *Corpus Linguistics: An International Handbook. Vol. I,* Berlin: de Gruyter, 706–737.

Xiao, Richard (2008), 'Well-known and influential corpora', in Anke Lüdeling and Merja Kytö (eds), *Corpus Linguistics: An International Handbook. Vol. I,* Berlin: de Gruyter, 383–456.

Index

Note: Major references are given in **bold**. Specific corpora, text databases and similar resources are listed under the entry for *corpus*.